Transforming Educational Administration

Meaning, Community, and Excellence

Robert J. Starratt
Fordham University

The McGraw-Hill Companies, Inc.

New York St. Louis San Francisco Auckland Bogotá Caracas
Lisbon London Madrid Mexico City Milan Montreal New Delhi
San Juan Singapore Sydney Tokyo Toronto

This book was developed by Lane Akers, Inc.

This book was set in Palatino by Ruttle, Shaw & Wetherill, Inc.
The editor was Lane Akers;
the production supervisor was Paula Keller.
The cover was designed by Rafael Hernandez.
Project supervision was done by Spectrum Publisher Services.
R. R. Donnelley & Sons Company was printer and binder.

TRANSFORMING EDUCATIONAL ADMINISTRATION
Meaning, Community, and Excellence

This book is printed on acid-free paper.

1 2 3 4 5 6 7 8 9 0 DOC DOC 9 0 9 8 7 6 5

ISBN 0-07-061239-0

Library of Congress Cataloging-in-Publication Data

Starratt, Robert J.
    Transforming educational administration: meaning, community, and
excellence / Robert J. Starratt
    p.   cm.
    Includes bibliographical references and index.
    ISBN 0-07-061239-0
    1. School management and organization—United States.   2. School
administrators—United States.   3. Community and school—United
States.   I. Title.
LB2805.S7445   1996
371.2' 00973—dc20   95-34015

About the Author

ROBERT J. STARRATT is professor and chair, Division of Administration, Policy and Urban Education, in The Graduate School of Education of Fordham University in New York City. His scholarly interests include the areas of Leadership, Curriculum, and Human Resource Development. Recent books include *The Drama of Schooling/The Schooling of Drama* (1990), *The Drama of Leadership* (1993), *Building an Ethical School* (1994), and *Supervision: A Redefinition* (with Thomas J. Sergiovanni, 1993).

*This book is dedicated to three teachers
who had a lasting influence on my life:
J. Joseph Ryan, who made me half-believe I had a mind
during a mindless adolescence; William Carrol,
who helped me believe I could be a writer;
and Frank Finn, who was my mentor for living fully.*

Contents

Part Two
ADMINISTERING MEANING

Part Four
ADMINISTERING EXCELLENCE

Foreword

We have witnessed the end of a generation, and the beginning of a new one. Arguably, the study of how to administer the education of youth goes back to the ancients, but in the modern era, that study has been dominated by an attempt to provide rationally and technically a system of controls for administering educational institutions. Thus, much of the work done in educational administration in this century has used, as its guide, a technical model for administration, by which I mean a model whose fondest hope was the engineering of schools so that they ran in the most efficient way. The dominant assumptions of such a technicist approach were, I believe, a profound faith in the "scientific method" and in empiricist research aimed at finding the underlying "laws" that might govern human behavior; a belief that there were, indeed, regularities and truths that could be discovered; and a trust that the discipline of administration, undeveloped as it might be, was one that could capture the ways and means of running organizations so that the "human resources" therein would be both satisfied and productive.

The modern foundations of educational administration, with some notable exceptions, have been dominated by a technical mentality that has attempted to see the study of administration as a scientific enterprise in which our students, teachers, and administrators were the "objects" of such study. However, occasionally the earth shakes and old generations are swallowed. Such is the case here. There is a resurgence of interest now in the field of administration as a human endeavor, one that must be linked to the critical and appreciative arts. Administration, and particularly educational administration, is studied now not so much as a system of technical regularities but more as a moral endeavor, in which people of good will try to achieve excellence in their practice.

The critical art is one of examining the system of which a person is a part. The educational system has been under considerable attack in recent years. Undoubtedly, it does many things well, but it also fails to serve many. It is clear that we often fail in serving those who do not approach the Western man—the white, Christian male. Certainly, a failure of enough resources is one reason why this is so, but I wish to argue that it is a failure of ideas that led to our problems. The great transformations of this century—feminism, civil rights, and others—were transformations of consciousness and transformations of ideas sparked by practices and action. The critical art, then, examines those structures, practices, and ideas that contribute to the current malaise.

This is a fundamental prerequisite, I believe, to being an administrator of schooling. I consider it necessary for an administrator to be able to reflectively and critically engage his or her practice, to ask in what ways do these particular structures, these ways of monopolizing the time and space of children, serve them well or poorly. Such is the stuff of administration. Although schedules, placements, curriculum, and teacher assignments are important, it is also necessary to reflect on the totality of the experience for children and young adults. If I were in their places, how would I feel? What would I want done differently?

In this text, Professor Starratt adopts, in many ways, the critical turn. He asks us to consider how administration is connected to issues of power, control, and a changing society. He looks at the evolution of schooling and asks why this evolution is so centered around an individualistic and competitive bias, why the structures reproduce those unfortunate divisions that mark our society. He suggests that the Western condition is marked by a loss of meaning, by the lack of a substantive public and common life, and by a one-dimensional conception of meritocracy.

The loss of deep meaning has to do with the purpose of our lives. Put bluntly, do we educate in order to provide trained workers who can keep the economy on track, or do we educate to develop a coherent social fabric composed of citizens deciding their destiny? Surely, we achieve meaning from belonging, belonging to a community of care. This community of care, in turn, is marked by a robust and active public life, in which questions of the common good are frequently and actively pursued. In turn, this common life is just that–common. It requires the participation of all, not just of an elite distinguished by its ability to score well on standardized exams. In his critical turn, Starratt asks us to examine such issues and to examine them at *site level,* where administrators, teachers, students, and parents can actively discuss them. He also asks us to consider how we might provide ways of living in a school that allows for a common life characterized by a community of both learning and caring.

Starratt also engages in the appreciative art. The appreciative art is to look at our strengths, our ways of being in the world, and our wonderful diversity in a unity. Here, we need to appreciate our students, and our teachers, and to value them for the worth they bring to us. We look for a community, a bonding of divergence aimed at achieving good for all. The appreciative arts seek to establish a way in which we can understand others in what could be a chaotic universe. They attempt to bring meaning to what it is that we do.

It is clear to me that schooling is more than just "learning." Rather, it is learning combined with the formation of a self-, political, and social consciousness, whether we are talking about grade school or high school. The appreciative art attempts to help form this consciousness so that we engage our students in thinking about their responsibilities as members of a civic republic and a community, as well as participants in a world of their own making. This, I think, might be the foremost responsibility of educational administrators.

This text is, then, a subtle blending of the critical and appreciative arts. It represents the new generation of thinking about administration in education. Instead of embracing a technical approach to his subject, Starratt has adopted a viewpoint that suggests that what is of importance in our lives is the meanings we create for ourselves. We pay attention to what is "meaning-full," and what is meaningful to us dictates how we construct our daily actions, whether it be to bond with others, to accomplish things, or to feel wanted. It is these types of conditions that inform the new school administration. In the old paradigm, the question administrators were told to ask was, "How do we keep things running smoothly?" In the new model of administration, the question we must ask is, "How do we make things meaningful?"

To this end, this author focuses on three inter-related dimensions of educational administration—the building of meaning, community, and excellence. Each is necessary in its own right.

For me, the building of meaning is the creation of institutions not engaged in the reproduction of apathy. These are educational institutions that provide a sense of purpose and a sense of mission. The idea of meaning is deep-seated in human endeavors; otherwise, we become lost in the routine of routines, in wondering how we got here and why we should continue. Yet, in the past, the fundamental meaning of schools has eluded many of us. We have seen the process of schooling as resulting in a diploma, which might lead to more schooling, which might result in another diploma, which might lead to a job. Lost here is the fundamental meaning of schooling: the creation of articulate, conscious, critical, and knowledgeable citizens who can forge a better life for their children.

Such meanings are not created and sustained in vacuums, however. The notion of community becomes central in this text as well, and this notion becomes the context for the creation of meaning. It is important to distinguish a community from a collection. Although we call many of our institutions, including educational ones, "communities," they are, in fact, collections of individuals. In many modern societies, individualism, not community, is the preferred state, and the individual—celebrated as the iconoclastic cowboy, the entrepreneurial tycoon, the artistic diva—provides us with our role model and, more important, our way of being. This is ultimately self-alienating: no one stands alone. Indeed, without reference to others, without a connectedness, and without a common sense of who we are and where we come from, we simply become roles and role players. A community is a memory and a vision and, ultimately, the source of meaning. It is a memory in the sense that it provides a collective history of those purposes it attempted to achieve; it is a vision of those purposes yet to come. The memory and the vision together provide a sense of belonging and meaning.

The building of meaning and community are intimately linked, in this text, to the achievement of excellence. This is an important concept and one that can be misrepresented in many ways. By excellence, I do not believe the author means stellar performance on the playing field or the winning of academic awards. I take excellence in this context to mean the attempt to achieve the (almost) unachievable. In educational administration, excellence is the continued building of community and meaning through the development of shared practices whose fundamental aim, redundantly, is the achievement of excellence. This is not a far cry from the assertion that there is no achievable "good life," but only the search for the good life. It is this search that makes us most fully human. It is the search that counts.

Shared practices are important. Practices are activities designed to accomplish, extend, or renew the aims and purposes we set for ourselves. The practice of medicine, for example, aims to accomplish the healing of the sick, extend its knowledge of the process, and renew its dedication to healing. The practice of administration does much that is similar. When the practice of administration is linked to the accomplishment, extension, and renewal of the building of community and meaning, it is called leadership.

The art of leadership is central to schooling. This text, I believe, talks about leadership. Leadership comes in many forms, from the purveyor of ideas intended to change old habits to the bargainer of beliefs. But it is a certain kind of leadership that this text extolls. This type of leadership is different from persuasion and is certainly not the type of situational gambits one often finds in the literature. Rather, I think, this leadership is a moral craft, one of compelling belief in a way of living that strikes the leaders and followers as more sound, as more appropriate. Perhaps this is what this text is about—leadership as a moral craft devoted to the building of excellence through community and attention. Excellence comes through pushing the limits of the possible, but this requires us to pay attention to what is possible and to see how indeed our communities might help this to happen.

In my view, leadership as a moral craft involves a number of attributes. First, there must be a sense of purpose, a vision in which the leader believes. Second, there must be action, a means of confronting established regularities in order to overcome them. Finally, there must be a sense of belief that what we do is indeed right and true. Each condition is a moral condition. Each requires a sense of commitment and obligation.

Becoming an educational administrator, then, is more than learning skills, although these are certainly important. Rather, it is engaging in a practice of excellence designed to create communities and to provide moral leadership. This is no easy task under what has been called the conditions of postmodernity: ambiguity, pluralistic values and the erosion of singular beliefs, and a world characterized as much by chaos as by stability. Yet, if we wish our children and our children's children to live well, we must create a sense of meaning, community, and excellence. This text directs you to that end.

William Foster
Bloomington, IN

Introduction

This book has been written out of a conviction that educational administrator preparation programs need to become more responsive to changes and challenges in the complex and dynamic social arena we call education. These changes and challenges are embedded in the social and political context of schooling, in new approaches to teaching as a profession, in educational public policy. One of the first courses in a graduate program in educational administration is usually a course on fundamentals of educational administration. This book is an attempt to help beginning administrators or those seeking state certification to become administrators get started on the right foot, in a program that will build on the perspectives developed in this course.

Many currently available textbooks on the fundamentals of educational administration present a selection of chapters dealing with various levels of education. The reader is exposed to the role of the federal government and the state government in policy setting, the operations of federal and state agencies in implementing policy and overseeing policy implementation at the local level, the role of the district central office administrators in directing the school system, the politics surrounding school board activities, the influence of special-interest groups on the local and state education policies, and so on. Other chapters deal with teacher unions, administering the budget, instructional supervision, public relations, and overseeing the physical plant. Such textbooks assume that the purpose of a fundamentals course is to provide a broad overview of a range of concerns that educational administrators encounter. Such courses, however helpful they may be in providing the larger picture, do not focus on the educational unit where most beginning administrators find themselves, namely, the individual school.

A fundamentals course should introduce the beginning administrator to the fundamentals of administering an individual school or of being a member of an administrative team in an individual school. Those who are moving into district office administration or into state education departments can learn more about their responsibilities in courses dealing with district- or state-level administration, although I would hope that those courses also point to the individual school as the place where their efforts will bear fruit.

Other fundamentals texts, even when they concentrate on the individual school site, tend to provide treatments of discrete functions of administration. Hence we find chapters dealing with special education, with extracurricular programs, with testing and counseling programs, with parent and community relations, with scheduling, resource allocation, communication, decision making, delegating responsibilities, dealing with legal and safety concerns, and so on. Again we find a diffusion of focus, a sampling of functions that, while touching on real concerns for school administrators, reveal the trees but provide little sense of the forest. We return to the question: "What is *fundamental* to educational administration?"

This book attempts to focus attention on three areas that we believe are fundamental to educational administration: meaning, community, and excellence. With clarity about their responsibilities in these three areas, administrators can provide a focus to their decision making, their resource allocation, their communication processes, parent and community relations, and their concerns for special education, extracurriculars, and so on.

School Administration in a Historical Context

There is an even more pressing need, however, for another change in the fundamentals course. Present courses tend to reflect limited and fragmented conceptual frameworks that derive from earlier historical and theoretical developments in the fields of education and educational administration. The recent work of Murphy and Beck provides an historical overview of the metaphorical themes that shaped understandings of principalship during the past seventy years in the United States.[1] Their study indicates how the ways of understanding principalship were influenced by historical events such as the Great Depression, World War II, and the success of the Soviet space program, as well as by themes emerging from the political and academic worlds, such as concern for social homogenization of disparate communities of immigrants, for scientific management, and for accountability for measurable student learning.

While Beck and Murphy point to the fluctuations of thought about school administration, the more serious critiques of Greenfield, Foster, Bates, Carr, and Kemmis, among others, challenge the scientific basis for administrative theory and for prescriptions for practice based on such theory.[2] This book stands firmly with their contentions that much of what has recently been considered "mainstream" educational administration literature makes unsupportable assumptions (1) that truly professional administrators make rational decisions based on facts derived from scientific research, not on subjective preferences; (2) that educational administrators work within (or can create) rational organizational systems; and (3) that they can control the school as an organization (and, indeed, have the responsibility and right to do so) by applying scientifically grounded knowledge to make the school work according to rationally derived goals.

This book asserts, in contrast, that educational administrators need to probe the assumptions, presuppositions, and values that stand behind the interpretations they make of what goes on in schools, and behind the decisions and actions they take in the course of carrying out their roles. Indeed, they need to see that their interpretations and decisions are rooted in the normative assumptions and beliefs that they hold about the general purposes of schooling.

In looking for emerging understandings of the principalship, Beck and Murphy summarize the sizable recent literature that indicates a shift of major proportions in understanding the context, the process, and the purpose of schooling.[3] This shift, in turn, implies new ways of understanding the principalship. In the 1990s, principals—and by implication other school-based administrators—will be seen as leaders, servants, organizational architects, social architects, educators, moral agents, and persons in a community.[4]

This book is in sympathy with this literature in its espousal of a more collegial style of relationships among a variety of educators who think of themselves as professionals, in its appreciation of the need for teacher leadership and full participation by teachers in renewal of the school, and in its focus on the human development of persons. The recent insistence that schools nurture the success of all students rather than sort the more able from the less able by means of standardized test results finds support in our treatment of excellence. The emerging understanding of knowledge as a social construct, as something that develops in social interaction focused on problems seen in specific contexts rather than knowledge as an external entity existing independently of the historically situated human subject, influences the development of several themes in the book. The book also supports the concern that professionalism go beyond a foundation in a distorted scientism of facts divorced from values to a recognition of the educational professional's profound value commitments to the human growth of children in a free and open community. Besides these emerging concerns and understandings highlighted by Beck and Murphy, there are other emerging influences within the larger culture that affect the way we think about education and educational administration.

Educational Administration Faces Cultural Challenges

Shifts in perspectives derived from feminine scholarship, fresh understandings of the influence of mythical thinking and ideology on our world view, openness to the importance of multicultural sensitivity, and convictions about the need to actively build community out of a mixture of pluralistic and sometimes antagonistic groups also influence the ways in which we approach educational administration in this book.

In addition to being grounded in much of the changed perceptions about schooling and about administering schools, the book is grounded as well in a judgment that the schools cannot continue to ignore the major social and cultural challenges facing American society. If the mission of the school is to prepare future members of American society who will live in the twenty-first century, the school must interpret and respond to major challenges facing that society in the present and in the foreseeable future. Those challenges appear to be threefold: (1) a loss, trivialization, or distortion of the deeper meanings that undergird human life; (2) excessive if not exclusive emphasis on the isolated individual as the primary social unit, to the detriment of serious consideration of the public community and its common good (at the local, national, and international levels); (3) as a consequence of the first and second challenge, the goal of "excellence" in education is superficial, one-dimensional, fundamentally accepting of a tacit social Darwinism (the economic and political survival of those who win in the economic and political struggle, at the expense of and in disregard of the losers), and separated from broader and deeper considerations of what constitutes excellence in a whole society or community of human beings. In framing a treatment of fundamentals of educational administration, therefore, it appears that we have to deal with these fundamentals, namely, how the school will respond to the challenge of dealing with meanings that undergird human life in the twenty-first century, the challenge of building a concern for and an understanding of the demands of community in public life, and the challenge of promoting a broad spectrum of excellences in the private and public lives of young people.

Overview of the Book

The book proposes a treatment of the fundamentals of educational administration as involving the administering of meaning, the administering of community, and the administering of excellence. Before moving into those three fundamental concerns, the book discusses some introductory concerns in an attempt to locate *educational* administration as a unique kind of administrative activity (and hence not to be governed by prescriptions derived from administration in other kinds of organizations, such as commercial or political organizations), and as an activity historically and socially contextualized (and hence not presented in a universal, a-historical theoretical construct). On the contrary, the first chapter points to the historical challenges facing schools and underscores the expectation that educational administrators are not simply to manage the schools through the crisis, but must find ways to transform the schools into workable learning communities. The second chapter offers a psychological and existential perspective on administration of a school in order to encourage personal reflection on how one performs in the role of administrator. Such reflection leads to an appreciation of the moral implications of educational administration.

The titles of the three major parts of the book, "Administering Meaning," "Administering Community," and "Administering Excellence," may set the reader off-balance. Normally one might suspect that "administered meaning," "administered community," and "administered excellence" are self-contradictory. An administered meaning smacks of manipulation (and therefore distortion) of meaning. An administered community suggests a community devoid of spontaneity, passion, conflict, or surprises. Administered excellence could mean a kind of uniform, mass-produced (and therefore not customized, one-of-a-kind, creative) excellence. The titles suggest the seemingly impossible challenges contemporary administrators face. How does an educational leader bring the plurality of meanings, one might say the cacophonies of meanings, being experienced in the school into some kind of large synthesis or world view? Likewise, how does the school overcome the individualism fostered by the culture at large and by the youth culture in particular and build a sense of a community so that everyone has some sense of responsibility for promoting the common good of that community? Finally, how does a school foster a sense of excellence that honors a variety of excellences—indeed, that understands the necessity of a variety of excellences for the fullest public life of the community? These are the fundamental issues that administrators must grapple with, must direct their attention to, must organize their activity around. The individual chapters in each of the three parts of the book suggest ways in which administrators can address these issues.

It is understood that many other concerns will occupy an administrator's attention (conflict resolution, budgeting, collective bargaining, scheduling, etc.) and that administrators function at other than individual-school-site levels. Other courses and other texts will treat these other concerns and levels. It is hoped, however, that this text provides large fundamental frames of reference that color the interpretation of and responses to these other concerns at whatever level one serves as an administrator.

At the end of each chapter, I suggest a variety of site-based, action research activities. The material in each chapter presents a way of looking at and thinking about what is going on in schools. The suggested activities are meant to develop understanding of these frameworks and ideas as they are expressed by students, teachers, and parents, or as they are exemplified in the practices and structures of your school. I expect that the action research of these assignments will teach much more than the textual material of that chapter. To read the chapter only, and not to engage in probing that material in the workplace, would be to miss the major learnings of the course. The book is intended primarily to frame the learning that participants will achieve *after* reading the chapter—in the activities suggested for their own workplace and in the sharing of findings and ideas with the others taking the course or unit.

A central tenet of this book is that administrative leadership is intellectual work. By that I mean that administrators need to *know* what they are doing, to understand the relationship between the work of the school and the challenges facing contemporary society. This book attempts to develop an understanding of historical, philosophical, and sociological frameworks that enable educators to interpret what the school is promoting and not promoting. I believe that the work of administrative leaders needs to be grounded in these understandings. To grasp what is implied in these historical, philosophical, and sociological frameworks is hard work, requiring focused reading, reflective, probing conversations with peers, and a willingness to challenge long-held personal assumptions. The purpose of this work is not to turn participants into professors, but to enable them to bring a large view of what should be happening in schools to their work. More than one study of schools in the recent past has concluded that they are mindless institutions. That conclusion does not say much about the administrators in those schools. Presently there is a groundswell for school renewal. That renewal will require, beyond an understanding of the dynamics of change, a leadership of ideas.

Another central tenet of the book is that the *student* is the producer of knowledge, not the teacher or the textbook. What participants take away from this book and the course in which it is used will be the knowledge and understanding they produce through active engagement with the text and through learning activities suggested by the text and the teacher. The book is intended to get participants to ask themselves challenging questions and to stimulate them to construct practical and workable responses to the questions.

The book suggests that administrators have to lead the way in restructuring schools, but it provides few suggestions as to how to do this. Although there are some suggested activities that are intended to explore specific elements of restructuring, the book is not intended to provide a blueprint for restructuring schools. Rather, it is intended to bring beginning administrators to consider *fundamental frameworks* that should shape the more specific work of restructuring. Furthermore, it would be irresponsible for me to suggest that beginning administrators will be ready to tackle the enormously complex task of restructuring after reading this book. I am assuming that they will be exposed to courses and seminars on the dynamics of organizational change, curriculum development, staff development, school community partnerships, the politics of conflict resolution, arbitration, and consensus building, for which, again, this book provides fundamental frameworks within which these elements of restructuring would intermingle. Even when the beginning administrator is finished with his or her preparation and certification program, the work of restructuring will require close attention to the contextual readiness of his or her school for the work of restructuring. Restructuring will be different in each school, and so it is inappropriate to suggest any one formula or sequence of steps as the way everyone should restructure their school. The preparation program simply provides opportunities to explore possibilities that might be appropriate in participants' settings. The work of restructuring will not fall from the sky in a ready-made package. Restructuring will happen only when people in each school decide to make it happen.

One final word before we jump into the text: I believe that educational administration is, like teaching, autobiographical. That is, we work as we live and have lived: we are the primary tool in the crafting of our administrative work, as Blumburg suggests.[5] We may adopt, for example, a particular strategy in resolving conflict, a strategy that we have seen described in a textbook. That strategy, however, will be colored by our personality, by our personal history of dealing with conflict, by our cultural roots, by our feelings toward the people involved in the conflict, by our class, gender, and ethnic biases, and so on. Although we strive to be objective in our dealings with others, each of us nonetheless brings his or her own interpretive frameworks to bear on his or her experience, such that it is difficult in any given situation to describe objectively what the facts are in the case. Differences of opinion and different conclusions and solutions are to be expected in a class on school administration. No one person—

not even the professor—has the perfect answer, or, indeed, even understands the question fully. Every class discussion and class project needs the participation of everyone because each person has something to offer. We need the perspectives of others to enrich our own learning. The full participation of everyone in the class will teach us the most important lesson of all about educational administration: that fundamentally it is about meaning, community, and the search for excellence.

Endnotes

1. Lynn G. Beck and Joseph Murphy, *Understanding the Principalship: Metaphorical Themes, 1920s–1990,* Teachers College Press, New York, 1993.
2. See Thomas B. Greenfield, "Re-forming and Re-valuing Educational Administration: Whence Cometh the Phoenix?," A paper presented at the annual meeting of the American Educational Research Association, Chicago, 1991; William Foster, *Paradigms and Promises: New Approaches to Educational Administration,* Prometheus, Buffalo, NY, 1986; Richard Bates, "Toward a Critical Practice of Educational Administration," in Thomas J. Sergiovanni and John B. Corbally (eds.), *Leadership and Organizational Culture: New Perspectives on Administrative Theory and Practice,* University of Illinois Press, Urbana, 1984, pp. 260–274; Wilfred Carr and Stephen Kemmis, *Becoming Critical: Education, Knowledge, and Action Research,* Falmer, London, 1986.
3. See Beck and Murphy, op. cit., pp. 178–195.
4. Ibid.
5. Arthur Blumburg, "The Craft of School Administration and Some Other Rambling Thoughts," *Educational Administration Quarterly, 20,* (4): 1984; 24–40.

Acknowledgments

McGraw-Hill and I would like to thank the following reviewers for their many helpful comments and suggestions: Terry Astudo, New York University; Lynn Beck, University of California, Los Angeles; John Bennion, University of Utah; C. Cryss Brunner, University of Wisconsin; Donald Carver, University of Georgia; Gary Crow, University of Utah; Philip Cusick, Michigan State University; and Cecil Miskel, University of Michigan.

Robert J. Starratt

PART ONE

The Nature and Importance of Educational Administration

Part One attempts to establish three presuppositions behind the development of the rest of the book: (1) the enterprise of education so contextualizes educational administration as to differentiate it from all other forms of management, (2) educational administrators cannot assume the legitimacy of the status quo in schools but must grasp the profound challenge to recover the essential meanings of education for the present and for the twenty-first century, and (3) educational administration involves the personally and professionally fulfilling work of reconstructing the educational process. This part establishes educational administration as a uniquely challenging calling. It is unique because no other type of administration faces the complex work of transforming the educational enterprise, and because understanding the sociocultural dynamics at play in schools is beginning to be seen as the key to building schools with intellectual and moral integrity. It is challenging because we expect so much from schools and because the job can bring out the worst, as well as the best, in all of us.

1

CHAPTER 1

The Unique Calling
of a School Administrator

In this chapter we look at what makes educational administration unique among types of administration. We also consider the present historical context of schooling in America in order to underscore the crucial importance of school administration in the schools of today and tomorrow. The chapter concludes with some questions for self-reflection for those who plan to assume the responsibilities and challenges of school administration.

THE SPECIAL NATURE OF EDUCATIONAL ADMINISTRATION

For the past thirty years or more, educational administration has been assumed to be one of several types of a fairly uniform activity labeled *administration*. This label was thought to encompass relatively similar characteristics. That is, if a person was a good administrator in one setting, presumably he or she would be a good administrator in another setting. Sometimes a more idealized form of administration was considered to be found in a specific type of administration, such as military or business administration. Indeed, it has been suggested in the United States and in other countries that school administrators ought to imitate business administrators, or, further, that schools ought to be run by people with training and experience in business administration.

This kind of thinking often is based on the assumption that there is a kind of science of administration, which, through empirical research extending over decades, has established certain universal principles and management techniques that can be applied in diverse administrative and organizational settings. This belief was well expressed in an influential volume edited by Thomas Sergiovanni and Frederick Carver:

> Research to date has revealed that human behavior, as a result of organizational life, manifests remarkable similarities as one moves from hospital, to school, to

retail store, to welfare agency, and to military unit. . . . Thus, while the school administrator is particularly concerned with one kind of formal organization, his vision may very well be improved by studying organizations in general.[1]

As early as 1911, Frederick Taylor sought to create a science of management based on his time-and-motion studies of a manufacturing process.[2] Elwood Cubberly was an early proponent of the application of scientific principles generated through empirical research in educational administration.[3] Later, the work of Herbert Simon rekindled an interest in administrative theory based on scientific research on the behavior of managers in organizations.[4] His work influenced the administrative theory movement in educational administration. Getzels, Griffiths, and Halpin each advocated the use of scientific research methods and theories from the social sciences to construct a theory and science of educational administration.[5] They believed that only in this way would educational administration gain the legitimacy and respect accorded to true professionals. Consequently, they stressed the rationality and objectivity that administrators, having been exposed to these studies, would bring to their tasks. Such rationality and objectivity would ensure professional judgment in circumstances of organizational life in the pursuit of rational goals.

Not every scholar, however, endorsed the scientism and rationalism of the mainstream theorists of the 1950s and 1960s. Studies by Lindbloom and others questioned the assumed rationality and objectivity of administrators in all organizations.[6] Cyert and March suggested that administrators exercise a *bounded rationality*: They may make decisions with goals in mind, but they cannot consider all the alternative choices available and then make the best choice among those alternatives according to an independently objective standard.[7] Administrators' understanding of the alternatives is limited by their own experience, training, and imagination, and by the pressure to make timely decisions. Administrators tend to choose a course of action that resolves the immediate situation in some way or another. These decisions, however, may not necessarily be the best decisions for the long run. Lindbloom also found that administrators tend to make short-term decisions that are not necessarily consistent with earlier short-term decisions, nor with those they will make the next day. Their decisions tend to be disjointed and incremental, rather than rationally consistent with long-term, prioritized goals.

Other studies by Apple, Bates, and Giroux report that, beyond the disjointed and bounded nature of the rationality found in the actions of educational administrators, one finds ideological assumptions and beliefs. These assumptions and beliefs are not subject to empirical proof. More important, they are rarely articulated and indeed consciously attended to, and hence are all the more influential.[8] These criticisms of the "administration as science" perspective are highlighted in order to caution the well-intentioned administrator to recognize that the job entails more than making decisions based on a rational assessment of the facts. Interpretation, bias, distortion, subjective feelings, untested beliefs, and assumptions are all at work in determining what one considers as facts, and indeed influence how one goes about gathering facts.

I am not suggesting that administrators surrender to the seeming impossibility of acting rationally and simply follow their own private hunches and beliefs. Educational administration requires a constant effort to introduce rationality into decisions. That rationality will not come exclusively from the individual administrator, but will come more from the individuals involved in the decision discussing the merits of alternative choices. Even then, decisions will rarely if ever be purely rational; to seek for that kind of rational purity is to chase an unattainable ideal. Rather, what administrators ought to seek are the most reasonable decisions under the circumstances—decisions for which others can take responsibility for because they have been involved in making them.

THE PRIMARY FOCUS ON MANAGEMENT

Besides the assumption of an ever-present rationality, there has been another harmful side effect from the effort to think of educational administration as one form of a general science or theory of administration. That harmful effect has been encouraging school principals to think of themselves primarily as managers rather than as educators. Such thinking has led administrators to concentrate on structures and procedures and the smooth running of the school organization. It has encouraged an emphasis on mechanical control and maintenance through reliance on administrative technique (good public relations, open communications, well-organized meetings, delegation of responsibilities with attendant accountability and reporting structures, etc.). Administrators often tend to forget that they are educators, and that the core activity of the school is teaching and learning. The organization of the school has to follow and support the efforts of teachers and students to maximize learning, rather than forcing the teaching and learning tasks into some preordained organizational structure.

It is important to emphasize, therefore, that one of the fundamentals of educational administration is that it is educational; in other words, educational administrators are educators. Their work is the education of youth. Their work is to explore more fruitful and effective ways of enhancing student learning with the learning community. Although it may be helpful to study the administration of other types of organizations, the school community should not organize itself according to organizational theories or strategies derived from other types of organizations. The organization of the work of education should derive from the activities of teaching and learning. The work of educational administrators is to create, develop, support, and encourage those organizational arrangements that flow organically from the core activities of the teaching and learning enterprise. In this sense, educational administration is unique among forms of administration and management; it is shaped and directed by the essential work of teaching and learning. As David Purpel put it: "Schools are not shops that require clever and ingenious bits of engineering to increase productivity and morale, but major social institutions where wisdom and courage are required to infuse practice with our highest hopes."[9] Educational administration does not have to resemble any other kind of administration, although in some instances it may. Therefore, when considering what is fundamental to educational administration, we do not look to the general lessons from research on organizations that are not primarily educational. Instead, we attempt to focus on the fundamental administrative concerns that arise from the work of educating young people.

Educational administration, however intense its focus on teaching and learning, is nevertheless different from classroom teaching. Classroom teachers have traditionally focused on the teaching of a specific academic discipline or on the teaching of several academic subjects to a specific group of children. Teachers kept this more constricted focus because their daily activities required them to deal, not with the problems of the whole school, but with teaching certain youngsters particular material. More recently, teachers' involvement in the restructuring of schools has come to be seen as essential. Hence partnerships are being forged between administrators and teachers as both groups become involved in reinventing schools.

Administrators must constantly think of the education of the whole community of youngsters in the school. This requires them to think of the scope and sequence of all of the learning activities occurring in the school, not simply as a collection of activities, but as activities that comprise a unity, a balance, and a harmony, activities that make up a fitting education for human beings living in *this* moment of history, in *this* society, who are preparing for a challenging and demanding future. Administrators need to engage teachers in discussing these larger issues. Undoubtedly, there will be times when teachers become leaders in these discussions. In other words, the administrator needs to think about and discuss with teachers what it means to be an educated person, and to have some sense of how all the activities of the school are nurturing the growth of youngsters toward becoming educated persons.

I believe that an *educated person* is a person who tries to understand, appreciate, critique, and participate in his or her culture, traditions, and history. Such a person is also one who can participate in the public life of the community, who understands the political and social mechanism by which the community governs itself, and who handles the necessities of everyday life competently. The definition of an educated person, however, will be historically and culturally conditioned: A young woman growing up in seventeenth-century Japan would be judged an educated person by criteria quite different from those used to judge the son of a patrician growing up in Athens in 400 B.C. The persons responsible for the education of youth in those cultures would have had an idea of what the culture and the political community required of an educated person and would have commissioned various teachers and artisans to provide instruction in the required subjects and skills.

THE LARGER VIEW OF LEARNING

Similarly, an educational administrator today, working with the school board and the school district officers, is expected to have a larger sense of what constitutes an educated person and to bring this perspective to the task of coordinating and harmonizing the various separate areas of learning. Although teachers are expected to have a detailed understanding of specific learnings in their curriculum areas, administrators are supposed to bring the work of individual teachers into balance and unity by coordinating the varied activities of the youngsters during the years they spend in school. For example, one might expect that an educated person in twenty-first-century America would have an understanding of the natural environment and of the importance of national and international policies enacted to protect this environment from excessive exploitation and deterioration. Hence an educational administrator would be concerned that, in various science and social studies courses offered in the school curriculum, such understandings would be nurtured, even though he or she might not know at what specific moment in any given course such considerations should be raised. Similarly, one might expect that educated persons in twenty-first-century America would have developed an appreciation of the cultural diversity of the region in which they were raised, and would have some understanding of the history and culture of communities that are culturally different from their own. Thus an educational administrator would be concerned that, in a variety of classes and extracurricular activities, multicultural sensitivity would be developed, even though the administrator might not know how to bring about such sensitivity in every particular instance.

From the teacher's perspective, we could say that the teacher has a large sense of what youngsters in a particular course are supposed to be learning, and also a wide variety of learning activities by which the youngsters can arrive at those learnings. One might say that each teacher, after a few years of teaching, carries the course in his or her head. Educational administrators, however, must carry around in their heads the whole school's learning agenda as an integrated and harmonious unity. One might say that a concert violinist carries the violin score of the symphony in his or her head, but that the conductor must carry the whole symphony in his or her head, so that the playing of the various instruments can be integrated. Such an analogy helps explain the difference between the consciousness of the administrator and that of the teacher. The analogy appears to illuminate the difficulty of the administrator's task when we think of the individual musicians not as the teachers but as the students who are just beginning to learn to play the various instruments. The administrator has to have some sense of how learning scales is an appropriate step in learning to play a symphony and, indeed, that both teachers and students need to keep the playing of the symphony in mind as they learn the mechanics of the instrument or the first simple melodies. It is the vision of what all individual learning activities, linked together and intertwined over the course of several years, are intended to produce that educators must remember. This vision includes the gradual emergence of mature, autonomous, intelligent, moral, and caring human beings, who will comprise a community full of promise for the future.

While keeping in mind the ideal of the *educated person* who understands the history and traditions of the community and is prepared to participate fully in the public life of the community, the administrator will realize that few youngsters will ever achieve the full and harmonious balance of understandings and skills contained in the ideal. Youngsters bring individual talents and liabilities with them to school. They have different interests and abilities, and different learning styles.[10] Teachers struggle to bring children to a minimal level of mastery in many areas, yet they will find that individual youngsters will perform better on some tasks than on others, and their readiness for some tasks differs from their readiness for other tasks. Some youngsters will come from homes where English is not spoken, and hence their learning activities may have to be structured to take this into account. Some youngsters may come from dysfunctional home environments, and thus their educational program may have to be supplemented with other support services. In other words, educators have to look at the total condition of the children and respond to it. They have to see that their ideal of an educated person is always contextualized by the youngsters being served. The symphony may not be Mozart's; for now it might be a symphony in fingerpaint, or the symphony of a child learning for the first time how to play with other children. In every instance, the educator must work with whatever the youngster brings to the learning situation, but the educator must never stop believing that each child is capable of something wonderful and heroic, and that he or she will never exhaust his or her possibilities.

THE CRITICAL IMPORTANCE OF EDUCATIONAL ADMINISTRATION

Besides understanding the uniqueness of educational administration, it is important to grasp the present challenges facing persons who would be educational administrators. For the past two decades there have been continual calls for school system reform. These calls for reform and renewal were based on the perceived decline of American competitiveness in the world economy and on the comparative test score summaries of students from various countries around the world. American students were far behind students from Asia and Europe in their knowledge of science and mathematics, according to results of standardized tests.[11] Industrialists complained of a shortage of literate and motivated workers. Economists pointed to the mediocre products that American companies produced in contrast with similar products from Japan and Europe. Despite differing cultures and differences in the way students were tracked throughout their school years, sweeping judgments on the inadequacies of U.S. schools were made. Other criticisms were also leveled against the schools, charging that they were functioning according to a model instituted for the industrial age rather than for the information age and the global realities of the twenty-first century. Students were not being prepared for knowledge-intensive work, or for the kind of cooperative teamwork and total quality commitment that emerging industries around the world were demanding.

However fair, intelligent, or distorted these critiques of the school have been is no longer the point. The point is that a massive, sustained effort is under way to renew or transform U.S. school systems. The external demands for a more literate, committed, and technologically sophisticated workforce comprise one source of influence on this effort. Another force for renewal is the awareness in the United States, as in some other countries, that we are fast becoming a multicultural nation in which minority communities are making up significantly larger percentages of the total population. This awareness requires changes in school systems in order to accommodate these communities and to honor cultural differences. It also requires a more mature understanding of community, citizenship, and democratic governance, as well as the education of youngsters in these understandings.

Other changes in perspective are already affecting the way we think about schooling: our view of the student and our view of knowledge. Whereas in the past the teacher was viewed as the primary worker in the school and students were viewed as passive clients who were supposed to do what the teacher told them, now there is much more credence to the view of the student as the primary worker in the school and the teacher as facilitator, coach, and resource person. Since this view of the "student as worker" is relatively new, the full pedagogical and curricular implications have not yet hit the educational community.

The other change is in the way that educators view knowledge. Knowledge is no longer seen as some objective entity out there, independent of a human knower. Rather, knowledge is seen as something that is created by humans—something historically and personally conditioned by the persons and context in which the knowledge is generated.

Both of these changed views point to the importance of learning as the active engagement of students in all the learning activities of the curriculum. Learning involves the students creating knowledge and understanding. Knowledge and understanding are something that students actively make; they are not something that passes into their minds already prepackaged like a can of tomato soup off the shelf of a grocery store; they are the result of the students' activity. This view is far different from the view of the student as a passive recipient of correct information handed to him or her by a teacher employing effective teaching strategies, which deliver the knowledge directly from the scholarly source to the student, uncontaminated by the teacher's or the students' personal histories and the circumstances surrounding the learning activities.

When we put these four influences together—the demand for technological literacy in order to function in the information society, the requirement for multicultural sensitivity and multicultural political literacy, the emphasis on the student as the producer of knowledge, and the recognition of knowledge as the historically contextualized product of human inquiry—then we have the ingredients for a transformation of schooling as we have known it.[12] These four changes in the expectations of schooling offer an agenda for administrative leadership that requires administrators to be authentic educators and to be creative inventors of responsive environments in which such changes can flourish.

This agenda would provide educational administrators with more than enough to do. However, as succeeding chapters show, this agenda is colored by other currents of thought within the larger civic culture—currents of thought that are forcefully affecting the curriculum and management of schools. These currents include the following: the understanding of the environment as the endangered natural habitat of the human race and the need to address environmental public policy; the discussion of schools as centers or hubs of an organized program of social services to families; the growing willingness of states to empower local communities to govern their own schools; the insights of educators who deal with disabled or challenged children concerning the customization of learning programs; the increased clarification of women's ways of knowing and the implications that this has for the learning agenda of the school; the greater understanding of the influence of parents on the education of their children. These influences provide even more potential for a creative transformation of schools.

The ingredients for reform are known, at least in general outline. The political mandate is there. Public opinion seems rather firmly behind school reform. Anyone familiar with large-scale organizational change, however, knows that the transformation of schools, one of the more conservative institutions in society, will require leadership on a broad and continuous scale for at least a generation. Persons at the forefront of these changes will find themselves embroiled in controversy with teachers' unions, with special-interest groups in the community, and with fiscal conservatives who oppose increased spending for schools. The task will require facility in building coalitions, in arbitration and conflict resolution, and in communicating an appealing vision of the human benefits to be derived from changes in the form and substance of schooling.

To exercise leadership in this climate of change will require deep convictions, strong commitments, and clear ideas about directions for changes in the form and content of schooling. There should be no illusions about this. The people leading the way in school transformation must be people who have thought and read their way through the complex issues at stake in school reform. They must be people who see a clear connection between the public program of schooling and the kind of society that will carry the human adventure into the future; that is, they will understand the human and technical challenges that the community faces and will bring the understanding of these challenges to bear on the design of the form and content of the schools they are redesigning.

Aware of the dangers and dysfunction of imposing policy from the top down, future administrators will also realize that their ideas about the shape and content of schooling must be tested in the forum of public debate. Such public debate is often a raucous, contentious, self-interested power struggle. One's bright ideas will be misunderstood, misinterpreted, distorted, ridiculed, and contested. One will be subjected to personal accusations, verbal abuse, betrayals, threats to one's job, and various forms of raw hatred. Through all this, one must attempt to keep people talking about the issues, appealing to people's better side, finding common ground, bargaining for more resources, bringing disparate interests together, and keeping one's dreams and hopes alive, month after month, year after year.

Such a prospect is not for the fainthearted or for the weekend enthusiast.

Rather, it is for people who see the possibility for a better life for children and youth, who dream of a better tomorrow for all members of their society, and who have the inner strength of their convictions and ideals, as well as the humility to know that they need to join themselves to the ideas, talents, and energies of countless others if their hopes and dreams are to be realized. The school administrator of the future will have to have a different mind-set and skills than the status-quo administrator of the past; the dramatic challenges facing schools call for a different kind of vision and commitment. Schools are not served well by people who go into school administration primarily for the increased salary, for the greater prestige and power in the community, or for a heightened sense of self-importance, all the while assuming that schools are more or less fine just the way they are. Those contemplating a career in educational administration need to make a sober assessment of their own talents, motivations, and dispositions for meeting the challenges in educational administration in the twenty-first century. Such an assessment is necessary before rather than after a decision has been taken to become an educational administrator. For those who do choose to pursue such a career, the foundational orientations provided in these chapters will expose them to the exciting possibilities.

ACTIVITIES

1. Write out your understanding of educational administration prior to reading this chapter. Compare your prior understanding with that of your classmates. Does that shared understanding of administration represent what you perceive as standard practice in the workplace?
2. Assume that the view of educational administration present in this chapter is to be used as the basis for standards of hiring and evaluating administrators in the near future. Assess your strengths and shortcomings for success in this kind of educational administration. What does this assessment suggest to you?

ENDNOTES

1. Thomas J. Sergiovanni and Frederick D. Carver, *Organizations and Human Behavior: Focus on Schools,* McGraw-Hill, New York, 1969, p. ix.
2. Frederick Taylor, *The Principles of Scientific Management,* Harper & Row, New York, 1911.
3. Elwood Cubberly, *Public School Administration,* Houghton Mifflin, Boston, 1916.
4. Herbert Simon, *Administrative Behavior*, Macmillan, New York, 1950.
5. Jacob W. Getzels, "A Psychosociological Framework for the Study of Educational Administration," *Harvard Educational Review,* vol. 22, no. 4, 1952, pp. 235–246; Daniel E. Griffiths, *Administrative Theory,* Appleton-Century-Crofts, New York, 1959; Andrew W. Halpin, "A Paradigm for Research on

Administrative Behavior," in R. F. Campbell and R. T. Gregg (eds.), *Administrative Behavior in Education*, Harper & Brothers, New York, 1957, pp. 155–200.

6. Charles E. Lindbloom, "The Science of Muddling Through," *Public Administration Review*, vol. 19, no. 1, 1959, pp. 79–88; Michael D. Cohen, James G. March, and Johann P. Olsen, "A Garbage Can Model of Organizational Choice," *Administrative Science Quarterly*, vol. 17, no. 1, 1972, pp. 1–25.

7. Richard M. Cyert and James G. March, *A Behavioral Theory of the Firm*, Prentice-Hall, Englewood Cliffs, NJ, 1963.

8. Michael W. Apple, *Education and Power*, Routledge & J Kegan Paul, Boston, 1982; Richard J. Bates, "Corporate Culture, Schooling, and Educational Administration," *Educational Administration Quarterly*, vol. 23, no. 4, 1987, pp. 79–115; Henry A. Giroux, "Curriculum Planning, Public Schooling, and Democratic Struggle," *NASSP Bulletin*, vol. 75, no. 532, 1991, pp. 12–25.

9. David E. Purpel, "Introduction," in D. E. Purpel and H. V. Shapiro (eds.), *Schools and Meaning: Essays on the Moral Nature of Schooling*, University Press of America, Lanham, MD, 1985, p. xvii.

10. See the well-developed work of Joseph Renzulli on the theory and practice of enrichment education: Joseph S. Renzulli, "A General Theory for the Development of Creative Productivity through the Pursuit of Ideal Acts of Learning," *Gifted Child Quarterly*, vol. 36, 1992, pp. 26–35.

11. See, however, the commentary by Stedman, who shows that American students rank among the best in reading and literature. His analysis, which should be read by every school board member coming up for election, also points to the influence of nonschool factors on low test scores. Lawrence C. Stedman, "Incomplete Explanations: The Case of U.S. Performance in the International Assessments of Education," *Educational Researcher*, vol. 23, no. 7, 1994, pp. 24–32.

12. Although he deals with these same influences using different sources, Arthur Wirth comes to much the same conclusion; see Arthur Wirth, *Education and Work for the Year 2000*, Jossey-Bass, San Francisco, 1992.

CHAPTER 2

Pathology and Health in School Administration

It is not surprising that educational administrators get a little crazy from time to time. The daily pressures of the job can drive anyone to distraction. The routine of many school administrators involves reacting to one crisis after another—now a drug bust outside the school, announced by three squad cars with flashing lights and wailing sirens; next an angry teacher complaining that someone parked in her parking space; then a parent on the phone complaining about racial prejudice toward her child; and the superintendent on the phone wanting test results that have not arrived as scheduled. Administrators career through the day, responding to demands, complaints, injuries, deadlines, and meetings that somehow never resolve the problems they were called to address.

Beyond the daily crisis management, there are the larger questions of purpose and accountability. Schools are supposed to serve multiple purposes, from teaching the basics of language and science and math to bringing about racial harmony, controlling childish impulses, solving the drug crisis, teaching good manners, preparing workers to keep America competitive in world markets, responding to the multicultural needs of their constituents, preventing violence within the school, keeping youngsters in school, communicating care and respect for children while at the same time giving failing marks and forcing them to repeat a grade, and most of all, ensuring that all the children can get into the top colleges. When one of these purposes is seen as not being achieved, it is the principal's fault. The public and the media say that administrators and teachers should be held accountable for improving the quality of learning in their classes. Usually this demand translates into raising the children's scores on standardized achievement tests, even though numerous research studies have shown that teaching to these tests has little to do with genuine student learning.[1] It is the principal who is held accountable for not keeping the teachers accountable to public demands. When anything goes wrong at the school, the public, the teachers, and the superintendent all assume that the principal is to blame. Rather early on the job, principals start to believe all this.

Even though there may be twenty, forty, and even eighty professional staff members in the school, with an additional six to twelve support staff—any of whom can make a mess of things at any given moment of the day—the expectation is that if the principal was *really* doing his or her job, messes would not happen. Despite the fact that perhaps half the student body does not particularly want to be in school on any given day, the principal is held to blame for student truancy and misbehavior: "If the principal were in charge, these things wouldn't happen here."

Moreover, the principal is blamed no matter which set of purposes he or she supports. If there is a high academic press in the school, the principal is criticized for overemphasizing academics to the detriment of other developmental social goals of the school. If the principal pursues greater involvement of the school in the socialization of youngsters, then the principal is faulted for neglecting academic achievement. If the principal strictly enforces the rules, he is a dictator; if he allows mitigating circumstances to soften the punishment for breaking a rule, he is a lax disciplinarian. The same principal is criticized for efforts to be sensitive to various ethnic and racial communities and for not being sensitive enough. Principals receive, simultaneously, praise and condemnation for encouraging a whole-language approach to reading and writing. Maintaining ability grouping and tracking is interpreted as serving the goals of equal educational opportunity or as opposing the very same goal.

Principals will always be subjected to criticisms, many of them contradictory. It is the nature of the job. When principals attempt to respond to every criticism they receive, they end up being caught in a frenzy of reactionary activity. The principal's job is steeped in ambiguity and unrealistic expectations. It is normal for most principals to feel uncertain and defensive in the face of this ambiguity and pressure. No one wants to be seen as a bungler, or incompetent, or stupid, either by superiors or by subordinates. We all try to create, as the Italians would say, a "bella figura," to exude a sense of confidence in our physical carriage, to offer a vague response with the appropriate furrowing of the eyebrows and touch of the shoulder. We put on a performance for those around us, a performance whose underlying message is: "I know what I'm doing; things are really under control; this is no big problem; not to worry, help is on the way." Even when we can focus on the essentials of the job, we are often faced with a small but messy problem that has no immediate solution. So we fudge our response and hope it will disappear by tomorrow, and carry on with what we think is the important work in front of us. Most conscientious principals will admit at the end of a busy day that there are still a dozen or more problems needing immediate attention, but that there simply is not enough time right now to deal with them. These problems are added to the next day's list, even though the principal knows that he or she will be lucky to deal with two of them by the end of the next day.

ADMINISTRATIVE PATHOLOGIES

What happens to some administrators, unfortunately, is that they develop unhealthy ways to cope with the pressure and the ambiguity. I shall exaggerate somewhat by labeling these unhealthy ways a "complex" or a "syndrome."

Thus, one can point to a power-wielding syndrome in some administrators. These persons, unsure of themselves and afraid to let others see their weaknesses, try to dominate and control others by asserting power over them. They use the authority of their position, subtly or explicitly, to threaten sanctions and public criticism of those who work with them in order to get them to do what they want. In an effort to cover up their own feelings of inferiority, they adopt an attitude of superiority, giving the impression that others are inferior in intelligence, judgment, or drive. Having people do their bidding feeds their need for power, makes them feel in control, and validates their sense of superiority.

Such power-wielding administrators are sick. They sometimes appeal to the sickness in their subordinates, a sickness that prefers an authority figure to make decisions for them. Healthy, adult professionals, on the other hand, want to have the discretion to make decisions on the job. That is what being a professional means: that you possess the expertise to respond to the client in this particular circumstance in ways that will be helpful. The professional's response is based on some diagnosis of need as contextualized by the present circumstances. Administrators removed from the immediacy of the circumstances cannot decide for the professional on the line what should be done. The power-wielding principal creates alienation and frustration among healthy, professional teachers on the staff. If they accept his demands, they may end up doing the wrong thing for the students. Students will resist and thus frustrate the very compulsion to control which drives the power wielder. If teachers do not accede to his demands, but pretend that they do (which is often the case), then again, the need to dominate and control will be frustrated.

Other principals exude what I call the "superfather" or "supermother" syndrome. This is a controlling compulsion covered over with smiles and warm fuzzies. These principals act like loving parents toward their children, making sure that the children are given clear instructions about what they are to do, making sure that they will stay out of harm's way, stepping in to fix something when a child makes a mistake, and protecting the child from outside criticism. These principals need to be needed. They do not know what to do when teachers go about their business with efficiency and dispatch without first checking with the principal to see if they are doing it right. Such principals try to keep teachers dependent on them for their feelings of self-worth. They often arrange parties and hand out awards to good teachers, especially to those who have listened to their advice, who check out their ideas with the principal first. Such "parenting" may be helpful to a first-year teacher, but the longer it keeps the teacher dependent, the longer it will take the teacher to grow into a mature professional.

Some principals exhibit a hyperrational complex. These principals have constructed the school in their own minds as a perfectly rational system. The goals of the school are clearly spelled out. Student outcomes are defined in measurable terms. Appropriate teacher interventions, described in the research literature as effecting these outcomes, are mandated. Teacher evaluation schemes are tied to evidence of the use of these teacher protocols. Staff development programs are designed around these protocols. Thus, the school is a rational system of ends and means, tied to rational ways of evaluating how well the means produce the ends, and to schemes for increasing the production of the desired ends. Such a system is supposed to guarantee maximum predictability and control. It is tidy, neat, and efficient. Memos from the principal carry the logic of this rational system. The expectation is that teachers and students will cooperate by functioning rationally within the system.

The problem is that teachers, students, and parents have other goals besides the achievement of the preordained learning outcomes the system establishes. They have affiliative needs, recreational needs, economic needs, and personal interests different from the prescribed focus of the school. Furthermore, the prescribed teacher protocols are too limited to apply to every child's learning style and interests in each classroom. Not every child is ready to learn the prescribed curriculum on every day or in every week. Teachers may need to attend to the emotional upset of a child who is experiencing difficulty at home. The hyperrational principal has no sympathy for these deviations from the preordained schedule. These variations do not fit into the teacher evaluation criteria and students whose interests do not coincide with the curriculum must be judged as failures.

Granted that the previous descriptions are exaggerated, the stereotypes can help us to realize that various forms of psychopathology may be present in the behavior of school administrators. As a professor in a graduate school of education, I never cease to be amazed by the stories my students tell me about administrators in their school systems. I find it hard to believe that school boards and superintendents tolerate such behavior, but often the pathology has been there for many years. Most veteran teachers can point to more than one administrator in their experience whose actions were immature, childish, or even pathological.

The moral is that administrators should know themselves well. With even a little candid self-reflection, most of us can recognize how we engage in small subterfuges, rationalizations, denials, and distortions to make ourselves appear in the right and other people in the wrong. One part of us is always at the back of our heads editing the tape of our present experience as it unfolds, offering a self-congratulatory and self-serving commentary on what is happening. We cover over a careless comment, a stupid mistake, perhaps even a really mean wisecrack with rationalizations such as "He provoked me," "She had it coming," or "Had I known *that*, I never would have done it." We protect ourselves from seeing our faults by these defenses; we make excuses for ourselves; we do not want to admit that there are times when we are not nice, when we are stupid, when we are boring or unlovely, or unconcerned for the feelings of others. We would be ashamed if people really saw us that way. We are afraid, in short, of not measuring up to our own and other people's expectations. We all need to feel good about ourselves, and in order to feel good about ourselves we distort our experience to make ourselves look good.

It is important to realize that everyone does this. This is healthy behavior, although of course the definition of *health* may be quite elastic in this context.[2] More mature persons come to admit their shortcomings more freely, especially if they have experienced unconditional love from someone else, someone who knows their faults and loves them nevertheless. The problem is not that we have these faults, or that we cover them up. The problem arises with the intensity and absoluteness of the coverup. In other words, as long as self-deception is relatively mild, it does not prevent us from experiencing reality in any major way. It is still perceivable by us, especially when we see ourselves as a character in a comedy.

I used to love Jackie Gleason's portrayal of the character Ralph Kramden, because I could see myself and others I knew doing the same foolish things Ralph did. The television show *All in the Family* also helped us to appreciate the outrageous ways we treat one another. A relative of mine whom I knew to be a racial bigot told me that his friends at work had started calling him "Archie Bunker." This led him to start watching *All in the Family*, where he recognized himself in the words and actions of Archie Bunker. He confided, however, that "Hey, I'm bad, but not *that* bad."

The problem with the power wielder or the hyperrationalist is that his or her distortion of reality is so absolute that it causes real harm to others. Such people cause others to adopt defensive strategies to protect themselves. Often these protective strategies detract severely from the work at hand. Sometimes a sick administrator can force both teachers and students to leave the school.

MAINTAINING PERSPECTIVE/ MAINTAINING HEALTH

Every school administrator needs to adopt measures for maintaining perspective, which is necessary for maintaining mental and emotional health. Space and time are key resources for maintaining perspective. Simply getting away for a few days provides the spatial distance to disentangle the small annoyances from the major issues. Taking time to reflect on our behavior and people's reactions to us may enable clarity about motives to surface. Feedback from others is also helpful. A trusted confidant can help us evaluate our behavior on the job. Another way is to ask for an outside evaluation of our performance by a neutral party. Some principals ask their teachers to fill out anonymous evaluation surveys every year in order to get a reading on the teachers' perceptions of the principal's performance.

Spending some time every month or two in self-reflection enables us to get in touch with what we are afraid of, what drives us, and what fulfills us. We need to be able to read ourselves, especially in situations of crisis or of stress. We need to take soundings of our feelings and uncover what is making us feel stressed or uneasy or afraid. Often an unattended intuition will be lying right below the surface of our awareness and will be causing some feeling of discomfort; sometimes a pause, a one-minute break from the matter before us, will allow the intuition to come to the surface.

THE SELF AS TOOL

Arthur Blumberg suggests that we ourselves are our primary tool in our craft of administration.[3] Our sensitivity to issues, our ability to carry around the whole school in our head, our ability to remember events from last week and see their connection to present events, our ability to be patient with the shortcomings of others, our ability to read the unspoken messages of parents and teachers, and our ability to see the connection of the present decision to the long-range plan—all these enable us to become this "primary tool" of our craft. If we keep that tool fine-tuned, we can serve the school well. If we know that tool well—its blind spots, its sore points, its biases, its dreams—we can deal with the matter in front of us with a minimum of unintended distortion.

THE SELF AS FILTER

Administrators need to understand that in every person's apprehension of reality there will always be distortion. The self is inescapably involved in interpretation. Our experiences are always being interpreted through language, custom, world view, personal beliefs, the pressures of present circumstances, and so on. We are historical persons. How we perceive the world, the very categories we use to name things, are given to us by our culture and our traditions.[4] Were we born in Tahiti in the twelfth century, we would interpret our experience quite differently than we do as contemporary Americans. Even the term "cold war" carries different connotations for us now than it did twenty years ago. Our history has changed; hence our view of the world has changed.

The self is always a filter; we gain a feel for the moment, a hunch about what the problem really is, an intuition about a course of action. We look at a piece of the reality in front of us and see it according to certain categories, metaphors, and perspectives; we see the details or we see the whole *gestalt*. What we apprehend in front of us puts us in touch with that reality, but what we apprehend simultaneously prevents us from apprehending another aspect of that reality at the same time. Every "reality" is multidimensional, and we usually perceive it under one dimension or another. If perception is always and necessarily partial for healthy people, then for those whose distortion of reality is deeper and more intense, the apprehension of reality will be even more limited. The defensive person, the fearful person, and the compulsive person will interpret their experience in ever more distorted ways. If we know our fears, our biases, and our compulsions, we can check the impulse to go with the first interpretation.

School administrators need to practice both an interpretation of trust and an interpretation of suspicion. An interpretation of trust attempts to find out what really happened. We trust that we can find the facts if we keep asking the right questions and following the rules of evidence. For example, a student with a discipline problem may be expressing anger over a poor self-image, or over parental abuse at home, or may simply have a problem with impulse control. The interpretation of trust assumes that the principal, the student, and the parent(s) can come to some meaningful interpretation of the problem, which will point in the direction of an appropriate solution or response to the problem.

An interpretation of suspicion assumes that sometimes the problem is much deeper, that the very language we use to frame the problem may be inappropriate or even self-serving. Freud practiced an interpretation of suspicion. He believed that people's actions often concealed a much deeper problem with their sexuality. Marx practiced an interpretation of suspicion. He believed that all of social life was a reflection of people's relations to the means of production, and that Western politics was a cloak for maintaining the economic status quo. Much of what can be called "postmodern sensibility" is based on an interpretation of suspicion, namely, that modernity's claims to rationality, progress through science, and history as the charting of the development of the human race have all proved bankrupt.

A more general practice of the interpretation of suspicion assumes that every interpretation will probably be distorted, that self-interest will unwittingly enter into *my own* as well as the other's interpretation of events. By "suspicion" I do not mean that I suspect the other person of malicious intent. Rather, I may have to look more deeply into the cultural assumptions behind my definition of the event, because my interpretation may be driven by a distorting ideology, and these assumptions may prevent a genuine interpretation of the event.

These considerations of administrative pathologies and everyday distortions of perceptions pose a critical challenge to administrators: namely, that we seek to probe the values and philosophical assumptions we bring to the job of running a school. We all are victimized by our ideologies, whether they be of the left, right or middle. We need to know what we stand for, and to ask whether we are ready to take responsibility for all the assumptions we make about schooling. This challenge calls us to an intellectual depth and to a critical moral stance with ourselves. To avoid this challenge puts us in danger of growing comfortable using the distorted interpretations we bring to events as an excuse for intellectual and moral indifference.

ADMINISTRATION AS AUTOBIOGRAPHY

Administration is autobiography. This is both good news and bad news. The bad news is that we tend to impose our neuroses on others, either through projecting or through acting out our distorted interpretation of events. The good news is that, at our best, we live as authentic human beings in our work. We write our history—though not all of it, to be sure—in our work. We take our place on the public stage of history in our work. We make our special contribution to the lives of others through our work. One way or another, we achieve our destiny through our work. Even with all our limitations, we achieve much of our human fulfillment in our work. This fulfillment comes as we give our best selves to the work in service to others.

From another perspective, administration is all relationships. The work of administration requires working with and through others. At its best it requires genuine working relationships, relationships of trust, openness, inclusion, flexibility, patience, compassion, caring, and laughter. In other words, the work of educational administration is human work; it requires a level of self-giving and relational cooperation that few other jobs require. From this perspective, everyone needs to grow and develop beyond defensiveness and insecurity to a fuller human involvement with others in the school community.

Studies of women in administration have enlightened us on this score.[5] As more and more women become school administrators and enter the professorate in school administration, this emphasis on authentic relationships, inclusion, involvement, and shared responsibility may not seem so foreign in a textbook on the fundamentals of educational administration.[6]

SUMMARY

In this chapter we see how important self-knowledge is to the work of school administration. The stress and ambiguities of the job can easily encourage defensive behavior. When the stress brings out insecurities in administrators, it can lead to pathological behavior. Keeping in touch with what drives and motivates us can enable us to avoid the sickness that besets some administrators.

The work of administration involves interpreting the daily events in the school. Interpretations need to be checked for accuracy. Again, administrators need to guard themselves from snap decisions based on distorted interpretations by opening up the decision-making process to the perceptions and interpretations of others, especially of those most affected by the decision.

Finally, we saw how the work of administration can be seen as a way of composing an autobiography. Many of the chapters of our life will be written in the work we do in education. That is where we will find our fulfillment, and make our contribution to the betterment of children's lives.

ACTIVITIES

1. Review your behavior on the job for the past three working days. Were there times when you reacted to people angrily or derisively? Were there times when you cut corners on your own standards for quality work? Were there simply some aspects of your workdays that you are not proud of? How did you rationalize your behavior when you did not act up to your own high standards? Is there a pattern of this?
2. Ask a colleague with whom you have a good relationship to point out one area where you could improve. How do you feel about your colleague's response?
3. Identify three examples of administrative pathology in your workplace. How do people in the workplace deal with each of these pathologies? Is there anything that can be done to improve the situation?
4. Identify three examples of administrative health. How do people respond to being treated this way? Is there anything that can be done to improve on these already healthy practices?

5. Devise a reasonable, simple plan to maintain your perspective as an administrator, including strategies for increasing self-knowledge.

ENDNOTES

1. See Linda McNeil, *Contradictions of Control*, Routledge, New York, 1988.
2. An excellent treatment of this issue is to be found in the work of Ernest Becker; see Ernest Becker, *The Birth and Death of Meaning*, 2d ed., The Free Press, New York, 1971.
3. Arthur Blumberg, *Administration as Craft*, Longmans, New York, 1989.
4. See the excellent treatment of this theme in Edward A. Shills, *Tradition*, University of Chicago Press, Chicago, 1981.
5. See Helen Astin and Carole Leland, *Women of Influence, Women of Vision*, Jossey-Bass, San Francisco, 1991; Sally Helgesen, *The Female Advantage: Women's Ways of Leadership*, Doubleday Currency, New York, 1990.
6. Two recent books by women professors of education bring a different perspective to the management of schools. See Lyn Beck's *Reclaiming Educational Administration as a Caring Profession*, Teachers College Press, New York, 1994; and Nel Noddings' *The Challenge to Care in Schools*, Teachers College Press, New York, 1992.

PART TWO

Administering Meaning

In this part we take up the first fundamental of educational administration, administering meaning. Schools have as their primary purpose the promotion of learning. Some of this learning involves memorizing information; we call this *superficial* or *surface learning*. Learning that involves understanding and insight is involved with meaning, with grasping relationships between the knower and the known, and between previously known and newly known. This kind of learning involves a making of *meaning*. Students are meaning makers. They invest their world with meaning. Human experience is continuously transformed as it becomes meaning-full, as it takes on significance.

Schools are supposed to stimulate the young to discover meaning in their world, in the world of nature, the world of human affairs, and the world of human relationships. Administrators are supposed to see that their schools intentionally nurture this process of discovering and making meaning, bringing students beyond the generation of superficial knowledge that is memorized in order to score well on tests. The meanings of nature, the meanings of the world of human affairs, and the meanings of human relationships fit into large patterns, which we call *world views*. These large patterns of meanings are embedded in cultures and are passed on in traditional habits of thinking that can censure and inhibit the creation of new meanings.

Educational administrators, working in tandem with their teachers, need to explore what meanings the school promotes, what meanings the school inhibits or censures, and what meanings are simply not considered. This task is, as we shall see, an enormously challenging one, but one which cannot be set aside by administrators. It is fundamental to their work as educators.

CHAPTER 3

Administering Meaning

In Chapter 1 we saw that school renewal is being influenced by four major issues: (1) concern for technological literacy in order to function effectively in the information society; (2) concern for multicultural understanding and multicultural political literacy; (3) concern for the student's active participation in the production of knowledge; and (4) appreciation of knowledge as an historically contextualized product of human inquiry serving human interests. All these issues implicate the school, for better or worse, in the administration of meaning. Technological literacy implies mastering the accessing and processing of information into meaningful propositions or inferences. Multicultural literacy implies understanding what things mean within a culture not our own, and constructing meaningful bridges between cultures that both honor differences and facilitate public discourse and public action. For students to produce knowledge, they must be able to posit that knowledge in meaningful frameworks or use it for meaningful interpretations of some aspect of reality. Knowledge as an historically contextualized human product implies that the teaching of that knowledge requires understanding of the historical and cultural context for the knowledge to be meaningful.

In this chapter we address some of the problems and possibilities in the administering of meaning. In so doing we touch upon some of the most difficult and profound issues involved in schooling. For many readers the task of administering meaning may begin to seem impossible. The chapter ends, however, with the development of a foundational position from which educational administrators can approach the administration of meaning. Subsequent chapters explore additional problems and possibilities in the administering of meaning. To begin, let us consider some definitions.

THE MEANING OF MEANING

Since we use the term *meaning* in several ways, it will help to know what we mean by meaning. Meaning can refer to what we want to convey, especially by language. Hence one can say, "What I meant by that remark was that I disagree strongly with your politics, even though I like you as a person." Meaning also refers to a person's intention in saying or doing something, when the saying or the doing has a symbolic or unspoken meaning. Thus, "It was clear to those present that he meant to humiliate the student in front of the principal." Another use of the term *meaning* refers to the denotation or connotation of words. Thus people ask, "What does the word *hermeneutics* mean?" or "What do teenagers mean when they say, 'That's cool.'?" Under other circumstances we use the term *meaning* to signify that something was significant, that it carried some symbolic content for us. Thus we say, "I found a deep meaning in the preacher's sermon."

In this chapter the term *meaning* refers to the cultural and personal meanings that are attached to or embedded in what students learn in school. Thus the social studies teacher may pose the questions, "What does the welfare system mean to you?" "How do you make sense of the American Civil War?" "Whose side would you have been on in the national debate over the Vietnam War?" "What does Newton's theory of gravity mean in the practical, day-to-day matters of your life?" "What does a free-market economy mean to a banking executive as opposed to what it means for an out-of-work coal miner?" All of those questions go beyond asking for factual information. They explicitly ask for a point of view, an interpretation, a placing of the topic in a perspective of some kind, relating it to some sense of values. That framework for meaning can be derived from the culture, from the study of other scholarly commentaries, as well as from personal experience.

A point of view can be absorbed without reflection from one's culture. Sometimes personal history colors one's experience, sometimes the perspective is dominated by one frame of reference—for example, an economic explanation of the Civil War or a Marxist interpretation of the welfare system.

Teachers' questions also ask for pieces of information. However, even in "factual matters," facts are described or explained by using frameworks of meaning. Hence one might respond to the question about the welfare system above that it is one way in which the state redistributes wealth. Another answer might be that it is the way the state keeps poor people in a condition of dependency. Both responses are "factual," but their factualness is established by larger frames of meaning.

In some instances, the meaning may derive from something personal. The historical reality of slavery means something different to a descendent of slaves than it does to a person whose descendents were never enslaved, even though both persons might "know" the same facts about the slave trade in the sixteenth century. The notion of sexual harassment means something different to someone who has experienced it than it does to someone who has not, even though both might give the same dictionary definition of it. Does this mean that one can understand the meaning of something only if one "experiences" it? No. Meanings attain a kind of public status that most people understand, even though each individual's understanding will also contain unique colorations and intensities. Thus, meanings have a public status and a personal status.

One can study what certain actions or rituals or symbols mean to people of a different culture and come to some understanding of their meanings. That understanding, however, will not normally have the depth and richness of meaning that it will have to someone from that culture.[1] Anthropologists who immerse themselves in a culture may come closest to that depth of understanding, but even anthropologists will confess that their understanding never fully grasps the deepest meanings of the cultural phenomena of the people they study.

It seems fair to say that people of a common culture can come to some public agreement about what words and symbols and gestures and natural objects mean. This is normally referred to as what those words, symbols, gestures, and natural objects *denote.* Thus, in certain English-speaking locales, a sign bearing the letters "W.C." denotes a public toilet, although a foreigner might not get the connection between the literal translation of *water closet* and a toilet. In the United States, the word *bathroom* carries the same denotation, although a foreigner who comes from a culture where the toilet is always separated from the bathing area might find the term confusing. Symbols inscribed on traffic signs are supposed to denote a univocal meaning to everyone, giving them directions on how to proceed. Numbers attached to grocery items denote the same price for everyone. Terms such as *due process, a binding contract, liability,* and *felony* denote precise meanings, especially for lawyers; such terms will soon enough come to have precise meanings for those who might need a lawyer. Terms such as weight, mass, velocity, bacteria, nervous system, immune system, crystals, acids, carcinogens, toxic waste, biodegradables, biosphere, taxes, profit, and insurance all have public meanings or cultural denotations. Clearly, schools are concerned with helping youngsters acquire these and a host of other public meanings, without mastery of which it will be difficult to engage in public life.

Words, symbols, gestures, and natural objects also carry additional meanings that color, shape, nuance, distort, elevate, or in some way add to the denoted meaning, the public meaning. This is the *connotative* meaning, which relates what is publicly signified to additional personal associations. Although some hypothetical persons who operate in a purely rational and logical fashion might apprehend the world only according to its denotations, most human beings develop a rich and complex web of connotative meanings associated with words, symbols, gestures, and natural objects. Psychologists play word-association games with patients to understand the affect they attach to objects or persons or experiences in their lives. Poets employ images rich in connotation to convey their meaning. Politicians utilize, for better or worse, language and phrases that carry undercurrents of coded meaning for their followers. At a seemingly more prosaic level, ordinary conversations between ordinary people carry rich and complex patterns of meanings associated with experiences, persons, and objects, and a language of metaphor, intonation, and inflection that punctuates those meanings. Listen in on a conversation between two people sitting behind you on a train, or sit at a bar and listen to the stories and interpretations expressed, and you will hear layers of connotative meanings riding on the denotative meanings that people attach to experiences. It will also become

clear that the connotative meanings often control or influence people's interpretations of events as well as their subsequent actions and decisions.

MEANING AND REALITY

One of the basic questions about meaning is its relationship to reality. Does the
meaning something has for us correspond to the reality of that something?
Were the meanings attached to American military interventions in Nicaragua,
Panama, Iraq, Somalia, and Haiti in correspondence with the realities of those
particular historical events? Most historians would say that, after all available
documentary and evidential sources have been considered, the historian tries
to provide an interpretation of what happened that is consistent with the cumulative record of evidence. Often, however, the sources themselves represent
interpretations by various witnesses of what happened and why it happened.
That is why history is always being rewritten, and why there will probably
never be a definitive history of any event.

The history of science, though shorter in time than the history of writing
history, illustrates this perpetual rewriting. Science gradually builds a clearer
body of knowledge, with each succeeding generation of scientists correcting the
errors and misinterpretations of its predecessors. Hence the meaning of scientific discoveries is constantly undergoing reinterpretation as new information,
new metaphors, and new frames of reference are developed.

In the field of literature, the arguments over meaning have perhaps reached
their extreme limits. Does the text of the author correspond to some reality
about human life beyond the text? Or is the text simply a revelation of the author's interior fantasy? Are all the characters "merely" a reflection of the author's own multiple personalities? Is the text, however, simply a reflection of
the social history of the time, reflecting prevailing attitudes toward commerce,
tradition, sex, war, nature, suffering, and a transcendent Being? Perhaps the text
does not even have an independent meaning of its own, but rather has meaning only within the mind of the reader. This later position places the reader as
the constructor or reconstructor or deconstructor of the text. The author's text
is simply material out of which readers make sense for themselves. Where, in
other words, is the text? Is the meaning of Joyce's *Portrait of the Artist as a Young
Man* to be found in the social realities of the Dublin of Joyce's day? Is it in
Joyce's interior battle with himself and his demons? Is it in the reader's reconstruction of Joyce's reconstruction of the social and religious realities of Dublin?
Is it in the reader's critical deconstruction of Joyce's story? Or is the meaning
somehow to be found at all of these levels of composition? Scriptural theologians ask similar questions about sacred texts.

The social sciences have been going through their own epistemological up-
heaval. Social scientists have questioned how much of social science is "real"
science, in the sense that the natural sciences such as physics and biology are
"real" sciences. Are social sciences, like the natural sciences, able to explain ob-

jective regularities in societies? Is social science able, in the process of reducing social phenomena to a few univocal variables such as class or power or gender, to explain those social phenomena objectively, or does the reduction cause distortion to the point of misrepresentation? Over the past thirty years the attempt to reduce social and human phenomena to quantifiable measures has increasingly come under attack, not only from philosophers and humanists, but from social scientists themselves.[2]

Social scientists argue whether a country's statistics on its gross national product count for more than a country's artistic production; whether a country's industrialization should count more than a country's agricultural base; whether urban life is better than village life.[3]

We see this argument carried on in the field of education itself, between educators who organize their educational programs to produce higher scores on standardized tests of basic competencies, and educators who propose a more "authentic" form of assessment tied to the local curriculum and more responsive to complex and multiform learning tasks. Educational research that attempts to measure statistically the impact of specific teacher protocols on learning tends to reduce teaching to decontextualized, uniform behaviors. This research is rejected by others, who argue that thick descriptive narratives of one classroom reveal more truth about effective teaching than a statistical study of several hundred teachers.

Thirty years ago it was generally taken for granted in the social sciences that, through the study of psychology, economics, sociology, and political science, we could understand how society and human beings work and therefore through social policy construct a social environment that worked better. These assumptions are now being questioned.

Moreover, there are serious scholars who propose that the social sciences have been used to serve, not the interests of science, but the interests of ideologies and power centers. These scholars argue that the production of knowledge through the social sciences has intentionally or unintentionally served political purposes while posing as objective scientific endeavors.[4] Some among these scholars do not object to social science serving political purposes, as long as those purposes are established by accepted policy decisions governed by constitutionally legitimate procedures.

The picture that emerges in all the intellectual disciplines is a search for a meaningful framework that will help us interpret the human condition, guide the application of what we know, and illuminate the moral implications of our knowledge. Such searchings seem to be fueled by an awareness that the uses of knowledge in public life, as well as the knowledge itself, require a framework of meaning that is intimately tied to questions of what it means to be a human being in today's world, what a good society consists of, and what are our mutual responsibilities to the creation of such a society.[5]

Although it is hazardous to quote a public figure as an authority, Hillary Rodham Clinton, the wife of the President of the United States, seemed to be engaged in 1993 in the same search. In the first year of her husband's presidency she spoke of a nation crippled by alienation, despair, and hopelessness, a nation in the throes of a crisis of meaning. "What do our governmental institutions mean? What do our lives in today's world mean?" she asks. "What does it mean in today's world to pursue not only vocations, to be part of institutions, but to be human?"[6] These questions illustrate the quest and the quandary of contemporary America. People seek for some large purpose to their lives, yet they are suspicious of those who propose such a purpose in a world populated by charlatans and gurus of questionable credentials.

MEANING IN THE CLASSROOM

Teachers in their day-to-day work administer the acquisition of meaning. Although they do not control the meanings their youngsters will discover, accept, or create, they may strongly influence those meanings. What assumptions do teachers make about what is meaningful and where and how meaning is to be found? That, it seems, is an essential question all educators need to ask: What is a meaningful interpretation of contemporary human society, one that on the one hand offers hope, and on the other hand owns up to the failed promises of modernity? Various interpretations are offered through the media, through popular culture, through the radical left and the extreme right. Do schools attempt a credible answer? Do they at least attempt to help students study the questions?

For an unreflective educator, what is meaningful is what is in the syllabus and the curriculum guides. Why it is meaningful is a question that hardly crosses his mind. If someone were to ask, the answer would probably be: "Well, the central office curriculum coordinators have determined what has to be learned, so that must be what is meaningful." A more reflective educator might respond: "Well, these learnings are what the experts in the field have determined to be most important. Science experts, historians, literary scholars, and so on have said that these understandings should be considered the essential and necessary scientific, historical, and literary understandings. Publishers consult these experts and translate their understandings into textbook chapters or course units, and our central office, or our departments, buy the textbooks."

Textbooks rarely, however, give a sense of the debates and uncertainties about where and how meaning and purpose is to be found. On the contrary, they tend to simplify the world of science and history and literature into "beliefs about the way things are."[7] There seems to be an underlying assumption of most textbook authors that: (1) there is *a* right answer; (2) they know the right answers; (3) they know how to bring children to learn these right answers; and (4) these right answers will help the children in their education and in the rest of their lives.

Schools which accept this unreflective rationale for teaching and learning accept the simplifications built into them, such as the following.

1. There is general agreement among "people who matter" (though not necessarily among experts) about what is meaningful, that what is meaningful appears in textbooks and curriculum guides, and that it is acquired by mastering the material (whatever mastery might mean) in the textbooks.
2. The role of the teacher is to explain the textbook when necessary, and to get the children, through a variety of pedagogical stratagems and inducements, to memorize the material to the extent necessary to get the right answers on local and standardized tests.
3. The role of the student is to accept the meanings provided in the textbook and curriculum guides and to repeat these meanings as right answers to questions on local and standardized tests.

Those who administer schools that accept this unreflective rationale for teaching and learning likewise accept the above simplifications. Further, they accept as their own responsibility to see to it that teachers teach this curriculum and that students are held accountable to produce enough right answers, as contained in this curriculum, to be promoted or graduated. Since the right answers are already known, it is simply a matter of getting teachers to develop sufficient motivational and explanatory techniques for students to "get" the right answers. Hence the principal and other supervisors of teachers work with teachers to help them develop their bag of tricks and strategies to lead students to the right answers as given in the curriculum.

The problem with this strategy is that meaning and its acquisition is determined largely by someone other than the teacher and the student. Whether the meanings include gender, racial, cultural, or class bias is never asked. When these questions are not asked, it is usually because of the assumption of legitimacy and power of the central office staff and of the publishing houses that their point of view concerning what things mean and how and where one finds meaning is the correct, the only, the most desirable, or the most politically acceptable point of view. When questions are asked and alternative meanings and methods of uncovering meaning are suggested,[8] then advocates of these previously silent assumptions of legitimacy and power attack the supporters of alternatives. Those who support the administrative status quo in schools support a process of administering meaning, but clearly in a pejorative sense. This type of administration denies access to meanings that are not included in the textbooks. The meanings that textbooks make available to students are prepackaged meanings representing a limited worldview. Those who defend this limited worldview are open to the accusation of attempting to preserve the present social, political, and economic status quo. If they succeed in controlling meaning in this way, they will surely place the nation's future at risk, for they will disempower the young to meet the intellectual challenges of a rapidly changing world.

If we find this possibility unacceptable, how do we as educators plan to administer meaning? If we allow ourselves to feel the full weight of this question, we might readily decide that a career that asks such difficult questions of us is not to be pursued. Who is willing to be responsible for this kind of work? More than a few who choose careers in educational administration never give these questions a thought. Are we to leave the schools in their hands?

Daunting as the question is, let us search for some approaches that may help us develop a foundation for this fundamental work of educational administration.

THE SOCIAL PRODUCTION OF MEANING

First, we need to develop a reasonable stand on the nature of learning and the discovery/production of meaning. Learning is not something that takes place in isolation. Learning takes place within language communities whose lives are fed by, led by, inspired by, and governed by traditions, world views, culture, and values. No individual learns independently of the community in which he or she lives. Even mature intellectuals who oppose their community's ideas, values, or traditions do so using the language and metaphors already available within the community.

Learning is a social activity that immerses the learner in a thick cultural stew of meanings. Add a little salt here and the meaning is colored by irony; add a little sugar and the meaning is colored by sentimental allusions. The knowledge makes sense only in a context of cultural presuppositions and assumptions and prior personal knowledge. At any given moment, the meanings within the knowledge a learner grasps are limited and even slippery. The knowledge represents a temporary, interpretive fix on a reality that is open to many interpretations. The production of meaning, whether by an individual or a group, is always limited and fallible.

Learning, therefore, is always interpretive, tentative, and subject to revision. No individual or group can achieve a comprehensive and exhaustive meaning of anything. The production or attainment of meaning is always cumulative yet limited, engaging yet partial, inventively new yet transitory. Learning becomes enriched when it involves more than one learner, because the insights and perspectives of others can fill out the limitations, partiality, and tentativeness of the individual's achievement. Differences of opinion and perspective reveal distortions; argument often requires returning to the material for a larger grasp of the meaning. The richest form of learning seems to take place in what the American philosopher Charles Pierce called a self-corrective critical community of inquirers.[9] Within a community of learners, we have a better chance of arriving at richer, more complex interpretations of what is real and what is meaningful.

This foundation for an educational administrator is supported historically by the philosophical writings of Pierce, James, Royce, and Dewey—all quintessentially American thinkers—all of whom have influenced educational and social thought in the twentieth century. We elaborate more on the school as a learning community in Chapter 6.

LEARNING AND HUMAN CONCERNS

A second foundation for this fundamental work of educational administration is a stance that continually relates meaning, knowledge, and learning to a sense of something intrinsically human. This position sees learning as centered around questions of importance to human beings as human beings. What is important to human beings are answers to questions such as: How should I live my life? How can I maintain my autonomy, my identity as a singular individual who takes responsibility for myself and at the same time belong to a community that grounds the meaning of my life? How should I govern myself? How should we govern ourselves? How can I get along with so-and-so, whom I don't like, who is so different from me? How can I find fulfillment in my work? How do I take care of my own needs while being responsive to people in greater need than I? How do I balance leisure with participation in public life? How do I make sense out of the complexity of economic and political institutions? How do I make sense out of the universe? What does it mean to say that I am responsible for what I know? The questions go on and on. They all have moral overtones.

For young children the questions are more concrete: How do I make this thing work? Why did she call me a name? How do I please my parents? How do I make friends? How do I make up after a fight? Where does thunder come from? Why do adults get so angry? Many of their questions are attempts to situate themselves in a safe and predictable world that provides them a sense of existential security.[10]

This foundational position asserts that learning is not neutral, not disinterested, not disengaged from the struggle to understand how to live as a human being. All of our relationships, whether with other humans, with animals, with inanimate nature, with institutions, or with primary groups, provide the natural and cultural space within which we define who we are. We bring to these relationships, furthermore, a vague but enduring sense that our humanity is at stake in the way we respond to whatever we encounter—that somehow we are obligated to respond to whatever we encounter. In benign encounters that response often is a spontaneous appreciation or wonder; in threatening encounters the response is flight or self-protection. When the immediate threat is removed, we go back to look again, to figure out how to arrange conditions to minimize that threat, so we can get on with our life.

There is a sense in which the pursuit of knowledge for its own sake expresses a noble human vocation. The life of the scholar, although it can be tainted with self-serving, nonetheless has a high moral purpose: to push back the frontiers of darkness and misunderstanding so that other humans may enjoy the fruits of new knowledge. The scholar nonetheless participates in the meta-narrative of learning and knowledge, namely, that humanity is on a journey in which we deliberately participate. Learning enables us to understand the journey and to understand *ourselves* as we engage in the journey. Learning is what makes the journey a human journey, by producing interpretations about who we are and what the journey means.

Seeing the connection between learning and human concerns lends depth to the work of an educational administrator. It provides a sense of purpose behind the work of the faculty and staff. It fuels the vision that guides the administration of meaning.

LEARNING AND THE CULTURAL PROJECTS
FACING CIVIL SOCIETY

A third foundation for the fundamental work of administering meaning is the relation of school meanings to the large cultural projects of our current historical era and the cultural projects of our past history. For example, we often hear political and economic commentators speak of a new world order. What cultural work is needed to nurture this new world order? What new understanding of politics and economics will provide the scaffolding for such an order? How can the world community take responsibility for the fragile ecosystem of the earth? How do we honor cultural differences in a crowded world that has shrunk in space and time? How do we settle conflicts in nonviolent ways? Although we cannot turn the fourth grade into a year-long discussion of the United Nations agenda, we need to find ways to link what we learn in school to the weighty questions facing humanity. We need to enable youngsters to feel the urgency of being prepared to participate in this agenda as adults. They need to feel connected to a significant discourse about the making of history. This sense of the significance of learning will also fuel the vision of the administrator of meaning.

LEARNING AND EVERYDAY LIFE

Finally, a fourth foundational position for the work of administering meaning is to relate school meanings to students' experience of everyday life, so that school meanings will be more securely grounded in life experience. This means not only relating school meanings to things such as family history, adult authority, family responsibilities and loyalties, family celebrations, and cultural and religious traditions, but also relating school meanings to family economics, the technology used in the home, and the experience of nature in gardens, the cycle of seasons, and weather patterns. School meanings can also be related to neighborhood patterns (housing density, traffic patterns, commercial enterprises, health agencies), family occupations, health issues, life and property insurance, government services (or lack of them), neighborhood conflicts, neighborhood heroes, varieties of architecture, and community projects. In short, the total physical, technological, political, economic, and social reality of the life of students outside of school can be a source of learning and can provide a grounding for the various kinds of learning prescribed in the official curriculum.

SUMMARY

With these four foundational perspectives on learning, knowledge, and meaning, we may begin to feel more focused in our fundamental work of administering meaning. Our work is shaped by the understanding that meaning is socially produced and therefore requires attention to the cultural groundings of meanings and to the collaborative work of a community of inquirers. Our work is shaped by the understanding that learning must be intentionally rooted in human concerns. Our work is shaped by the understanding that the learning in the school must be connected to the major cultural projects facing our society. Our work is shaped by an understanding that learning needs to be connected with the realities of everyday life. These understandings provide a framework for discussions with teachers about what is being learned in classrooms. They help to frame evaluations of the current curriculum and strategies for enriching that curriculum. They help to frame conversations with parents about what is important in the education of their children. They help to redefine what is meant by school effectiveness.

These four foundations of learning do indeed provide a sense of direction. But the landscape of meaning has not been cleared of all uncertainty. The landscape of meaning is presently a contested one. Educators find themselves in a period of historical transition between world views. In the next chapter we survey this contested landscape in order to see both the problems and the possibilities for administering meaning.

ACTIVITIES

1. How do you respond to the suggestion that you administer meaning? What are the meanings that you try to promote throughout the school?
2. Talk with your teachers about the textbooks they use. Ask them to explain the assumptions the textbooks seem to make about the way students learn. Ask them what important topics are left out of the textbooks. Ask them whether the textbooks contain a point of view about human values.
3. Identify one or more teachers in your school who are relating classroom learning to the human questions suggested by the second foundational position—learning and human concerns. Talk with them about the kind of meanings they are encouraging youngsters to uncover.
4. Are any of the subjects or courses in your school related to a "cultural project facing civil society"?
5. Prepare a presentation for parents, using the four foundational positions on learning described in the latter half of this chapter.
6. Are your classrooms and instructional spaces set up around the notion that learning is a social production? How would you change them to make them more conducive to this notion?

7. In your journal, reflect on how you would like youngsters in your school to interpret who they are and the meaning of their life's journey.

ENDNOTES

1. See Clifford Geertz, "From the Native's Point of View: On the Nature of Anthropological Understanding," in Paul Rabinow and William Sullivan (eds.), *Interpretive Social Science: A Reader,* University of California Press, Berkeley, 1979.
2. For example, see Jean-Francois Lyotard, *The Postmodern Condition: A Report on Knowledge,* translated by G. Bennington and B. Massumi, University of Minnesota Press, Minneapolis, 1984; Michael Foucault, *The Archeology of Knowledge,* translated by Alan Seridan, Harper Colophon, New York, 1972; Richard Rorty, *Philosophy and the Mirror of Nature,* Princeton University Press, Princeton, NJ, 1979; Robert Stake, "Overview and Critique of Existing Evaluation Practices and Some New Leads for the Future," paper presented at the AERA Annual Meeting, San Francisco, 1976; Bruce Jennings, "Interpretive Social Sciences and Policy Analysis," in Daniel Callahan and Bruce Jennings (eds.), *Ethics, The Social Sciences and Policy Analysis,* Plenum Press, New York, 1983, pp. 3–35.
3. See, for example, E. F. Schumacher, *Small Is Beautiful,* Harper & Row, New York, 1973; *A Guide for the Perplexed,* Harper & Row, New York, 1977.
4. See the scathing critique of sociologists by C. Wright Mills, *The Sociological Imagination,* Oxford University Press, New York, 1959. Thomas Kuhn's influential book, *The Structure of Scientific Revolutions,* University of Chicago Press, Chicago, 1970, changed the way the world viewed the objectivity of scientists. See the work of Jurgen Habermas in translations: *Knowledge and Human Interests,* Beacon Press, Boston, 1971, and *Legitimation Crisis,* Beacon Press, Boston, 1975; as well as the classic exposition of this philosophical rethinking of the social sciences by Richard J. Bernstein, *The Restructuring of Social and Political Theory,* University of Pennsylvania Press, Philadelphia, 1976, for a more philosophical treatment of this trend.
5. See Robert Bellah, Richard Madsen, William M. Sullivan, Ann Swidler, and Stephen M. Tipton, *The Good Society,* Alfred Knopf, New York, 1991.
6. Quoted by Michael Kelley, "Hillary Rodham Clinton and the Politics of Virtue," *The New York Times Magazine,* May 23, 1993, p. 25.
7. See Elanor Duckworth's interesting discussion of knowledge as beliefs, in *"The Having of Wonderful Ideas" and Other Essays on Teaching and Learning,* Teachers College Press, New York, 1987, pp. 50–63.
8. Cf. the debate over the introduction of multicultural perspectives in school curricula. Arguing for a greater space for multicultural concerns are Sandra Nieto, *Affirming Diversity ,* Longmans, New York, 1992; and John Ogbu, "Understanding Cultural Diversity and Learning," *Educational Researcher,* November 1992, pp. 5–11. Arguing against such diversity are Arthur

Schlesinger, Jr., *The Disuniting of America: Reflections on a Multicultural Society*, W. W. Norton, New York, 1992.

9. Richard Bernstein offers a compelling argument for this notion of a community of inquirers in an essay, "Pragmatism, Pluralism, and the Healing of Wounds," in his *The New Constellation: The Ethical-Political Horizons of Modernity/Postmodernity*, MIT Press, Cambridge, MA, 1992, pp. 323–340.

10. Ernest Becker provides a penetrating analysis of these human questions in his *The Birth and Death of Meaning*, 2d ed., The Free Press, New York, 1971.

CHAPTER 4

Contested Meaning:
Postmodern versus Modern

One of the hazards of school administration is becoming caught up in managing change, or in negotiating changes imposed on the school by outside forces. That is, we become so caught up in the processes of managing and negotiating that we do not fully appreciate the substance of the changes themselves. Many of the changes now proposed tend to be incremental and relatively superficial—for example, peer supervision as an alternative to administrator supervision, which may or may not assume traditional curricula and traditional pedagogy; student performance appraisal formats that alter testing protocols but not the curriculum being "performed"; "schools within schools," which place decisions in the hands of teacher teams about pacing and sequencing an unchallenged, traditional curriculum. Administrators' attention to the administration of meaning can be framed entirely by the demands of negotiating the numerous organizational or cultural problems these changes occasion. This focus on accommodating organizational changes leaves little time to step back and consider the larger sweep of cultural changes taking place in the world of ideas.

"History is what takes place behind our backs."[1] Indeed, the chroniclers of present-day events, whether journalists or anchorpersons, are rarely able to distinguish between superficial events and events of lasting historical significance. We grasp what is happening "behind our backs" only when we have time to place events in perspective, to link events with a discernible pattern, and thus to form an interpretation that connects our micro-narrative to the larger macro-narrative or even to a meta-narrative. Particularly in times of cultural transition, we are apt to dismiss the early signs of change as ideosyncratic, temporary aberrations in the smooth flow of public order. Thus the first changes in accepted standards of taste, esthetics, political behavior, or lifestyles, as well as changes in scientific paradigms and philosophical perspectives, are usually greeted with resistance, ridicule, condemnation, or various other forms of censure. After a while, however, certain cultural shifts begin to become more accepted, more legitimate, more "sensible," and eventually are judged to be significant, promising, and enlightened.

We seem to be at a historical point when we in education need to take account of what has been happening "behind our backs," so to speak, in art, philosophy, social theory, technology, the sciences and humanities—in short, in the way leading scholars have been fundamentally refashioning the way we look at our world. Earlier frameworks, presuppositions, and bedrock principles have been challenged, modified, discarded, or reworked. While an overarching sense of the emerging certainties may yet escape their grasp, these scholars assert that the old certainties are clearly inadequate, misguided, inappropriate, or invalid. These old certainties make up what we have come to accept as the modern world view. The assumptions behind this modern world view are, by and large, the assumptions behind the certainties being taught—directly or indirectly—in our schools. Indeed, in most instances, proposals for school reform are based on the familiar beliefs of the modern world view. The legislatures, business groups, and educational professionals proposing these reforms appear to be unaware of the shift that has been going on for well over half a century in art, philosophy, the sciences, the social sciences, and the humanities. The shift has indeed been taking place behind their backs.

Peter Drucker, a man usually a step ahead of his contemporaries, summarizes the shift rather dramatically:

> Within the next decades education will change more than it has changed since the modern school was created by the printed book over three hundred years ago. An economy in which knowledge is becoming the true capital and the premier wealth producing resource makes new and stringent demands on the schools for educational performance and educational responsibility. A society dominated by knowledge workers makes even newer—and even more stringent—demands for social performance and social responsibility. Once again we will have to think through what an educated person is. At the same time, how we learn and how we teach are changing drastically and fast—the result, in part, of new theoretical understanding of the learning process, in part of the new technology. Finally, many of the traditional disciplines of the schools are becoming sterile, if not obsolescent. We thus also face changes in *what* we learn and teach, and indeed in what we mean by knowledge.[2]

POSTMODERN VERSUS MODERN

What is this shift that has been taking place behind our backs? One way to comprehend the shift is to contrast the basic assumptions of modernity to the new questions and challenges of postmodernity. In using the terms *postmodernity* and *modernity* and their associated adjectives and synonyms, we must be aware, as Richard Bernstein cautions, that in contemporary usage these terms are slippery, vague and ambiguous. He goes on to say:

> There is no consensus of agreement about the multiple meanings of these treacherous terms. Furthermore there is the paradox that many thinkers who are labeled "postmodern" by others, do not think of themselves as "postmodern" or even use this expression. . . . I think it is best to use the expression

"modern/postmodern" to signify what Heidegger calls a *Stimmung,* a mood—one which is amorphous, protean, and shifting but which *nevertheless exerts a powerful influence on the ways in which we think, act, and experience* [emphasis added].[3]

What follows is an attempt to capture the main differences between these moods, to highlight some generalizations supported by the mood of modernity in contrast to generalizations supported by the mood of postmodernity. We shall not attempt to discuss the positions of various philosophers in any great detail, but we want to be able to recognize the underlying mood which seems to be influencing the ways we think and act. Hence we will summarize each mood in order to grasp the enormous shift that has taken place and is still taking place, and to grasp the implications for education.

THE MOOD OF MODERNITY

The basic tenets of modernity might be summarized as follows.

- Science and technology, intrinsically good, are the fuel that drives society's engines.
- "Objective knowledge," embedded in scientific discovery and technological invention, represents the only (legitimate) knowledge of the world. This objective knowledge enables us to know life's realities.
- The individual is the primary unit of society; any theory of society must start with the sanctity of the individual, and with individual rights and responsibilities.
- The individual, through the exercise of reason, is the source of intellectual and moral knowledge.
- The individual, guided by reason and self-interest, will make economic choices the cumulative effect of which, when combined with the choices of other reasonable and self-interested individuals, will result in the most widespread happiness of most of the members of that society.
- Under the aegis of science and human reason, human life is becoming progressively better.
- This progress is best guided by an intellectual elite who have developed expertise in the physical, social, and human sciences, and hence are best equipped to manage society's public affairs through their rational administration of state and corporate institutions.
- Democratically elected representatives of the people will direct these elites to pursue the common good of society (or the nation, or the people).

It is helpful to elaborate on some of these tenets of the mood of modernity in order to see why the postmodern mood rejects them. We look at the tenets dealing with individualism, the impact of scientific rationality on our relationship with nature, our understanding of human nature, and the progressive character of modern history.[4]

INDIVIDUALISM

In the modern world view, the individual occupies center stage. No longer do traditional authorities determine what is right or true. In the theory or ideology of individualism the individual, by the exercise of reason, determines right and truth, either by deductive logic or by scientific proof.

The postmodern view counters that the individual is neither the primary source of knowledge nor the primary judge of truth. Individuals are embedded in cultures and language communities. What is accepted as knowledge is socially constructed by these cultures and communities. Similarly, what is defined as morally right or wrong is determined by the community. Postmodernists may not necessarily be happy with the location of knowledge and morality within the community—indeed, many go to great lengths to demonstrate that this knowledge and morality is an expression of power by elites within the culture—but they do contend that the community, *for better or worse,* is the source of what is seen as true and right.

The modern mood posits the individual, not the community, as the basic social entity. The community is seen as merely a gathering of individuals. These individuals pursue their self-interest within limits spelled out and agreed to in a social contract. Thus, each individual surrenders some of his freedom to the state in return for protection against the intrusions of others on his basic freedoms. (Most of the thinking about these matters was done by men, with only men in mind, thus the use of the masculine.) In the economic sphere, the individual pursues personal gain in the free competition of the marketplace. As the recipient of a bounteous economic productivity, the individual can achieve self-realization in consuming a cornucopia of commodities. Through some presumed "hidden hand" behind the free market, each individual adopts a self-seeking, instrumental stance toward others and yet upholds a commitment to social harmony. When that harmony breaks down, the theory assumes, the state assumes responsibility for the external regulation of social behavior.

From a postmodern perspective, however, the theory of economic and political individualism is disproven in practice. Political pressures by competing interest groups continually lead the state's regulation of social behavior toward concessions, compromise, and political expediency, rather than to a pursuit of an agreed-upon common good. Those without political influence are not protected by the state. Only when they organize to represent their interests (through workers' strikes, civil rights protests, voter registration drives, women's political action groups, etc.) does the state respond. The state, in short, is not the impartial overseer of a free-market, basically self-governing society; the state, rather, is seen to be much more of a *product* of those who control the "free" market. The common good of the community does indeed emerge from the self-interested activity of men in a free market, the postmodernist sarcastically observes, because the common good is defined by those who control both the market and the state. "What's good for business," as the saying goes, "is good for America."

THE DISENCHANTMENT OF NATURE

Along with individualism, the modern mood enshrined rationality and its most advanced expression, science. Modernity believed that science enables humans to understand the laws that govern the operation of nature. As more and more knowledge has been accumulated about the natural environment, the abstract categories and vocabulary of science have come to dominate the language and the imaginations of humans as they stand apart from and confront nature. The truth about nature is contained in scientific findings dealing with atoms, molecules, chemical compounds, and magnetic forces. These truths negate the primitive's world of spirits and totems, forces and mysteries, which require a reverential stance toward nature, and brand such reverence as childish "anthropomorphism." The poetry of brooding coastal waters, dancing stars, howling winds, raging storms, singing brooks, winter trees as bare ruined choirs, is entertaining, perhaps, but when all is said and done, these images are simply a subjective projection of the poet's fantasies. Science gives us "real" knowledge, knowledge about how to control nature: dams to control flooding, pesticides to control crop infestation, and antibiotics to control disease. Beyond the knowledge of how to control nature, we possess the knowledge of how to exploit nature for commercial purposes. Technology creates both the tools with which to exploit nature and the processes by which nature can be repackaged in consumable forms.

There are several postmodern responses to the scientific approach to nature. One is that science, through its continuous splintering into subspecializations, has so dismembered nature that it is impossible to gain any large sense of how natural systems work. The dividing up of the natural sciences into specializations, while providing knowledge about how microsystems work, has thereby destroyed an understanding of how the larger systems of nature work. Ironically, the rationality of scientific specialization leads to the impossibility of understanding the whole. This rationality is further challenged at the level of particle physics and at the macro level of large systems, where scientific study encounters indeterminacy.

Another critique of the modernist expectations from the scientific study of nature and its subsequent technological mastery over and exploitation of nature is that it has tended to develop in humans either a detached, indifferent attitude or, worse, an adversarial, superior attitude toward nature. With mass production and the artificialization of nature, humans lost direct contact with the primary natural processes of growth, decay, and regeneration, and lost the sense of the interdependence of natural processes in the environment. Nature ceased to provide the modern person with metaphors for understanding his or her own natural processes. What may be worse, science may have destroyed man's sense of dependence on nature, or any sense of stewardship toward natural environments. Humans have come to accept increasingly artificial environments as their natural environment. Their environment is more and more a mediated environment. In such mediated environments, free-floating image and stimulation (e.g., MTV and the advertising media), not stable meaning frameworks for sustained human striving, become the primary social and psychological realities.

THE DISENCHANTMENT OF HUMANITY

The success of the natural sciences led the human and social sciences to attempt to imitate them. More and more of the social, cultural, economic, and political world was subjected to scientific analysis. To reduce the complexity of the social and cultural world, however, the scientific method had to search for a very few variables or categories that could explain at least most of the social and interpersonal behavior of humans. Social scientists applied the methods of the natural sciences to dissect the personal and social worlds by means of reductionist categories such as "drive," "need," "instinct," and "motive." Organizations were viewed as large machines driven by a few variables such as authority, profit, hierarchy, status, goals, and efficiency. Laws of the market were derived for economics. The human and social worlds became rationalized. That is to say, all social and interpersonal behavior could be analyzed and broken down into rational explanation. The social world became disenchanted. The Emperor's new clothes were seen to be fabricated out of a fictional cultural thread. Social science could explain pretty much everything that happened in society. It was a matter of power, of socialization, of mass propaganda, of market forces, alienation and anomie, of self-serving political alliances, of the necessary bureaucratic organization of life to serve the goals of efficiency, predictability, and order.

Under the microscope of the human sciences, even human beings became disenchanted. Once their "problem" had been diagnosed, scientific or technical solutions could be applied to return people to a state of equilibrium where desire was balanced by release. There was no mystery to creativity or genius or madness; the human soul or spirit was a fiction. The existence of a subject encountering other subjects in interpersonal dialogue was denied by the explanations of reductionist psychology and social psychology. Humans as economic agents were reduced to consumers and producers, all quantifiable in economic formulas. Humans as political agents were looked upon as electors whose self-interested votes were gathered by political rhetoric and simplistic platitudes. Humans as citizens became objects of public policy and must be uniformly obedient to the dictates of the state. Humans as biochemical objects were seen as systems of neurologically interrelated cells. In short, humans were reduced to an assemblage of things; they no longer existed as "natural" unities in their own right. The notion of a human person disappeared into component systems of drives, microbes and cells, neural reactions, a unit of purchasing power, a unit of production, a unit of taxable income, an assemblage of carbon, hydrogen and oxygen and small amounts of other minerals.

Thus, according to the postmodern critics, we have the ultimate irony of human beings finding themselves estranged from themselves by the very process of attempting to understand themselves. Either the human person, the self as a unity, is a subjective fiction unable to stand up to rational and empirical criteria for being defined as real, or the claims for rationality are undercut by a humanism grounded in an irrational or arational intuition of the truth about human beings. In the critique of postmodernity, one or the other or both of these assertions have led to the legitimating of nihilism, egoism, and anarchy. Such attitudes are expressed by artists and architects in the playful intermingling of esthetic elements previously claimed to be rationally incompatible; in a recreationally defined, consumer-driven social Darwinism; in a cynical mockery of the orthodoxy of work and achievement through a manipulation of either the stock market, the banking system, the legal system, the political system, or the welfare system. At their worst, these attitudes have been used to justify tribal and international warfare by means of terror and weapons of mass destruction.

THE MYTH OF PROGRESS

Modernity assumed that history is a unidirectional process moving forward or upward. Civilization was seen as advancing by stages. Relatively self-subsistent tribal societies steeped in superstition and tradition gradually became united with other groups and "advanced" to urban centers, which developed trade, monetary systems, more cosmopolitan culture, more centralized governing structures, and more specialized legal and police systems. Civilization then "advanced" to nation states and empires; government became separated from religion, and commerce was largely in private hands. National identity was thought to hold primacy as tribal, religious, and ethnic cultural features evanesced. Everyday life became interwoven with and regulated by a complex of social institutions. These advances, of course, went hand in hand with advances in rationality, science, and objective knowledge of the world. Human beings were thought to be better off: Infant mortality declined due to advances in nutrition, water purification, medicine, and sanitation; housing, transportation, education, and the productivity of the workforce all improved. In other words, as history unfolded and moved forward, guided by advances in human knowledge and science, people became happier, wiser, and more fulfilled.

The modern world view saw science and technology, now wedded to capitalist industry and invention, moving forward under the banner of democracy, leading to greater freedom for the individual, greater rationality in civic and international affairs, and greater harmony among peoples. It is not difficult to understand how these myths of individualism, technical rationality, and progress hardened into an ideology that placed the industrial West in a superior position to the "underdeveloped" rest of the globe and rationalized economic, political, and military expansion into those lands to bring them the blessings of this "higher" civilization. It was the West's manifest destiny to bring progress to the colonies.

The postmodern mood is profoundly conscious of the failures of the myth of progress. This myth cannot stand up to the evidence of two world wars and numerous regional wars that have unleashed massively destructive weaponry against both combatants and citizens. It cannot stand up to the evidence of extermination camps, ethnic cleansing, torture chambers, widespread political imprisonment, state surveillance of all citizens, intimidation, and terrorism (both real and symbolic). Beyond the violence of war and national oppression, one finds widespread evidence of impulsive and random cruelty among racial, ethnic, and religious protagonists. Almost daily, reports of domestic violence and child abuse compete with the now-familiar headlines of widespread drug abuse, prostitution, and pornography. Gun-carrying children have replaced stereotypical gangsters as impulsive killers in the popular imagination.

The engines of progress—business corporations, government institutions, and cultural institutions, and the elites who run them—are often shown to be subject to a scandalous lack of rational or moral integrity. Hardly a day passes without some report of corporate fraud, government venality and deceit, vindictive use of power, disregard for the environment, religious bigotry, inattention to public safety, unsafe products, false advertising claims, price rigging, insider trading, sexual harassment, or reckless investment by "trust" institutions. The public is exposed to behavior expected from the low life lurking in the seamy atmosphere of the underworld, now being exhibited by supposed beacons of the community. "This is progress?" ask the postmodernists.

In response to the modernists' faith in reason, science, the benevolent hidden hand of the free market, the progress of history, and the freedom of the individual, the postmodernist questions the trustworthiness of any absolutes or any orthodoxies. Indeed, one whole side of postmodernism can be summed up in a profound sense of betrayal and hence in a series of "don't trust . . ." statements:

- Don't trust the government.
- Don't trust the banks.
- Don't trust the market.
- Don't trust the police.
- Don't trust your doctor.
- Don't trust your priest, minister, rabbi, mullah.
- Don't trust your lawyer.
- Don't trust the university.
- Don't trust logic, statistics, scientific proof.
- Don't trust the corporation you work for.
- Don't trust mass-produced products.
- Don't trust advertising.
- Don't trust politicians.
- Don't trust the media.

- Don't trust anybody.
- Don't trust your mind or your emotions.
- Don't trust language.
- (Most of all!) Don't trust yourself.

This sense of alienation articulates a mind stripped of all illusion. There are no absolute truths, no universal principles. Nothing is pure; all is tainted by uncertainty, egoism, calculated manipulation. The postmodern person knows the truth, and it is not kind or gentle.

Yet the postmodern truth is not the whole truth. The modern world has not been a complete failure, a narrative only of terror and betrayal. The landscape is also dotted with successes, with examples of moral courage, with instances of generosity and sacrifice, and the small but significant kindnesses that ordinary people extend to one another. Some corporations exhibit great concern for their workers and their customers; some are producing quality products and exercising social responsibility. Science and technology have produced many breakthroughs in medicine and manufacturing that have benefited millions of people. Many government agencies have provided many good services to people. Not all politicians break their campaign promises. The evils of the modern world, although frighteningly real, have to be weighed against the evidence of human goodness that flourishes despite the evil.

Nevertheless, the way we look at the world has shifted profoundly. Although we still believe in human ideals, we are not as confident about their eventual realization. We recognize the need for courage and long-term commitments to a future that is by no means guaranteed. Now that we have some sense of the shift away from naive optimism to awareness of the struggle, where do we as educators go from here? How do we attend to the task of administering meaning in a world so uncertain about which meanings to embrace?

A first step requires acknowledging that the landscape of meaning provided by the modern world view has been blasted by the postmodern critique. There remains the hard work of absorbing the "new realities," as Drucker calls them, of creating a synthesis of the new and the old world views (with the awareness that not everything in the old world view should be discarded, and that not everything in the new should be accepted), and of bringing the mission and purposes of schooling into alignment with this new synthesis. Then comes the inventive work of constructing an appropriate curriculum and pedagogy for the school of the future.

The redesign of schooling cannot wait for a research-and-development team of education experts to design a prototype of such a new school in a laboratory somewhere over the course of a five-year period. Schools have to be redesigned even while they are functioning in the old ways. It is like redesigning an airplane while it is on a protracted series of flights. When the plane lands, a new set of wings is fitted on. At the next landing a new tail rudder replaces the old one. On the next landing, new engines are installed. In flight, the pilots and navigators carry out their new training protocols and fine-tune the new systems as they go. That is not, of course, the way the airline industry is run, but it is the way the educational industry is run. School administrators responsible for administering meaning have to manage this refitting, retooling, and retraining while the school is in flight, and when it lands for the summer or between-semester breaks they have to replace dysfunctional pieces and install new ones.

I am not proposing any specific new designs, but I will suggest, in the next chapter, that educational administrators can administer the pursuit of meaning in this time of transition primarily through engaging teachers and parents in the process of creating a vision for their school. I will also suggest that the beginnings of a way out of the ruins and despair of a discredited modernism is already at hand, even though the shape and direction of its flowering is inchoate and indeterminate at present. To anticipate, let me say that the way out is to *go forward,* neither clinging stubbornly to the absolutes of modernity, nor jettisoning wholeheartedly the agenda of the Enlightenment. Rather, the way forward is to explore new understandings of the natural, social, and human worlds, and to bring new meanings to the learning process itself.

ACTIVITIES

1. Before you read this chapter, would you say that you were a modern person, or a postmodern person? What kind of a person are you now? Write about that in your journal.
2. In your journal, list all the people and institutions that you had decided not to trust, well before you read this chapter. If you believed in the world view of modernity, how did your trust erode? Share your reflections with your study group.
3. Identify at least five examples of the modern world view that is still prevalent in your school or agency.
4. If the individual is *not* the source of truth and of moral judgment, where does that leave you, Mr. or Mrs. Administrator? What does this suggest about collaborative decision making and collaborative learning? What ought to be done at your workplace?
5. In your study group, devise a way of bringing the perspectives of this chapter to your teaching faculty so that they in turn can reassess their curriculum and pedagogy.

ENDNOTES

1. This statement is attributed to the German philosopher Hegel by the French philosopher Jean Paul Sartre, as recounted by William Barrett in *Time of Need: Forms of Imagination in the Twentieth Century,* Harper Colophon, New York, 1972, p. 3.
2. Peter F. Drucker, *The New Realities: In Government and Politics/In Economics and Business/In Society and World View,* Harper & Row, New York, 1989, p. 232.

3. Richard J. Bernstein, *The New Constellation: The Ethical-Political Horizons of Modernity/Postmodernity*, MIT Press, Cambridge, MA, 1992, p. 11.

4. In this overview of the modern and postmodern world I have been assisted by the work of many scholars, notably Ernest Becker, *The Structure of Evil*, The Free Press, New York, 1968, and Richard Bernstein, *The Restructuring of Social and Political Theory*, University of Pennsylvania Press, Philadelphia, 1976. This overview reflects earlier material developed in *The Drama of Leadership*, Falmer Press, London, 1993.

CHAPTER 5

Vision: Hope amidst the Ruins

As we examine the various implications of the fundamental responsibility of school administrators to administer meaning, we begin to grasp the considerable challenge it presents. This is intellectual work. It requires that administrators give a lot of thought to the cultural, intellectual, social, and political purposes of schooling. It also requires that administrators look at these purposes in the light of the cultural history of the past hundred years, and in the light of a rapidly eroding faith in the promises of modernity.

Administering meaning implies that an educational administrator knows what questions make up the search for meaning in the lives of the community at large and especially of the learning community we call school. We saw in the last chapter that the meanings embedded in the modern world view have been challenged and at least partially discredited by the postmodern critique. Hence, at least some of the questions that make up the search for meaning in school have to do with the tensions, transitions, and connections between these two world views.

Despite the need to rethink and re-create the learning process in today's schools, educators are challenged by some to return to a world of earlier certainties, whether those certainties are grounded in science and rationality or in a religious tradition, albeit a civil religion of small-town friendliness and redemption through hard work. They are challenged by others to emphasize intellectual skills, technological literacy, or a simplistic patriotism whose only horizon is economic superiority in a global market. None of these choices offer an appropriate interpretation of the challenges the country faces in the twenty-first century, and none provide a framework for school policy. This is not to say that schools should not promote friendliness and hard work, technological and economic literacy, as well as patriotism. These elements of the school agenda, however, need to be placed in a broader framework, one defined by the quest for and creation of those meanings that deal with the larger human journey, which transcends national boundaries, economic competition, and the desire for ever more sophisticated technology. A concern to understand and partici-

49

pate in that larger journey both as individuals and as communities ought to frame all else that we do in schools. That concern is both an intellectual concern and a moral concern. It is a moral concern because our efforts to treat this journey as a purely rational or scientific one have left the world of public affairs to be decided primarily on the grounds of economics and power, with intellectuals either providing conventional rationalizations for the way things are or standing off on the sidelines offering ineffectual complaints.

VISION

I propose that an essential work of administration is to construct a preliminary vision for the school and then to engage the rest of the school community in the process of developing a common vision for the school. This would be a fundamental way of administering meaning.

The development of a collective vision of where the school should be going is fundamental to the work of an educational administrator. This kind of activity involves both process and content. Developing a collective vision involves sharing ideas, clarifying and understanding the various points of view reflected in the community as well as the beliefs and assumptions underneath those points of view, negotiating differences, and building a consensus. Developing a collective vision also involves the content of that vision. Administrators may not possess the total content of this vision—no one does—but they should be willing to lay out a first attempt at articulating the content of a vision.

The term *vision* is much touted in the literature on political, corporate, and educational leadership.[1] Vision is seen as one of the essential ingredients of leadership. It refers to the projection of an ideal or desired state of affairs, a direction the organization should take, a supreme value or cluster of values that energizes the organization, a core meaning tied up with the essential identity of the organization, the dream of the organization's founder. The empirical studies of Bass[2] confirm that the leader's vision can mobilize the energies and commitments of the followers. Bennis and Nanus suggest that the leader's vision holds up a standard of excellence that motivates the members to attempt to reach.[3] Burns suggests that the transformational leader elevates the members' concern above self-interest toward something larger than themselves, a collective aspiration or commitment to a cause or value.[4]

One problem with popularizations of the notion of vision is that the above generalizations are presented in an ahistorical fashion. Educators can easily be led by this literature on visionary leadership to construct a vision of schooling based only on the flawed philosophical assumptions and broken promises of modernity. Indeed, many contemporary vision statements constructed by educators are steeped in such assumptions.[5] Schools, however, do not stand outside the larger social history in which they are situated. An enormous shift has occurred—and is still occurring—in our beliefs of the promises of modernity. The very notion of vision is suspect in the postmodern era. Any vision of the possibilities of schooling must take that shift and its attendant skepticism into account.

A credible vision of education must on the one hand acknowledge the limits and failures of the promises of modernity, and yet, on the other hand, respond to the public's anticipated skepticism of a vision based on purely personal convictions about the nobility and potentially transcending quality of the human adventure. A vision of education that reaches beyond the postmodern critique of modernity must be based, paradoxically, on the very reasoned inquiry, scientific study, and scholarly theories that postmodernism has attempted to discredit. Even cynical administrators who want to keep their jobs know the importance, if only for good public relations, of citing "research findings" to legitimize any proposed changes in the school. The public needs at least the appearance of rationality in its institutions.

Fortunately, within the natural and social sciences, as well as the humanities, there is emerging a view of nature, of society, of the human person, and of knowledge itself that reverses the reductionist determinism of earlier natural, social, and human sciences. These developments can be found in the recent work of many scholars, work which, to my mind, has been ably summarized by Frederick Turner.[6] Although a thorough presentation of this work is beyond the scope of this chapter, a brief summary is offered to point out how dramatically these emerging views recast the human adventure, and therefore the kind of education that is called for.

EMERGING VIEWS OF NATURE, SOCIETY, AND THE HUMAN PERSON

The new view of the natural universe is one of a free, unpredictable, self-ordering evolutionary process. Throughout the long history of cosmic and terrestrial evolution, the basic theme that all natural scientists find is *reflexivity* or feedback. It appears as though the universe is continually experimenting, discarding what does not work, and keeping what does. The experiment is nonlinear and therefore generates new future states, which while folding earlier forms into themselves are not predictable, but only describable after the fact.[7]

The generative feedback process is exemplified in the evolution of life forms, and perhaps most clearly in our own evolution. The feedback principle shaped our biological development, and indeed it is the origin of our own reflexive self-awareness and self-reflection. Humans seem to be naturally designed for learning and for creativity. Human reflexivity enables us to speed up the creative process, so to speak, of the universe's slow process of reflexive experimentation. Collectively engaging in the feedback of our own learning and creative experimentation through the free exchange and criticism of ideas, we can assist the journey of an intrinsically spirited (intelligent) cosmos into fuller transcendence of itself.

Psychobiology, neurology, paleogenetics, paleoanthropology, archeology, and other scientific specialties point to deep structures in the human brain and body that exhibit this reflexivity. Between the last phases of human biological evolution and the initial phases of human cultural evolution, there appears to have been an overlap of between 1 to 5 million years. During this time we were in the process of domesticating ourselves. The overlap of more than a million years suggests that our own cultural evolution was a major influence on the genetic material that in its later stages constituted our human species.[8] In other words, cultural and genetic evolution during this time engaged in a mutually shaping relationship; indeed, cultural evolution may have driven biological evolution. What emerged was a species equipped to learn through creative exploration and expression. What is natural to the human species suggests the kind of education that should stimulate and develop this talent.

What also emerged during this evolution was a naturally satisfying response within the human brain to beauty. Traditional archeology tended to present human prehistory in pictures of hulking males hunting and making tools. More recent paleoanthropology complements this picture by identifying women as the culture bearers. Their legacy was weaving and sewing, language and conversation, the daily rituals of gardening and cooking, children's lullabies and evening storytelling—in short, the gradual creation of a reflexive esthetic sense.

The theme of reflexivity is also postulated for the planet earth itself in the Gaia hypothesis.[9] This theory proposes that the enormous networks of mutual interactions between the organic and inorganic elements of the earth's surface make up a living, reflexive, organic system. As in the case of a small living organism, this larger organism reacts to threats it perceives in its environment. Humans make up part of this organic system; we are dependent on this ecological environment, and tamper with it at our peril. Gaia is our "mother"; we are part of this larger whole and bear responsibilities to that larger source of our life. If we damage the source of our life, we may in turn be destroyed as one of nature's experiments that failed.

Some physicists even postulate an anthropic principle, which is reflexivity extended to a cosmic scale. This principle of quantum theory stipulates that for the universe to become actual, it had to produce a human knower whose observation of the universe would force the universe to collapse from the realm of the possible into actuality. Thus is knowledge implicated in the evolution of the universe toward the human.

This thinking is a far cry from the reductionism and determinism of earlier forms of science. Turner sums it up well:

> In the new science of the late Twentieth Century, theoretical physics can find common ground with oriental mysticism; free, self-organizing systems are plausible not only in the human world, but throughout the world of matter; our common inheritance with the higher animals has become for us a source of strength and health, not a restriction on our freedom; and our human creativity now appears to be only the intensest form of the generous creativity of nature. Meanwhile, we have begun to see how a more sophisticated technology can act in harmony with nature and even begin to heal the scars that our earlier and cruder technologies have bequeathed us.[10]

We hear echoes of this observation in remarks by Vaclav Havel, on the occasion of his receiving the Philadelphia Liberty Medal on July 4, 1994:

Paradoxically, inspiration . . . can once again be found in science, in a science that is new—post modern—a science producing ideas that in a certain sense allow it to transcend its own limits. I will give two examples. . . . [He cites the anthropic cosmological principle and the Gaia hypothesis and then continues.] The only real hope of people today is probably a renewal of our certainty that we are rooted in the earth and at the same time, the cosmos. This awareness endows us with the capacity for self-transcendence.[11]

We might add that this new awareness offers us the ground for a vision of the education of humans.

A NEW UNDERSTANDING OF KNOWLEDGE

Besides the transformation of modernist science toward a new view of the cosmological history of the universe and human evolution, there has emerged a new understanding of knowledge itself. Within the postmodern mood we discover a series of insights concerning the nature of knowledge as a social and cultural construct, the understanding of learning as involving the learner in knowledge production, the understanding of learning as inescapably involving the self's own narrative, the relation of learning/knowledge to cultural production, the relation of learning to self-realization and self-creation, and the relationship of learning to communities of language and communities of memory, and hence to the meta-narratives of communities. These insights are embedded, to be sure, in the large theme of reflexivity elaborated above, but they need to be developed sufficiently for us to see how they can become additional ingredients of our vision of a new way of educating.

KNOWLEDGE AS A HUMAN AND
SOCIAL CONSTRUCT

We saw in the previous chapters that knowledge is no longer seen as a one-to-one correspondence with "the thing out there independent of the knower." Rather, knowledge of some external reality is understood as a conceptual or metaphorical interpretation of that reality, a partial grasping of some aspect of that reality. That partial grasping, however, involves the internal mental operation of a cultural being, a member of language community, a person with a life history and previous learning experiences, and a historical context in which the learning is taking place (a context that is favorable or unfavorable, threatening or nurturing, anxiety-filled or relaxed, with friends or strangers, easily related to recent experiences or something totally new, etc.), all of which predispose the knower to apprehend that external reality within a tapestry of prior meaning, value, and affective frameworks. What is known, then, is something that, while it exists in relationship to an external reality, is a human and social construct. It is a human construct in that it is produced by a human being with specific prior human and cultural experiences. It is a social construct in that it is shaped by the language and culture of the society that the knower inhabits. It is in relationship to external realities such that any action based on this knowledge must take that reality into account. If I jump out of a twenty-story building, my knowledge of the realities of gravity tells me to expect certain consequences.

SPATIAL AND TEMPORAL IMPLICATIONS
OF KNOWING

In the previous chapters we have also seen that knowledge is not an isolated piece of information, but rather that every piece of knowledge means something in relation to the larger meaning paradigms within a culture. A rock painting in a cave of a kangaroo in the Northern Territories of Australia will mean something to an Australian Aboriginal tribal elder, and something quite different to a European tourist. To an archaeologist or anthropologist, the same rock painting will mean something different than it will to a white, Australian schoolboy. In the act of apprehending the significance of the rock painting, each person also tacitly positions herself in relation to that rock painting. For some, it positions them as members of a culture quite different from the aboriginal culture. For others it positions them in time, as observers of a race of people whose cultural artifacts date back around 40,000 years, suggesting that the observers themselves are somehow part of that 40,000-year journey.

When I learn something in science—say, the physics of gravitational force—tacitly I know something about myself in relationship to that piece of information. I know something about how gravity affects me. I know that I am in a gravitational field that places me in relationship to the heavenly bodies of our galaxy. Similarly, when I learn something about the food chain in certain oceans, I know, again tacitly, something about myself, about how I live in a natural environment of various kinds of food, and as part of a food chain that sustains the food I eat. In other words, everything I learn about the world I live in teaches me, though usually at a subliminal level, something about myself. Knowledge positions me in a place and a time within a network of relationships.

KNOWING AND SELF-KNOWLEDGE

In a real sense, then, we can say that whenever I learn anything, I am simultaneously and *of necessity* learning something about myself. And if, in the continuing process of learning, I am repositioning myself again and again in relationship to temporal and spatial realities and to my culture, I am continuously reproducing myself—the self I am coming to know as more and more involved in a variety of relationships to the realities of the world I am learning about. For example, if I make a new friend, then there is something new about me: My experience is now enlarged by my friend's experience; my responsibilities to other people are realigned to take account of my responsibilities to my new friend; my new friend discloses a new appreciation of myself that I didn't have before. A new enemy may also challenge me to create and understand new aspects of myself. If my ethnic community is Italian, Irish, or Chinese, then as I learn the history of my people, I take on a growing understanding of myself as belonging to a specific cultural and political history; I become enlarged by belonging to a cultural and historical community. I am not alone; I am part of something much bigger than myself.

As I re-create myself during new learning about my world through my participation in a language and cultural community, the results are not always beneficial to my growth as a human being. If the cultural world view of the language community that educates me believes that nature is an inexhaustible resource available for exploitation and consumption, then the meaning of the food-chain lesson may create a self-understanding that justifies my relationship to nature as an exploiter. If the world view of my language community believes that women are inferior to men, then what I learn about women in history and in literature may create a self-understanding that places me in a domineering relationship to women. In other words, the world view that stands behind the explicit curriculum of the school carries all kinds of messages which in turn form the self-understanding of the individuals who learn that curriculum.[12]

Usually learning in schools implies that we are learning about reality as it is, rather than learning about how our cultural community has come to interpret reality.[13] If schools communicate that what we learn is the way things are, then we come to identify school learning as objectively defining reality. Gradually, this kind of fixing of reality into what schools teach us about the culture's interpretation of reality leads naturally to our expectation that this is the way reality *should* be, or at least that this is the way reality always has been and will always be. To change the way reality is presented in school (e.g., by changing the relationships between classes of people, or between the sexes, or between the races; by changing the definition of biological life; by providing a contrary interpretation to a moment in history) can be seen as a violation, a dangerous interruption of life's natural regularities.

KNOWLEDGE AS INTERPRETATION

One of the insights driven home by the postmodern mood of suspicion is that language and knowledge are not neutral. Categorizations fix people and things in hierarchies, in superior or subordinate positions in relationships to other people or things.[14] Think of the terms "welfare" and "tax incentives." The first term carries many negative overtones; the second connotes quite different relationships between the state and private individuals. Both, however, signify financial benefits bestowed on some people by the state in the interests of the common good. In our culture one is supposed to be ashamed to be on welfare; receiving tax incentives, on the other hand, is a sign of privilege. When youngsters learn these things in school, they are positioning themselves in a meaning system that has already made cultural judgments on their position in the social order. Such knowledge creates self-definition. In reproducing such knowledge, youngsters reproduce definitions of themselves.

Those definitions are, as implied in the very language the school teaches them, relational. Hence, my self-definition places me in some kind of pecking order in relation to others in the classroom and in the community. Whether the distinctions are related to wealth, gender, sexual preference, race, ethnic heritage, physical size, neighborhood, age, IQ scores, athletic ability, assertiveness, aggression, etc., youngsters pick up the value preferences within the culture and the subculture which the school teaches. This is the tacit curriculum, which even teachers are not usually aware they are teaching.[15] What is worse, the students are not aware of how much they are picking up of the points of view, biases, stereotypes, and ethical judgments of the culture. The process of self-definition and hence of self-creation seems to proceed effortlessly and without conceptual explanation. For the youngster, life simply unfolds and presents new information and experiences every day.

This does not mean that some of the learning is not painful. However, it is usually administered in such a way that it seems simply to explain impartially the way the world runs. There is no singling out of an individual as an object of someone else's evil intentions. The individual is simply part of a group (women, poor people, Orientals, corporate stockholders, etc.) that exists in this relationship to the rest of the members of society.

It must be understood, as well, that the process of learning involves the continuous re-creation of the world. With every new understanding, I add something new to the tapestry of my understanding of the world. Sometimes tacitly, sometimes with brilliant clarity, this new understanding causes me to realign the relationships between the various elements of this tapestry. These new understandings of the world are not something I create out of nothing. They are new understandings shaped by the language, images, and meta-narratives of my cultural and language community. When I learn, for example, about the Neuremberg trials after World War II, and the crimes for which the accused were on trial, I am learning something new about the limits imposed by the international community on the conduct of warfare. I have to realign my understandings about warfare, about the rule of law, about racial and religious intolerance, about the depth of cruelty and barbarism humans are capable of. In all of this I am learning about the world I inhabit, and imbibing moral lessons that shape later interpretations of warfare and the possibilities of my involvement with warfare, about intolerance and my complicity in it, about the rule of law and my support for it.

I am also learning an interpretation of history from within my own historical community. Had I been born in Germany, I would, perhaps, be offered a different interpretation of those events in history. As I grow older and study other military campaigns involving my country, I also learn that some "war crimes" never are prosecuted because the political chemistry needed to prosecute them is suppressed. I learn that intolerance includes subtle as well as overt forms of violence, and that the law tends to serve those who control its exercise. My relationships to the "realities" of warfare, law, and intolerance continue to shift, and as they do, a different me emerges, yet it is a me that continues to be shaped and to some degree controlled by my cultural community.

Another aspect of knowledge is that it becomes a tool for future knowledge. Through knowledge acquired earlier, I come to new experiences with ways to interpret those experiences, almost with expectations of what those experiences will mean. Prior knowledge predisposes me to interpret new things in the categories of prior interpretations. Prior knowledge becomes implicated in the new knowledge; I rarely, if ever, come to an experience without sensory and perceptual habits and dispositions that shape what I know. Knowledge of the way certain games are played enables us quickly to interpret how other games are played. However, knowledge of cultural definitions of kinship, masculinity, sportsmanship, authority, heroism, and the like provide me with an even deeper understanding of the ritual and symbolic meaning behind the games. Beyond the shaping influence of perceptual habits are habits of belief. What I know is what I believe.

Modern physicists challenge us to recognize that our theories about the physical world affect those realities. When we use a wave theory to study the motion of particles, they behave like waves. When we use a particulate theory, they behave like particles. In one sense we produce the knowledge and then the knowledge produces reality, including ourselves.

This dialectic, of course, does not take place in a social vacuum; rather, it includes corrective feedback loops which tell us whether the knowledge we are producing and using to produce other realities is related to what appears to be "out there." Teachers, parents, and peers will let us know whether our knowledge and our interpretations are crazy or not. The fact remains, however, that in this continuous process of creating knowledge, we continuously create our world. Sometimes the world that is created gets out of control, as it did in the death camps of Nazi Germany and in the gulag prisons of Stalinist Russia. But those uses of "knowledge" only show us unmistakably how the process works. In the United States, the constitutional checks and balances between the executive, legislative, and judicial branches of government (as well as a free press and public-opinion polls) provide some assurance that the social reality our knowledge produces will not lead to extremes. Similarly for the scholarly community, the open exchange and critique of new knowledge is supposed to control the realities that knowledge can produce.

RECAPITULATION

At this point, perhaps we should pause and see what we have in front of us. We saw in the previous chapter the landscape of contested meaning: the disillusionment, cynicism, and skepticism engendered by the postmodern critique of the promises of modernity. In the search for a new vision of education in the present chapter, we have discovered that the critique of postmodernism, though telling, has not been fatal. Science has survived—though considerably less arrogant, and with a more profound respect for the mysteries it explores. The state has survived—though considerably more transparent. Human reason has survived—now more open to multiple interpretations, and seen as both limited and inventive. And the individual has survived—seen now in a more organic relationship to the natural and cosmic environment, and with greater social responsibilities.

Meaning itself has survived—understood now as emerging from a more dynamic relationship between open-ended values (not deterministic principles) embedded in self-correcting, reflexive natural and social realities, and the human person who constructs and performs meanings out of experience with those natural and social realities, meanings that yet rely on the cultural and language communities for their legitimation. We thus understand knowledge as a cultural product which in its very transmission affects the self-understanding of learners, which in its apprehension by the learner becomes integrated into an individual and personal world view and which in turn produces interpretations and shapes new realities.

With these understandings, we can perhaps begin to build a vision of the possibilities of schooling. I suggest that we build this vision around one focus: the students, not the teacher, as the primary workers in the learning process. This focus, to be sure, is embedded in our changing understandings of the natural, human, and social world being developed in the natural and social sciences and the humanities. A focus on the students as the primary workers, however, will enable us to create the basic ingredients of our vision of schooling.

THE STUDENTS AS WORKERS

Schools are currently organized under the assumption that teachers are the primary workers. Through their instructional strategies—their work—it is assumed that they produce learning in the students, learning which can be replicated by the student on standardized tests. Behind this view of teachers' work in schools lies the assumption that knowledge is "out there" somewhere, waiting to be packaged by a curriculum designer and a textbook writer and then explained, treated, and passed along by the teacher. The techniques of teaching—the teacher's "bag of tricks"—consist in the shaping of the lesson material so that students will "get it"—will be able to repeat the definition, use the words of the vocabulary lesson in a proper sentence, apply the mathematical formula to a series of simple problems that resemble the model problem, memorize the textbook explanation of the mercantile system, describe the eating and hunting customs of native peoples of the Arctic, and so forth. In this arrangement, the student is thought of as a passive recipient of nuggets of information being "delivered" by the teacher.

To be sure, there has to be some activity on the part of students, just as there has to be some activity on the part of anyone being fed (chewing, swallowing, etc.). But the teacher is the one who selects what is to be learned, how it is to be learned, how the learning is to be evaluated, and according to what measurable standards of mastery it will be judged. Even where the teacher is urged to help students relate the present learnings to prior learning, or to personal experiences, the focus is on a motivational strategy, not an epistemological value. The point is not for students to construct or produce something that is personally and singularly their own, but to see their own experience as simply an example of the abstract textbook learning defined in the curriculum. Testing and grading convey the message: The personal life of the student does not count; the replication of a predetermined piece of material is what counts. It is as though students are expected to leave their own lives at the schoolhouse door; they— or at least their minds—belong to the school during the school day. It is what the school determines is to be learned that matters, nothing else.

If we make the student the worker, then this form of schooling has to change. The student now enters more actively into the learning process. Learning is the active engagement of the student, including all the sensitivities, points of view, talents, and imagination that he or she possesses, with the material under study, whether it is a short story, an algebraic operation, a question in biology, a comparison of the technique of Matisse with that of Pissarro, or their own poem about the season of spring. In the process of learning, and as a result of their active engagement with the material, students will be asked to produce something that expresses their learning.

That product can take many forms. It can be an illustration of the algebraic operation by an example from engineering, or an essay describing the historical circumstances leading up to the discovery of that algebraic operation by the mathematician who originated it; it can be a mathematical explanation of a biological reaction to certain chemicals, or it can be a freehand drawing of the same reaction, using colored pencils. The student's performance can be a written essay comparing the techniques of two painters through metaphors derived from music, or it can be a self-description of how the student feels when he or she is in a Matisse mood or a Pissarro mood. In any of the above examples, the students' products would have to show some valid insight into the material under study, an insight that might include but should go beyond the simple textbook terminology and definitions. Where warranted, the teacher or other students could ask for more elaboration of the meanings embedded in the student's product. More summative types of assessment of student learning can then be made on a complex performance in which students portray a multidimensional understanding of several important elements in the curriculum.

In the process of learning and performing what they have learned, students would be encouraged to reflect on how that learning affects their understanding of themselves. Students will hear their peers express their personal appropriation of the material under study, and thereby learn how various interpretations of the material help to enrich and complement their own understanding. The teacher can enter into the conversation to point out more generalized public understandings of the material under study which the students might have missed, and, when appropriate, point out divergent interpretations which groups in the community hold about that material.

Students' Work

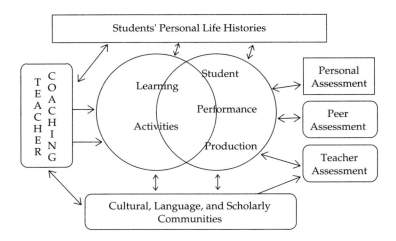

I find that visual diagrams sometimes help to portray the meaning of an abstract exposition. As we see in the diagram, the core activity in the students' work is learning and the expression of that learning in performance. Sometimes these activities will take place simultaneously: The learning will occur in the performance. At other times, some of the learning will precede the performance, and other learning will take place during the performance. Perhaps it is best to say that learning and performance always should go together. Summative performances may be used to exhibit the learning of many smaller elements and details that go into the more complex and dynamic construction of the summative performance. For example, the presentation of a scientific demonstration may reveal the learning of many smaller details, such as measurement skills, representational skills, organizing skills, analytic learnings, definitional learnings, contextual framing details, etc. The playing of a Bach piano piece would reveal mastery of the keyboard, mastery of melodic structuring, as well as an interpretation of the Bach piece itself.

The performance activities in which the student engages, through the feedback of his or her awareness, and the comments of peers, are building the knowledge in the student. For example, in composing a poem, a student is learning the essential ingredients of poetry: metaphor, rhythm, meter, allusion, mood, etc. The activity may involve a number of trials before the student is satisfied that the poem is "finished." Hence, the production and performance of the poem is not coterminal with the whole learning activity. The production of the poem indicates whether and how well the student is mastering the craft of poetry. The same might be said for a student performing a science experiment. The initial attempt to measure the distortion of light that is reflected through water might involve a certain amount of trial and error. When the student has manipulated the measurements enough to gain a consistent measurement, then she can "perform" the experiment and demonstrate her findings in a way that enables others to evaluate how well she has mastered the physics involved in that experiment.

Notice in the diagram that, above the learning activity and performance circles, we find the student's personal life history. The two-directional arrows indicate that student learning is influenced by the student's personal life history as well as that the student's learning is shaping and creating that life world, just as the performance is expressing that personal world and shaping it as well.

If a student has lived near water, swum in it, fished in it, thrown pebbles in it, then the experiment with light may have some features that are more familiar than if the student has little or no experience of water (although the apparent distortion of one's arm in the bathtub is hard to miss). If students are asked to write a poem about autumn, children living in climates with four distinct seasons (such as Canada or New England) will write a different poem than will children from a tropical climate. Below the learning activities and student performance circles, the influence of cultural and linguistic communities in which the student lives is indicated. A Japanese student may compose a poem about autumn in the *haiku* style that is common in his culture. A Spanish-speaking student may use soft, flowing consonants in her poem, an influence from the sound of her language. Japanese students engage in cooperative learning activities differently than their American counterparts do. A teenage boy from a blue-collar family may resist the activity of writing poetry, for such activities may be considered feminine in his family.

To the left of the learning activities in the diagram, we see the teacher's primary involvement. The teacher has an eye *both* on the academic material to be mastered *and* on the student's personal history and culture. With both realities in mind, the teacher can design learning activities that will lead the student to the essential learnings of the academic material. The teacher also assists the students in rehearsing the skills that will come into play in the learning activity, as well as explains the structure and the sequence of the learning activity.

To the right of the learning activities and student production, we see the activity of assessment. The three sources of assessment, the student's own assessment, peer assessment, and teacher assessment, are seen as essential to the learning itself. The reflexivity involved enriches the learning, amplifies, and corrects it when necessary.

As the student is engaged in the learning activity and performance, he or she is reflecting on how the activities are working out, checking out the expected results with the actual results, looking for the intelligibility embedded in the activity. Peers likewise comment on how the activity is progressing, or on the actual finished product. Their questions and comments help to point out things the student may have missed, or reinforce his or her own understanding of what is working in the activity. The teacher likewise plays a part in providing feedback to the student as he or she progresses through the activity and performance. When the activity is a group project, all three voices in the assessment are feeding information back to the group.

Thus we can see how the students' work is influenced by the teacher, by personal life histories, by the communities in which the students live, by the scholarly communities that have produced the material that goes into the learning activities, and by their peers. Nevertheless, the knowledge that is acquired is produced and expressed by the students in their active engagement with the material.

THE WORK OF TEACHERS

Teachers can help their students understand at increasingly deeper levels of sophistication that knowledge is something humans create in order to help them interpret and deal with the realities confronting them. They can help youngsters develop a habit of self-reflection in their learning, asking continually what the learnings mean to them, how it affects their understanding of themselves, how it teaches them to be in relationship to their world, how, possibly, it teaches them responsibilities toward that world. Where learnings involve conflict between various students' understandings of the material, or interpretations of the personal import of the lesson, teachers can use these opportunities to challenge stereotypes and cultural biases, and to create appreciation for divergent perspectives and different cultural traditions.

When appropriate, teachers can introduce themes from a community's meta-narratives as ways of expanding and deepening the meanings the students have created. For Americans, such themes may include freedom, equality before the law, human rights, due process, economic competition, etc. These themes are embodied in stories concerning the settlement of the country by the Pilgrims, the founding of the country on democratic principles inscribed in the Constitution, the histories of various ethnic migrations to this country, stories of the early political struggles of various communities, epics about heroes (and villains!) in various historical moments of the community, etc.

Introducing these meta-narrative themes can, at least for older students, lead to discussions about ideological uses of such themes to justify dysfunctional social and institutional structures that create destructive and unjust relationships between groups of people. The new meta-narratives derived from the Gaia hypothesis and the anthropic principle can be introduced, as appropriate, to place the students' learning within a deeper tapestry of meaning and moral value.

From the right-hand side of the diagram on teachers' work, we can see how coaching, assessing, encouraging, motivating, managing, and learning is linked to the students' work in the learning activities and performance/production of knowledge. At the far left and the bottom of the diagram, we see the teachers' work of mature interaction with the civil and cultural community and with the scholarly community in order to understand the challenges facing the commu-

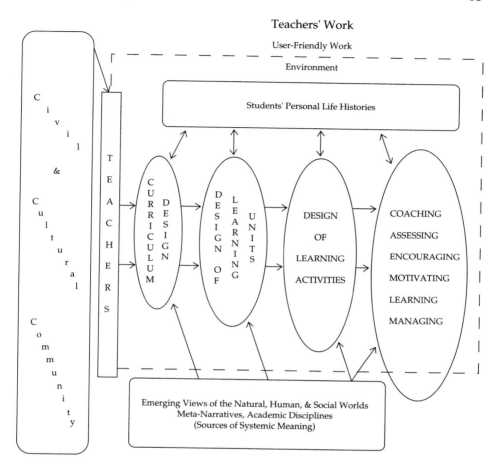

nity, to understand the perspectives being developed in the sciences and humanities, to explore the meta-narratives of the culture and the advances in the academic disciplines.

The teachers' work also involves using this conversation with their language, cultural, and scholarly communities in reconstructing the scaffolding of curriculum design. This design, of course, is also constructed with the students' active involvement in the learning process in mind. Based on the large design of the curriculum (which would incorporate cross-disciplinary themes, multidisciplinary perspectives, reflective critiques of problems in the civic communities, relationships to the personal experiences of the students themselves, etc.) teachers' work will also involve the design of smaller curriculum units with concomitant learning activities to flesh out the larger skeleton of the overall curriculum design.

Moreover, as the diagram suggests, the teachers' work is to create a user-friendly, stimulating environment which encourages and nurtures the work of the students. This aspect of their work will involve teachers working with administrators on the institutional structures and processes that govern the school as a whole. All too often the work of teachers in the classroom is negatively influenced by an institutional environment that, in its impersonality, authoritarianism, and severity, alienates students before they can ever get to their own work. Teachers need to work with administrators to make this environment more user-friendly—themes we will take up in detail in Part Three.

The primary work, however, has to be seen as student learning. The students' learning is not a product of the teachers' work. The students' learning is a product of the students' work. Teachers might be considered as coaches. As in the analogy with athletic contests, the players win or lose the game, not the coaches. Players can suffer from poor coaching, and so can students. But the end result of the performance is much more in the players' and the students' hands.

ADMINISTRATORS' WORK

Having mapped out the work of students and of teachers, we come now to the work of administrators, as shown in the accompanying diagram. If we are convinced that the primary work of the school is conducted by students in their learning and production/performance of knowledge, the work of administrators ought to be organized to support this primary work. This might involve administrators in supportive conversations with three groups of people. Parents, school board members, community leaders of all kinds, and central office administrators make up the first group. The conversation with them ought to involve discussion of community issues about which the students should be learning. Likewise, there should be discussions about the mission of the school, and how the school relates to the cultural and social capital which children bring to the school. All of these conversations ought to feed into the gradual building of a vision and a mission statement for the school. In these conversations, however, the administrators are not simply taking soundings from the community; they are actively promoting their best ideas about the purposes of schooling. In other words, they are not simply assessing public opinion; they are also helping to shape public opinion.

The second group of people whom administrators engage in conversations are the teachers and students of the school. These conversations should bring the central concerns of the civic and cultural community before the teachers. Often these concerns express the larger cultural projects facing the community, projects the students should be studying. The conversations should likewise engage the faculty about the emerging perspectives on the natural, social, and human worlds and about the nature of knowledge and learning. As educators, teachers ought to be talking about these things, but often the administrators have to initiate these discussions. The end result of these conversations should

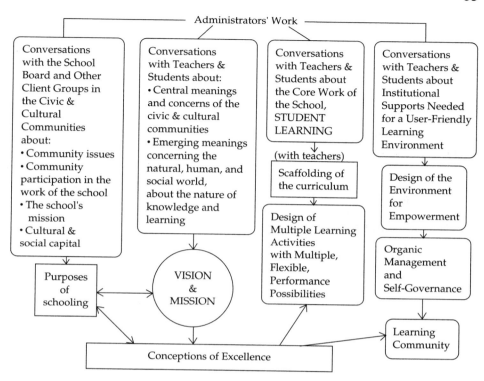

Administrators' Work

| Conversations with the School Board and Other Client Groups in the Civic & Cultural Communities about:
• Community issues
• Community participation in the work of the school
• The school's mission
• Cultural & social capital | Conversations with Teachers & Students about:
• Central meanings and concerns of the civic & cultural communities
• Emerging meanings concerning the natural, human, and social world, about the nature of knowledge and learning | Conversations with Teachers & Students about the Core Work of the School, STUDENT LEARNING | Conversations with Teachers & Students about Institutional Supports Needed for a User-Friendly Learning Environment |

(with teachers)

Scaffolding of the curriculum

Design of Multiple Learning Activities with Multiple, Flexible, Performance Possibilities

Design of the Environment for Empowerment

Organic Management and Self-Governance

Purposes of schooling

VISION & MISSION

Conceptions of Excellence

Learning Community

be the fashioning of a vision and a mission statement for the school, a statement that ought to be revisited every three or four years.

With a vision of where the school should be going, and a more specific mission statement that expresses that vision, teachers and administrators can begin discussions about the core work of the school, namely, student learning. Here is where the third group of people, the students, ought to be involved. Even in the early grades, administrators need to talk with students about their involvement in their learning. Out of these conversations with students and teachers ought to emerge the work of curriculum design and the subsequent design of multiple learning activities. The conversations with students and teachers should include assessment of the institutional environment of the school, an exploration of ways in which the school can be more user-friendly. Strategies for institutional transformation will be discussed in later chapters, but it is important at this point to indicate the connection between institutional change and improved student learning.

Underlying all of these conversations and emerging from them should be various conceptions of excellence—excellence in academics, to be sure, but excellence in many other areas as well. Thus we begin to sense how the work of administering meaning flows into the other two foundational concerns of educational administrators, administering community and administering excellence.

SUMMARY

This vision of the possibilities of education is a vision—not of certainty nor of self-righteous posturing—but of a chastened sensibility, with full awareness that our noble heritage and self-transcending mission have been and continue to be thwarted by our own propensity toward self-seeking. Our vision emerges from a knowledge that the reconstruction of our culture, politics, and economics will not fall ready-made from the sky. Rather, the building of a more humane school for a more humane society will involve struggle, argument, false starts, dead ends, frustrations, and betrayals. However, the effort will also call out the best that is in us and in our companions in the struggle, and will bring a sense of self-fulfillment and deep bonding with those we come to recognize as our brothers and sisters.

Obviously this kind of language almost topples over on itself with the weight of the dramatic consequences it tries to capture. Attempting to frame an educational vision of such enormous proportions, given the American propensity toward pragmatic, "just-get-me-through-the-day" solutions, is a difficult agenda. We run the risk of taking ourselves too seriously, of becoming preoccupied with global problems while missing the small joys embedded in the daily exchanges between people. We are not used to performing in Wagnerian operas on a daily basis; ours is much more the performance of a Gilbert and Sullivan ditty. The vision, therefore, must be framed in the language of exalted collective ends, yet celebrate even the small steps we are capable of taking individually, in our place and in our moment of time. And yes, we will need lots of comic relief in order to sustain a large vision of the struggle for a humane future. How that vision is worked out may become more apparent in succeeding chapters.

ACTIVITIES

1. Have each person in your study group select a book from among the readings in the new science suggested in this chapter (or other readings) and report to the group on the book. Let the study group educate itself in the new science.
2. During the coming week, engage one or more science teachers in conversation about the new science, to see how much they know about it.
3. In your journal, reflect on what the new science means to you personally.
4. Briefly visit some classrooms this week to see how much active learning is going on.
5. Talk to some students and ask them which school activities they like most.

Analyze their responses relative to the level of involvement those activities ask of them.

6. Think of a specific grade or year in your school, and the various subjects students are studying. Invent a student performance or production for each subject in that grade or year. Share that with a teacher in that grade or year.

ENDNOTES

1. For a sample of this literature, see: James MacGregor Burns, *Leadership*, Harper Torchbooks, New York, 1978; Bernard M. Bass, *Leadership and Performance Beyond Expectations*, The Free Press, New York, 1985; Warren Bennis and Bert Nanus, *Leaders*, Harper & Row, New York, 1985; Jay A. Conger, *The Charismatic Leader*, Jossey-Bass, San Francisco, 1989; Robert J. Starratt, *The Drama of Leadership*, Falmer Press, London, 1993; Noel M. Tichy and Mary Anne Devanna, *The Transformational Leader*, John Wiley, New York, 1986.

2. Bass, op. cit.

3. Bennis and Nanus, op. cit.

4. Burns, op. cit.

5. An exception may be found in Fred M. Newman, *Student Empowerment and Achievement in American Secondary Schools*, Teachers College Press, New York: 1992, pp. 194–200.

6. Frederick Turner, *Rebirth of Value: Meditations on Beauty, Ecology, Religion and Education*, State University of New York Press, Albany, NY, 1991. A sample of additional sources includes: Sir John Eccles, Roger Sperry, Ilya Progogine, and Brian Josepheson, *Nobel Prize Conversations*, Saybrook, New York, 1985; Stephen W. Hawking, *A Brief History of Time*, Bantam, New York, 1988; Vladimir Lefebre, "The Fundamental Structures of Human Reflection," *Journal of Social and Biological Structures*, **10**, 1987; James Lovelock, *Gaia: A New Look at Life on Earth*, Oxford University Press, Oxford, 1979; Lynn Margulis and Dorian Sagan, *Microcosmos: Four Billion Years of Microbial Evolution from Our Microbial Ancestors*, Summit, New York, 1986; Ilya Prigogine and Isabelle Stengers, *Order out of Chaos: Man's New Dialogue with Nature*, Bantam, New York, 1984; Ingo Rentschler, Barbara Herzberger and David Epstein (eds.), *Beauty and the Brain: Biological Aspects of Aesthetics*, Birkhauser, Boston, 1988; Thomas J. Scheff, *Microsociology: Emotion, Discourse and Social Structure*, University of Chicago Press, Chicago, 1990; George A. Seilstad, *At the Heart of the Web: The Inevitable Genesis of Intelligent Life*, Harcourt Brace, New York, 1989; Danah Zohar and Ian Marshall, *The Quantum Society*, Flamingo, Harper Collins, London, 1994.

7. Turner, op. cit., p. 16.

8. Turner, op. cit., p. 6.

9. James Lovelock, *Gaia: A New Look at Life on Earth*. Oxford University Press, Oxford, 1979.

10. Turner, op. cit., p. 46.
11. Vaclav Havel, "The New Measure of Man," *The New York Times,* July 8, 1994, p. A27.
12. For a review of research on this point, see Newman, op. cit.
13. This distinction is highlighted in Newman, op. cit.
14. See Paolo Freire, *Pedagogy of the Oppressed,* Continuum, New York, 1970.
15. This curriculum and its deep cultural assumptions are documented by many scholars. To mention a few: Robert Dreeben, *On What Is Learned in School,* Addison-Wesley, Reading, MA, 1968; Philip W. Jackson, Robert E. Boostrom, and David T. Hansen, *The Moral Life of Schools,* Jossey-Bass, San Francisco, 1993; Paulo Freire, op. cit.; Orit Ichilov, *Political Socialization, Citizenship Education, and Democracy,* Teachers College Press, New York, 1990; C. A. Bowers and David Flinders, *Responsive Teaching: An Ecological Approach to Classroom Patterns of Language, Culture, and Thought,* Teachers College Press, New York, 1990; Thomas S. Popkewitz, *A Political Sociology of Educational Reform,* Teachers College Press, New York, 1991.

CHAPTER 6

The Pursuit of Meaning in a Learning Community

In previous chapters we underscored the problematic nature of the construction of meaning in the postmodern era. Educational administrators have a fundamental responsibility to administer the pursuit, exploration, construction, performance, and critique of meaning. The question is how they can carry it out in a time of transition, when our culture is struggling to replace or transform the certainties that have sustained a whole cycle of its development? Clearly, the public does not want a radical leadership that will discard all the familiar formulas associated with schooling. The traditional mission of the school is to teach students to understand the natural, human, and social world in order to know who they are, how they can participate in public life, what their responsibilities are to the natural, human, and social worlds, and thereby to find fulfillment by participating in these worlds. In this time of transition, a fundamental task of educational administrators is to infuse that traditional mission of the school with a new meaning that melds the emerging perspectives from the sciences and the humanities with the truths behind the old certainties.

Earlier we focused on the analysis of core meanings in modernity and how they have shifted. We saw how the postmodern critique and the new science are leading us toward a revised understanding of the dynamic relationships between human life and the natural environment; between the political, economic, and cultural forms we create and the way these forms can be used to dominate and control, as well as to enlighten our sense of moral striving; between the constructive and performative sides and students' active involvement in school learnings. This new understanding constitutes the ground for a new vision of education. By the work of building that collective vision, educational administrators engage in the initial stages of administering meaning. In this work they initiate a conversation among teachers about the basic meanings behind what they teach, and the meanings that are implied and assumed in the curriculum.

Having explored the importance of vision for the administering of meaning, we turn now to a central metaphor that organizes that vision, the metaphor of the school as a learning community. As we do so, we recall the conclusions that help us to define the characteristics of such a learning community.

- Learning must be situated in a critical community of inquirers who accept that knowledge is always partial and fallible and who support the enrichment of knowledge through sharing of meanings, interpretations, and learnings among all members of the community.
- The learning agenda of the school must be continually related to something intrinsically human—to the exploration of questions important to human individuals and social life.
- The learning agenda of the school must be related to the large cultural projects of our current era as well as to the cultural projects of our history. Thus, school learnings are connected to a significant discourse about the making of history.
- School meanings must be continuously related to students' experience of everyday life.

In Chapter 5 we saw that the central work of the school is the students' work, the work of learning and of the performance of learning. The idea of a learning community thus implies a community of students who are actively engaged in producing knowledge and understanding, not simply as individual productions, but as productions of groups within the community. A learning community also implies roles for teachers and administrators, who must consider themselves as involved in continuous learning about the work of the school and the relation of schooling to society. A school as a learning community, however, does not exist in a vacuum. As a social institution, it is accountable to various stakeholders. The question of accountability has to be settled early on, for it determines how the learning community will conduct its business.

THE QUESTION OF WHO IS IN CHARGE

To whom is the learning community responsible? That is, who is in charge? Schools are not independent corporations; they are agencies of the state. Even private schools must have some kind of legal charter, which is granted by the state.

One would like to assume, as well, that schools belong to their local communities, and therefore are answerable to their local communities. This is true to some extent, at least in the United States and, I understand, increasingly so in England and Australia. Local educational authorities (LEAs) such as school boards can be sued by local parents for not providing customary educational services to their children, or for neglect of their legal responsibilities. The state, however, is considered the primary authority in education and may step in to mandate new services, new curricula, new tests, and new funding arrangements. Of course, the state is governed by people elected by the electorate, so they must ultimately be answerable to those who elect them, as well as to the courts who monitor the protection of civil and human rights.

Two other voices also exercise influence over school policies, the voice of the scholarly community and the voice of the business community. The scholarly community produces and legitimates the disciplines of knowledge. These disciplines of knowledge ground the production of textbooks and learning materials and technologies which, for better or worse, define the formal curriculum of schools. Textbooks are necessarily updated to take account of developments in the field. They are also updated to take account of political developments in the fields of scholarship, for example, the inclusion of feminist views of historical events, or samples of literature by minority authors. Local communities do not have the right to promote racism and sexism in their schools' curriculum, just as they do not have the right to insist that their geography courses teach that the sun revolves around the earth. The scholarly community can require, by virtue of the authority of its scholarship, that the school's curriculum represent the best knowledge and understanding of the natural, human, and social worlds that the scholarly disciplines have produced.

This is not to say that local controversies over the curriculum can be settled simply by referral to scholarly sources. Religious and ethical beliefs held by various groups in the community may lead them to object, for example, to theories of evolution as taught in biology classes, or to the curricula of health and sex education classes. Educators embroiled in such controversies need to turn to scholarly research in both theology and ethics, as well as to constitutional authorities, in order to work out some response to these objections. The weight of the scholarly community should be a strong influence in the conversation, even when it may not be the decisive voice.

Another influential voice in this whole question of the schools' accountability is the business community, including trade unions and associations of craftspeople. In general, these communities are concerned with the preparation of youth for employment, including the development of a good work ethic in youth and their grounding in the basic skills required in the world of work. As we approach the twenty-first century, these basic skills now include computer literacy, collaboration, inventiveness, and flexibility, as well as language and computation skills, problem-solving skills, and higher-order-thinking skills.

Schools need to take these different voices into account, whether they choose to retain the traditional bureaucratic format or to restructure in the direction of a learning community, for these groups make up the matrix of major influences over the substance of the curriculum and how it is learned. In other words, schools are accountable to the local community and must respond to local concerns and to the challenges, limitations, and opportunities offered by that local context, whether the context is a multicultural inner-city community or a wealthy suburb.

Schools are also accountable to the state to provide mandated services, and to observe the legal restraints and obligations imposed by state statutes. States can also hold schools accountable with respect to the integrity of knowledge as represented in the academic disciplines. Schools are accountable to the whole civic community in so far as they are to prepare youngsters for participation in the public life of that community. Work and employment are central concerns in the public life of the community, and hence basic preparation for the world of work is necessary.

ACCOUNTABILITY TO STUDENTS

Schools, however, have a basic choice. They can passively allow these various voices to define their agenda, or they can actively define their own agenda while taking these voices into account. Educational administrators should choose the latter, active form of self-determination for their schools.

I want to argue that schools are made up primarily of students and should take their reality into account first and foremost. Students are not owned by the state, the local community, the scholarly community, or the business community. They are not owned by the school, either. They are human beings in their own right who are beginning a life journey that for all of us is altogether too short. They are in school to help find out who they are, what their potential is, find out to whom they belong, to whom they are responsible. They are in school to learn something about human freedom, about heroism and its opposite, to explore the comedy and tragedy in human life, to explore the various examples of human fulfillment, to explore and learn to understand and respect their natural and human environment.

At the heart of all education is the belief that the truth we seek through the process of learning will set us free: free to be the best selves we can be; free to love the truths about ourselves and our fellows and our natural world, and free to turn away from the destructive elements those same truths reveal; free to bend our backs and our minds to the work society needs us for; free to express and celebrate the truths we discover. This belief does not deny the struggle such a learning process involves; rather it sustains it.

The self-definition of a learning community ought to be grounded on this belief. The learning community then enters into conversation with the local and state concerns, and into conversation with the scholarly and business communities. The conversation is not, however, between a lackey and an owner; it is a conversation between partners, between colleagues who have the same human stakes in the learning process.

ACCOUNTABILITY IN A DEEPER SENSE

There is another level of accountability that may be in conflict with the accountability to the four communities mentioned previously (local, state, scholarly, and business communities). This is an accountability to the historical moment and its tensions. We have already alluded to the school's responsibility to be aware of the transition from the modern to the postmodern mood, and to the emerging perspectives on the natural, social, and human worlds being developed in the sciences and humanities. I believe schools have to be accountable for this awareness, for it signifies an accountability to the historical moment.

There is another major tension in our historical moment that schools need to take into account, especially if the school community intends to become a genuine learning community. I speak here of the phenomena of mass administration and mass production and their threat to the life world of humans.[1] This tension needs to be addressed by educators as they try to build a learning community.

THE LIFE WORLD VERSUS THE ADMINISTERED WORLD[2]

The life world is the world of natural human relationships: the face-to-face life of people within a family and extended family, the world of intimacy and friendship. In native societies (often patronizingly labeled "primitive"), the life world encompasses everything: the child's birth in the home, the raising and socialization of children, education in the myths and traditions and history of the community, rites of passage at various stages of life, religious rituals, the world of work and commerce, and immersion in the rhythms of nature and the seasons.

With the coming of modernity, especially in the nineteenth and twentieth centuries, another kind of world began to emerge—a more artificial world of the state and of commerce. Public life became fragmented, compartmentalized, and rationalized through the public administration of the state. The state began to regulate banking and education; food production; the use of airwaves, travel, and commerce; law courts; and the dumping of garbage. The world of commerce became separated from the home. Workers worked in factories and firms where work is governed by goals of efficiency and maximization of productivity, not by kinship relations or the rhythms of nature.

The world of mass production and mass administration gradually but relentlessly intruded more and more on the life world of family and neighborhood. The government increasingly regulated the life world through laws governing marriage and divorce, compulsory schooling of children, the provision of health care and public housing, the administration of pension funds, and the monitoring of retirement incomes. The commercial world commodified more and more of the life world, replacing family agriculture with the supermarket, herbal healing with the chemist, the village square as the hub for news and gossip with newspapers, society columns, talk shows, and television newscasts. Even romance became commodified through dating services, wedding consultants, honeymoon packages, and marriage counseling. Day-care centers, child psychologists, and social workers took over much of the socialization of youngsters. Television replaced family and neighborhood story tellers.

The life world of face-to-face relationships where human beings engage in conversations, negotiate conflicts, express how they feel about aspects of their lives, where people laugh and joke with each other and commiserate over common sufferings; the life world where people make things for one another, such as clothing, meals, and toys for children; the life world where people experience nature first-hand through planting and watering and weeding and harvesting, where youngsters see birth and dying as natural events, where one can arrange flowers and eat food one has grown in one's own garden; the life world of sickness and recovery, of tragedy and pain and loss, of the joys of intimacy, the satisfactions of friendships, the loyalties of family, the singing and dancing to celebrate days of remembrance, and days of sacred events—this life world has been increasingly "colonized," as Habermas has said, by the artificial world of rational order, by the manipulation of desire and fantasy through advertising, by the reduction of individuality to predictable uniformity in state policy formation, by the quantification of interpersonal relationships and work and leisure, which are then entered into cost–benefit formulas and calibrated in the development of economic and political policies. The mind-set of this artificial world affects the private citizen and the business executive, as well as the public official.

This is not to say that the natural life world is all sweetness and light. It is also a world of jealousies and hatred, of parental violence against children, and of madness and cruelty. That part of the life world deserves public regulation and therapeutic attention. But we should remind ourselves when reading the educational reform proposals of state and corporate blue-ribbon committees that their worlds are also affected by greed, lust for power, self-serving rationalization, and not a little insanity.

The colonization of the life world by the artificial world of mass administration and mass commodity production and consumption has clearly affected all aspects of the school. Students experience being treated as things, as intellects that are expected to absorb required information and then to reproduce it, untouched by their own sentiments and experiences, on exams. Achievement in school means meeting uniform standards set for everyone, not a personal response to the curriculum. Students are to be controlled. Their sexuality is an embarrassment. Their physical energy is distracting. Their rebellion is to be smothered. It is as though they are the adversary. Students hear the unspoken message: "No thinking for yourself, thank you. We don't need your uniqueness or your creativity, only your conformity to our agenda."

What results from all this? A massive alienation of young people from schooling. Students recognize the trivialization of learning. Academic studies have less and less to do with their life world. Their hopes and fears, their longings and uncertainties are not addressed. Instead their schooling experiences are managed, controlled, commodified, and artificialized by those in authority.

Educational administration, as well as teaching in this artificial world of mass administration and mass production, is understood as management of inputs and outputs, efficient delivery of services, and productivity in terms of test scores. It makes perfect sense to officials of government and industry to colonize the schools, demanding that schools serve national economic policies. In their minds, schools are there to further the interests of the state and of commercial enterprise, for that is what for them, defines, public life. Hence school administration is expected to mirror government and business administration, and schools are expected to resemble the efficiency of corporations.

Educators should think twice before accepting this view. We have altogether too many examples of corporate executives and government officials who have colluded to monopolize the market, denude the environment, savage urban populations, and defraud their clients, while at the same time skirting the law and lining their pockets. We ought to be skeptical of the sanctimonious demands of the corporate world that education be held accountable to the public. Recommendations that schools be managed according to "accepted business procedures" should make us tremble. Where did such a sanitized and self-serving view of big business come from?

These proposals would reduce schooling to predictable, controllable, uniform elements of policy implementation. State and commercial executives would define what skills are required, and the schools would be expected promptly to turn out compliant workers with the required skills.

Another possibility, of course, is that educators will build genuine learning communities that connect the world of teaching and learning with the life world of the community. I am not suggesting that it is possible to return to the organic community of the primitive life world. The world of state government and commercial enterprise is here to stay. The two worlds, however, do not have to be antithetical; they could in fact enhance the values of each other. The life world, after all, requires some administration—family budgeting, negotiation of conflict, and distribution of labor. Commercial transactions in the life world are an everyday reality. Technology has enhanced some aspects of the life world, as, for example, in the availability of cultural productions through electronic media and the enhanced communication with family members on any part of the globe. However, nonexploitative dialogue between these two worlds, dialogue that serves the human interests of people, requires a profound transformation of the assumptions behind the world of mass administration and mass production.

I believe that unless educators confront the colonization of the life world by the logic of mass administration and mass production, their efforts to build a genuine learning community will be frustrated. The learning community can counteract that type of thinking by establishing continuous connections between the learning being promoted in the school and the life world of the students and of the community. This learning will probe both the possibilities and the dangers of living in a mass-administered society and a world of mass production and consumption—especially the dangers that arise when that world is severed from concern for moral striving, personal responsibility, responsibility to the environment, and the human quest for both freedom and community. In other words, within the learning community the curriculum should include the work of uniting the two worlds, allowing neither the artificial world of mass administration and mass production to dominate the human agenda, nor the humanistic agenda to ignore the demands of nation building and economic productivity.

ESSENTIAL ELEMENTS OF A
LEARNING COMMUNITY

A learning community tries to learn to live together in a defined space, with specific local challenges, problems, and opportunities , given specific resources. Sustained social interchanges among familiar people in a familiar terrain with recognizable landmarks nurtures the sense of connectedness, much the way village life does. Even in large cities, the local neighborhood serves the same purpose. Some communities build themselves around a religious center or place of worship. Some build themselves around a university and share in the intellectual and cultural life it supports. Some build around ethnic origins and traditional culture, such as the Chinatowns, the Little Italys, the Germantowns. Some build around a common race, such as The Harlems, The Watts, the South Sides.

Toni Morrison captures the special feeling of place that an urban neighborhood can have for a long-term resident in her description of Harlem in the 1920s:

> Daylight slants like a razor cutting the buildings in half. . . . Below is the shadow where any blasé thing takes place: clarinets and lovemaking, fists and the voices of sorrowful women. A city like this one makes me dream tall and feel in on things. Hep. It's the bright steel rocking above the shade below that does it. When I look over strips of green grass lining the river, at church steeples and into the cream-and-copper halls of apartment buildings, I'm strong. Alone, yes, but top-notch and indestructible—like the City in 1926 when all the wars are over and there will never be another one. . . .
>
> Nobody says it's pretty here; nobody says it's easy either. What it is is decisive, and if you pay attention to the street plans, all laid out, the City can't hurt you. . . .
>
> Do what you please in the City, it is there to back and frame you no matter what you do. And what goes on on its blocks and lots and side streets is anything the strong can think of and the weak will admire. All you have to do is heed the design—the way it's laid out for you, considerate, mindful of where you want to go and what you might need tomorrow.[3]

Schools are nested in neighborhoods or include youngsters who come from many different neighborhoods. For six or seven hours a day, schools that are learning communities become extensions of these neighborhoods; they become a place with defined spaces, with familiar people, and with friends and enemies. Students in learning communities develop a sense of being connected to their learning community. That connectedness implies trust, loyalty, and responsibility for relationships; it becomes a micro life world, an extension of the feeling of family and kin.

Learning communities can become extensions of neighborhood and family when they recognize and honor the life world of children in these neighborhoods and families. Children come to school brimming over with interesting experiences, funny stories, and frightful exposures to human spitefulness; they come with unformulated questions, curiosity about things in their life world they don't understand. Learning communities take the time to listen to young-sters' stories and to their questions. They find ways to relate the curriculum to that life world.

If schools are to teach the larger connections—connections to our ancestors, to the biosphere, to the cultural heroes of the past, to the agenda of the future—they must begin with the connections of everyday experience, the connections to our peers, to our extended families, to the cultural dynamics of our neigh-borhoods, and to the politics and economics and technology in the homes and on the streets of the neighborhood. In other words, they have to learn to un-derstand the life world of their immediate environment, how people relate to authority, to beauty, to nature, and to conflict. They should be led to appreciate all the connections in their immediate environment, for that environment is a metaphor for the field physics of the human, social, and natural worlds.

Youngsters who begin to understand these connections also begin to rec-ognize, at least tacitly, the interdependence of everything in that place. This helps to overcome the alienation from place bred by the individualism of modernity (the assumption that one is free to choose one's place—that one is not accountable to or for one's place). The learning community teaches again and again that you have to be responsible for your place. That means knowing the history of the place, as well as the present life-sustaining resources of the place. It means situating yourself in a place and understanding yourself in re-lationship to the natural and social ecology of that place. It also means taking account of the future of that place, joining with others to discuss the possibili-ties and dreams they might share.[4] Hence, a learning community will seek to strengthen the bonding and participatory processes necessary for membership in that community.

CORE PROCESSES OF THE LEARNING COMMUNITY

Every school that restructures itself as a learning community will be unique. Each school will have a particular chemistry of subcommunities from which its students come, a specific mix of talents and interests among the teaching staff, a variety of local limitations and resources in the neighborhoods surrounding the school, and so forth. Nevertheless, learning communities will manifest some common, core processes. The following are at least a beginning listing of them.

1. *Learning takes place in a caring environment.* This means that every child feels he or she is cared for as a valuable member of the school community, that others believe he or she has something to offer the work of the community. This kind of feeling of being cared for will take time to build. Youngsters will learn to listen to one another, how to disagree without hurting, and how to cooperate and collaborate on learning projects. The same goes for teachers, both in their dealings with students and with one another.

The caring environment should also encourage caring for what is being studied and the knowledge being produced and performed. This core process will involve intentionally and programmatically teaching youngsters how to cooperate on projects, how to resolve conflicts, how to take charge of and organize their work together, how to set up ground rules to guide their work together. Furthermore, especially in multicultural learning communities, youngsters will need to spend time becoming acquainted with the cultural traditions and perspectives of their classmates, and appreciating the unities that bridge the cultural differences among them.

2. *Learning involves lots of storytelling.* Telling stories is a natural way for humans to communicate. Learning the art of storytelling provides continuous practice of the grammar and rhetoric of the language. It also facilitates the mind's development of imaginative power through the use of specific images and metaphors in the story. It also nurtures the mind's development of temporal sequence and cause–effect relationships. Storytelling, most of all, provides a foundation for conveying and exploring meaning. Often it provides the link between the lesson of the curriculum and the life world of the student.

3. *Learning in school is related to home and neighborhood experiences.* The home and neighborhood represent the life world where students relate and apply their science and history lessons, where they discover reflections of their art classes, where they mine the stories of their families and neighbors, and where they test their understanding of their school learning with adults. Homework assignments should include projects to discover all the uses of electricity in the home, including the wattage and voltage used by the various appliances; projects to gather family history from family elders; projects to map their neighborhood, with attention to scale and to identification of key locations; projects to identify neighborhood heroes and characters, including discussions of the values they exemplify; projects to study the commercial businesses in the neighborhood, with an attempt to describe how they manage their finances; projects to interview local politicians and their positions on various issues in the community; projects to meet with local artists, musicians, and writers, to learn about their work and the meanings they are exploring; projects to explore the weather patterns of their region and how these affect the growth of vegetation in their area; projects that explore the various careers in their communities, with perhaps a statistical breakdown of the types of work that people in their neighborhood do; projects that study how local banks interact with their neighborhood, giving attention to how loans are secured, how much money the bank makes on various types of loans, who benefits most from using the local banks, etc.; projects that study the local newspapers and the types of editorial positions those newspapers take on a variety of positions; projects that study the various utilities in the neighborhood and how they function; and projects that study various tax-supported public services in the neighborhood. The list is limited only by our imagination.

In all of these projects related to family and neighborhood, students will exercise the academic skills of careful observation, storytelling, organizing, and summarizing, as well as various mathematical skills. They will also deepen their learning of much of the content of the school curriculum in science, history, and humanities, and make a connection between the academic learnings and their life world. They will also be learning much about the complications of a mass-administered society, and the mass-produced services and commodities that saturate their homes and neighborhood. Along the way, they will encounter human beings engaged in the daily work of making a living, making do, getting by, and striving for some kind of moral consistency and legitimated meanings in their lives. This kind of exposure to human realities should become food for reflection and discussion with teachers and peers in the school, discussions of values, lifestyles, and human qualities that they find appealing and not so appealing.

Much of this doing of science and history and art in the home and neighborhood can be done with relative dispatch. Some of the projects will require more extended time, perhaps released time during school hours. The details of scheduling a curriculum that requires this grounding of learning in the life world of the community and the exploration of the way a mass-administered and mass-produced world works will differ from school to school. Obviously, setting up these kinds of learning projects will require prior conversations with parents and community leaders. Also, assessment of this kind of learning will require some changes from current forms of assessment. Teachers who design such projects will know the kind of learning they expect from such projects and should be able to build in various criteria for assessment.

4. *Learning should lead to some product or performance.* This can be an individual or group product or performance. In either case, it should be a product or performance that is shared with others. Whenever possible and appropriate, the product or performance should be useful to the community of the school and to the community at large. In this respect, I mean useful in the broad meaning of the term: A project might involve an attempt to propose, for example, a more environmentally appropriate way to dispose of the community's waste; an entertainment that enriches the cultural life of the community (such as a musical production, a poem, a film); a design for a different kind of shopping mall; a report of an evaluation of some community service that could be improved; or simply a story about an unsung hero of the community.

The performances and products of the younger members of the learning community might not seem to have significant usefulness. Nonetheless, young children are very creative in coming up with ideas that engage their peers in helpful ways. Youngsters can create one-act plays that portray in story some human value, or even, through imaginary characters, demonstrate a scientific principle. Again, what constitutes a learning product or performance is limited only by our imaginations. The point is to have youngsters make connections between the learnings of the formal curriculum and then make something with those learnings. It is the making that brings the ideas, skills, and understandings into a visible reality that will be much more real than the producing of the "right" answer on a multiple-choice exam.

This connection of learning to production and performance personalizes the learning. It allows the student to own the learning. It also shows the student that learning can be useful, that it does have consequences beyond getting grades. And in the process, the student will be producing a self with much

greater clarity because she or he, the learner, will be putting her or his finger-
prints on something tangible as a result of the struggle to learn something.
Other people will see this product or performance and thank them for it. The
student will realize that she or he can actually do something that makes a difference or a contribution—something that other people appreciate.

   5. *There should be periodic and continuous reference to an exploration of meta-narratives.* By meta-narratives I mean the larger stories we tell one another about
the central ideological and mythical elements of the culture. Clifford Geertz's
definition of culture can help to set our focus here. Culture, says Geertz, is

> ... an historically transmitted pattern of meanings embodied in symbols, a sys-
> tem of inherited conceptions expressed in symbolic forms by means of which
> men communicate, perpetuate and develop their knowledge about and atti-
> tudes toward life.[5]

Against the backdrop of these larger stories of the culture, all our smaller
stories make sense or non-sense. In this core process of periodically exploring
the meaning of our meta-narratives, teachers and students can look at what
they are coming to understand by the following core terms in our culture. (They
are presented in no particular order.)

(a) *E pluribus unum*	(b) Science	(c) Wealth
(d) Community	(e) Responsibility	(f) Work
(g) Human rights	(h) Friendship	(i) Justice
(j) Freedom	(k) Democracy	(l) Competition
(m) Truth	(n) Beauty	(o) Goodness
(p) Death	(q) Time	(r) Self-worth
(s) Nature	(t) Love	(u) Heroism
(v) Patriotism	(w) Power	(x) Parenting
(y) Law	(z) Authority	

That is my list; others would cross out some terms and add others. Every learning community ought to come up with some kind of list of core terms that they
all agree to explore from time to time with their classes.

   Such discussions would not be the kind of abstract discussions of Socrates
and his friends. Rather, teachers would raise a theme as it emerged from the material the students were engaged in at the time. Students and teacher would attempt to uncover deeper meanings underneath the narratives being offered at
the time, by either the students or the curriculum. Students might be encouraged to compose a poem or a musical piece to express their thoughts and feelings about a particular meta-narrative. Teachers might pause to refer to a story
from Greek mythology, from Cervantes, Shakespeare, or Faulkner, or from one
of the great storytellers of another culture that illustrates or problemitizes an aspect of the meta-narrative theme. Students might be encouraged to ask an older
member of the family to talk about that theme, or to recount a story they heard
within their extended family that illustrated the theme.

   The point of these periodic reviews of meta-narratives is not to come up
with one, absolutely perfect definition of the concept. Rather, it is to bring home
the lesson that these themes are interwoven with the great questions about life

with which every community must wrestle. These themes circulate within the practical, everyday way a community and the individuals in it define themselves and perform themselves. If the members of the learning community are to learn how to be human beings, they too will have to wrestle with the meanings and the practical consequences embedded in these meta-narrative themes.

6. *The learning community should periodically explore the really big questions.* These questions include: What does it mean to be human? What does it mean to be a community? What is the meaning of life, of suffering, of death? What does it mean to be a global society? In what do I find my ultimate fulfillment? What is my relationship to the universe? Again, the purpose is not to answer these questions definitively. Rather, students at various points in their development should be brought up against these questions, and asked to respond from within their own experience and understanding. Of course, assessment of these responses should be handled with great sensitivity and tact.

Every other year or so, administrators and teachers should oblige themselves to respond to these big questions. They should be encouraged to share and discuss their responses as ways to authenticate their own search for meaning as members of a learning community. They will also need to explore appropriate ways to raise these questions with their students. Such discussions will help them recognize that from time to time the material under study in their classes may lend itself to a diversion into one of these larger questions.

ORGANIZATIONAL CONCERNS

Learning communities can be organized in any number of ways. Many large schools are now restructuring themselves into a tapestry of small schools-within-schools, structured around grade clusters or age clusters, or around large unifying themes. Size seems to be an important consideration. The unit in question should be small enough to promote quality interactions between teachers and students. Some of these units also look to duration as an important feature; they build in continuity over two or three years, so that teachers will come to know their students very well and can facilitate their development more responsively. Some schools will use the city or region as their classroom; others will focus on in-depth concentration on a profession or career (say, in music, science, or design); others will focus on replicating features of village life in the school by constructing their own money, their own cottage industries, their own governance and judicial structures, and their own cultural events. Again, the organization of learning communities is limited only by our imaginations.

ADMINISTRATORS' WORK

In the administration of meaning, the work of the administrator is to build and support the kinds of learning communities that are suggested by the main elements of this chapter. There is no way to build a learning community. Much depends on what the local circumstances are, the chemistry among the faculty and the students, and the willingness of parents and community leaders to investigate other possibilities in the shape and process of the school. I do not offer any magical formula that guarantees success. We are still in the process of inventing genuine learning communities, so there are various examples in most regions that we can turn to, even though no one model will transfer exactly to another school.[6] Ultimately, each school will have to invent itself as a learning community.

This chapter attempts to lay out the essential ingredients of a learning community. In Part Three we explore how such a learning community actually works as a community; how it governs itself; how it empowers people within the community; and how it structures and designs itself. As we will see, the foundation we have built in Part Two will connect nicely with the ideas in Part Three.

ACTIVITIES

1. Cite examples from your school that demonstrate how the world of mass production and mass administration intrude on the life world of your school.
2. Redesign your school as a learning community. Share that design with some of your colleagues at work, and record their reactions and suggestions.
3. In your study group, share your individual designs of a learning community. Compare similarities and contrast differences. What common elements can you agree on?
4. What are the major obstacles to turning your school into a learning community? As an administrator, what are some strategies you can employ to overcome these obstacles?

ENDNOTES

1. For examples of the use of this terminology, see Jurgen Habermas, *Toward a Rational Society*, translated by Jeremy J. Shapiro, Beacon Press, Boston, 1970, and *Knowledge and Human Interests*, translated by Jeremy J. Shapiro, Beacon Press, Boston, 1971. See also Anthony Giddens, *The Constitution of Society*, University of California Press, Berkeley, 1984.
2. This section is adapted from Robert J. Starratt, *Transforming Life in Schools: Conversations about Leadership and School Reform*, Australian Council on Educational Administration, Melbourne, 1993, Chap. 2.
3. Toni Morrison, *Jazz*, Plume/Penguin, New York, 1992.
4. Donald Oliver, in his *Educational, Modernity, and Fractured Meaning*, State University of New York Press, Albany, 1989, and C. A. Bowers, in his *Elements of a Post Liberal Theory of Education*, Teachers College Press, New York,

1987, both speak eloquently of restoring the learning of connectedness to a neighborhood and bio-region, as well as the attendant responsibilities such learning engenders.

5. Clifford Geertz, *The Interpretation of Cultures,* Basic Books, New York, 1973, p. 89.
6. See the examples cited in Gregory A. Smith (ed.), *Public Schools That Work: Creating Community,* Routledge, New York, 1993.

PART THREE

Administering Community

In Part Two we explored the paradoxical notion of administering meaning. We saw that in ignoring the larger historical and philosophical issues, educational administrators administer meaning by default. That is, they administer schools in which meanings largely left over from the modern world view are allowed to drive the curriculum and the assessment in the school. In these schools, administrators seem to take no responsibility for the teaching of obsolete and dysfunctional meanings in their school. A new appreciation of what is involved in administering meaning places the administrator squarely at the forefront of the reinvention of schools for the twenty-first century.

In Part Three we turn to the second fundamental of educational administration, administering community. In this part we explore new understandings of community, which transform the traditional separation of the individual from the community into a necessary union of the individual and the community. One needs the other; they are organically mutually sustaining. Furthermore, the individual finds personal fulfillment in living for the community. One of the essential characteristics of a community is that it governs itself; another is that it manage its affairs in such a way as to sustain and nurture the very core meanings by which the community defines itself. Central to self-governance and organic management is the process of individual and communal empowerment.

CHAPTER 7

Administering Community

In this chapter we take up the second major theme of the new fundamentals of educational administration: administering community. As with the first theme, we find ourselves initially entangled in a paradox. Communities are unique realities. They are embedded in specific contexts of place and history, made up of a unique mix of people with various interests, abilities, talents, and limitations. Communities need lots of space for spontaneity, invention, affection. Administering a community sounds like manipulating, controlling, and parceling out in some logic of production something that is very elastic and dynamic.

"Community" tends to signify a group of equals who are bonded together in friendship, kinship, and shared values. One does not administer friendship or kinship in the sense of creating or controlling it. Friendship, kinship, and shared values come before administration. Administration arises out of communities as they deal with the everyday problems of living and working together. We can speak of administering a social environment for the promotion of friendship, kinship, and shared values. One can administer a process for building and maintaining community. Such a process involves coordinating the work of various groups so that the areas where they overlap do not become sources of conflict. The process involves developing a communication network so that everyone in the community knows what is going on in the community. It involves future-search seminars, long- and short-range planning, attention to policy formation and implementation, as well as some assessment of the community's projects. Hence, the paradox is partially resolved, but only partially. A community becomes a community because the people of the community, rather than the administrators, make it a community. Administrators are neither a necessary nor a sufficient cause of community. Yet their influence on the quality of community life is thought to be substantial.

The theme of community, though it does not occupy center stage in the literature on school renewal, has been championed by some well-known scholars. In some cases, the theme of community emerges from a focus on caring as a primary value in the educational process. The work of Lynn Beck and Nell Noddings can be cited as examples of this point of view.[1] Others, such as Becker,[2]

Bricker,[3] and Ichilov,[4] deal with community in connection with the democratic purposes of schooling. Still others, such as Purpel and Shapiro[5] and Starratt,[6] connect the building of community in schools to the moral purposes of schooling. Bryk and Driscoll,[7] Gregory Smith,[8] and Ralph Peterson[9] link concern for community in schools specifically to the making of a learning community. Perhaps the most influential recent book is Tom Sergiovanni's book, *Building Community in Schools*.[10] Sergiovanni provides a good discussion of community, using the distinction between *gemeinschaft* and *gesellschaft* as developed by the German sociologist Ferdinand Tonnies in the late nineteenth century. That distinction echoes the distinction I made in Chapter 6, where I distinguished between the life world and the world of mass administration and mass production. Sergiovanni also develops the beginnings of a moral grounding for community, and then goes on to link community with the dynamics of the learning community.

In all of these recent works, however, there is the assumption that within our culture the very notion of community is nonproblematic. Perhaps the work of Bowers, although not so much concerned with community as I define it here, goes to the root of the problem by attacking the cultural assumptions behind the classical liberal world view, assumptions about rationality, about the individual, and about the direction of human history as progress.[11] These assumptions, as we saw in Chapter 5, have been seriously critiqued by postmodern philosophers and social theorists. Bowers, however, attacks these assumptions primarily because of their disastrous cumulative effects on the ecology of the planet, and calls for a change in perspective that would locate humans within an ecological web of intelligence and life much closer to the Gaia proposal mentioned in Chapter 5. At present, I want to continue to develop a new sense of community that takes the critique of the postmoderns seriously and yet which builds on the fragments of legitimate insights left after the devastation of their critique.

In this chapter, we try to gain a clearer focus on what we mean by community by situating the problem of community within the postmodern context. The chapter then explores the roots of the tensions between the individual and the community and the educational implications of these tensions. The centrality of a richer understanding of citizenship and governance derived from a reconstructed notion of community is treated as a prelude to a commentary on the centrality of education for citizenship and self-governance. Finally, the chapter suggests specific attention to community as an essential curriculum of the school, discussing ways in which educational administrators can administer this curriculum. Following chapters take up other ways of administering community, that is, through the process of empowerment and through processes of organic management and design.

MEANINGS OF COMMUNITY

In the previous chapter we considered community more as a means to an end than as an end in itself. The learning community was organized for the production and performance of learning and knowledge. Learning was the end; community inquiry and performance were the means. Even though we insisted on the social nature of knowledge, its imbeddedness in community, we nonetheless emphasized the social and personal dynamics of *learning*. The general goal of learning defined the kind of community this was to be; it provided its central task and shaped the processes of achieving its central tasks. Now, however, we want to consider community as an end in itself. Whereas the learning community had as its goal the production of knowledge, the community we are talking about now has as its goal the production of community itself. The major learning outcome now is the learning of community—how to be one, how to sustain community in the face of divisive conflicts and centrifugal forces, and how to become more of a community.

We can think of community in many ways. We can think of community as a utopian ideal we strive for. We can think of community as the given ground for our collective activities. ("I belong to St. James's parish and I attend St. James's school." "My family has always lived in the community of Cobberville, where I go to school.") We can think of community as a quality of the relationships we share in a group; we say that we have "achieved community," however imperfectly and temporarily, through a collective activity. Or we can think of community as something that is always in front of us, something we attempt to perform every day, yet something we never fully exhaust (the way a loving couple can say to each other every day, "This day I marry you," and never exhaust the possibilities of the relationship; the way John Dewey spoke of democracy, as something we progressively achieve but whose possibilities we never fully realize). It is this last meaning of community that I believe provides the focus for this fundamental purpose of schooling. This last meaning fits our historical and political realities more accurately and is more consistent with the scientific understanding of the evolution of life and the postmodern sense of the construction of social knowledge.

COMMUNITY AS A MODERN PROBLEM

Once again, let us take an idea journey so that we can understand the depth and complexity of the issue. With this understanding we can explore the rich possibilities for reinventing schools for the twenty-first-century demands on community. As with our treatment of meaning, we need to see community in the light of the transition from modernity to postmodernity.

One of the major beliefs of modernity was that the individual was the primary social unit. This belief held that individuals create artificial social contracts by which they agree to surrender some of their freedom to a thus artificially constructed state in return for protection from others' invasion of their rights to property and the free pursuit of their own self-interests. From the philosophies of Thomas Hobbes and John Locke there emerged a theory of "possessive individualism," as Charles MacPherson ably documents.[12] Thomas Popkewitz, in *A Political Sociology of Educational Reform,* and Gregory Smith, in his edited book, *Schools That Work: Creating Community,* both treat MacPherson's work as illuminating the basis for modernism's ideology of individualism and the effects of this individualism on school arrangements.[13] Individuals were thought to possess themselves as their own private property. Hence their talents, such as intelligence, business acumen, creativity, and artistic potential, belonged to them independent of their relationship to the community. These talents were to be developed for the self-realization of the individual, for his or her material betterment. This belief in possessive individualism was tied to a social philosophy of *laissez faire*. As Popkewitz comments:

> A common theme of possessive individualism is that society is improved through the efforts of its individual members to better their [own] positions through participation in the polity, through work, and through the exercise of the entrepreneurial spirit.[14]

Through a hidden hand of economic and political providence, society would somehow progress under the collective efforts of individuals, using their owned talents for self-serving purposes within a free marketplace of economic and political striving. In such a view of society, community is relegated to the perimeter of social concerns. In this perspective, community is simply made up of self-serving individuals who use the community for their own individual purposes.

The modern move toward individualism was a reaction against the smothering of individuality and individual initiative by more traditional communities of the tribe or clan, or of the medieval feudal communities, governed by religiously legitimated orthodoxies and hierarchically arranged systems of power and class. Within those communities, individuals were assigned a place, were expected to function within that place, and were required to *keep* that place. Individual social advancement or free inquiry were smothered by custom, tradition, and religious authority. The fear of this kind of domineering community is still with us. Not a few contemporary scholars in the field of education are wary of introducing the theme of community into schooling for fear that a strong community will stifle dissent, smother creativity, and ostracize difference. They warn about romanticizing the notion of community and the danger of seeing only its potentially beneficent effects.[15] Bricker[16] attempts to strike a middle ground between individualism and communitarianism by situating knowledge as socially grounded in society, and therefore as providing individuals the rules of rationality and the knowledge that enables them to make free choices. It is clear, however, that he places himself within the classical liberal position when he states in his last chapter that: "Autonomous persons should be understood as being neither totally emancipated from society, nor totally bound to it; rather, by making use of the opportunities provided to them by society, *they are able to live lives of their own*."[17] What contemporary critics of community in schools fail to see is that individualism has been romanticized as well. The free, autonomous person who lives a life of his or her own does not normally live the life of a hermit. We are at a point in our cultural and political history where the ideologies of individualism and communalism are increasingly seen to be dysfunctional. There is a search for a more mature realization of community, in which mature individuals can be at home and indeed be free precisely as members of a supportive community. Dewey was ahead of his time when he said: "I believe that the individual child is a social individual and that society is an organic union of individuals. If we eliminate the social factor from the child we are left with an abstraction; if we eliminate the individual from society, we are left only with an inert and lifeless mass."[18]

The postmodern critique of individualism revealed that, by its own relentless, reductionistic, rationalizing of the individual, as well as the rationalization of knowledge itself, modernity has shown the individual to be a *fiction*, and that in two senses of the term. By studying the person from a variety of scientific subspecialties, modernity "demonstrated" that:

- The individual was an isolated economic unit that could be predicted and controlled as both a producer of wealth and a consumer of commodities.
- As a political being, the self-interested, power- and security-seeking individual could be reduced to a vote, to a recipient of public services, to a producer of tax revenue, to an object of public policy, and to a statistic in the prison system, the health-care system, and the food-stamp program.
- In psychology, the individual could be reduced to an organism of drives, needs, and wants, controlled by positive and negative reinforcement or by subconscious mechanisms.
- In social psychology, the individual was simply a positive or negative influence on the activity of the group; or a predictable pattern of behavior depending on the type of socialization he or she was exposed to; or a free-floating self, shaping itself in response to the perceptions of others in the immediate social landscape.
- In biology and its subspecialties, the individual was a system of neurons, microbes, and DNA genetic factors.
- In physics, the individual consisted of a reaction to and a component of various energy field forces.

In the drive to rationalize the physical and social universe, science reduced the individual to compartmentalized units either of subsystems or of macro systems. Under the collective analyses of modern sciences, the individual human being as an objective, unitary reality effectively disappeared. The individual as subject, as the interior person behind the social and cultural masks, evanesced. The individual, in short, was a fiction, an imaginary composite, which, on the surface, might appear to enjoy free will and interiority, but which, under the objective scrutiny of the natural and social sciences, was reduced to much simpler components.

Moreover, the sociology of knowledge interprets the individual as a socially constructed phenomenon. In that sense, knowledge itself is a fiction (from the Latin verb *facere*, to make): It is something made. The word *fiction* is often given the meaning of "purely fictitious," something purely imaginary and fanciful. However, fiction can also mean something that is made as a tool to understand. In that sense, the terminology used to describe the individual—the self, the human person, the soul, the subject—can be seen as socially useful symbolic terminology constructed within a sociocultural context to identify and name a human reality, an identifiable, dynamic unit of a social group. It is the group's or species' way of identifying members of the group. In naming this unit a self, a person, and a soul, the group names something that may be a quality of that unit (intelligence, autonomy, flexible adaptability, reflexivity, etc.); in naming it that, however, the group also confers reality on that unit. The group creates the individual, so to speak, as a self.

The individual, once aware of being named a subject, a person, a soul, or a member, comes to reproduce that quality in himself or herself. The individual responds to the expectations of the group. The individual is socialized into becoming a subject, a source of various activities, by the group. As the individual responds to this socializing process, the individual creates him- or herself as *this* individual, a member of this group who call themselves humans. Thus, modernity again ends up, through its analysis of the sociology and the anthropology of knowledge, asserting that the individual is a fiction. Now, however, the insight goes much deeper. The individual is seen not so much as a fiction made up of simpler units, but a fiction that, while initially called forth by the group (especially by its parents), subsequently creates "her-self," "him-self," makes and remakes that self through continuous cultural and social interactions with the group.

Although this theory of the total fabrication of the individual, first by the group and then by the individual in continuous interaction with the group, may appear to deny the creation of an individual soul by God, as some theologies would seem to require, it is important to remember that social theorists are not talking to theologians or thinking from within theological frameworks. Rather, they are attempting to capture, within the empirical methodologies of social science, what goes on in the ordinary socialization process of children.

The problem of modernity, however, is that it successfully socialized the individual also to become *independent* from the group. In freeing the individual from the tyranny of the group, it also orphaned the individual, casting him out into a wilderness of other predators, leaving him to learn the hard lessons of survival on his own, forcing him to enter into a social contract with other predators, but leaving him alone with only his immediate nuclear family as the source of intimate exchange. (I use the masculine form here intentionally, for this kind of socialization has been applied especially to men.)

NEW UNDERSTANDINGS FOR
RE-IMAGINING COMMUNITY

We end up at the latter part of the twentieth century with not only the community as a problem, but with the individual as a problem as well. Some would have us go back to the premodern notion of community, in which individuality and autonomy were absorbed in a communal identity. But that would be to miss a historic opportunity. With our growing understanding of the interconnection of all natural systems on the planet, our growing understanding of the

interconnection of living systems with cultural systems, our growing awareness of the interconnection between human intelligence and the tacit or inchoate intelligence in the universe as it has reflexively evolved, we are poised
to create ourselves as new kinds of communities and new kinds of individuals.
We are closer now to knowing how to create an ecology of community that promotes the richest form of individual human life and to knowing how to create
an ecology of individual striving that promotes the richest form of community
life.[19]

In other words, the challenge of building a richer form of community in our
schools is a reflection of the challenge facing our society at large, namely, the
widespread creation of richer forms of community life. As we said earlier, this
will not require wholesale rejection of the achievements of modernity, or an anarchy of isolated critical enclaves (whether of the right or of the left) in revolu-
tion against the excesses of modernity.[20] True, we can no longer naively accept
the promises of modernity; they have been too conclusively destroyed in the
political and economic experiments of the nineteenth and twentieth centuries.
Neither can we return to a premodern state of affairs, attractive as Aristotelian-
ism appears. We can only move forward, learning the lessons that both Aristotle *and* history teach us. This journey will require, however, a transformation of
our limited understanding of both the individual and of the community.

COMMUNITIES OF MATURE INDIVIDUALS

Achieving or performing community is only partially realized, at best. It involves a struggle. Why? Because we, although incomplete as individuals, want
to be the center of attention, respect, admiration, and control. We are naturally
pulled by an instinct for individual survival. We desperately need, as Giddens
suggests,[21] a sense of ontological security, a sense that the world is not going to
snuff out our life in the next moment, or the next day. We want to be secure in
our basic physical needs for food and shelter. We want the world to be predictable. For the world to be predictable, we must control it. We must arrange
it to suit our needs. We do this by inventing science. Science, we think, places
us in the driver's seat. Knowledge of nature enables us to control it.

We also need to feel secure in our social world. We are always checking that
social world to see how it is responding to us. The tape at the back of my head
is always running: "How do I look? Am I saying the right thing? Am I being no-
ticed? Are these people friendly or unfriendly, attentive to me or bored with
me?" I must control my social world, for that world is what defines me. It can
disapprove of my actions and punish me by redefining me as stupid, dumb,
crazy, or bad.[22]

The pulls toward self-sufficiency and self-gratification are strong. They are
some of the survival instincts we inherit by being a child of nature and of the
cosmos. The universe appears indifferent to our needs and desires, unforgiving
of our excesses, and capricious in inflicting the calamities that fall upon us from
nature. My life can be snuffed out in an instant by an earthquake, destroyed by

a mosquito, ruined by a drought, or made miserable by a bacterial invasion. The universe will not weep over my demise or my misfortune. Some humans never make it past the first three weeks of life; some are born with severe physical or mental disabilities. Nature respects only one law: Adapt or disappear. Dysfunctional species disappear. Add to the impersonal disinterest of the universe and to the struggle for survival of all life forms a social environment of competition for scarce resources (whether those resources are oil, money, or a mother's attention), and we begin to recognize the depth of the survival instinct and its roots in the psyche.

Yet there is a second instinct, which is more mature and therefore more intelligent and more human: the instinct toward connection, toward the other, whether that other is a spouse, a companion, an extended family, a clan, or a nation. This instinct is a more intelligent and creative development of the survival instinct. It is an instinct carried in the learning of atomic, chemical, and organic structures: Connect, bond, unite, and become stronger through complexification. Complexification leads to increased adaptability and creativity for new forms of self-reproduction. That bonding at the inorganic and organic level grows toward the reflexive self-awareness of attraction. From that reflexive self-awareness of attraction grows the creativity of making *oneself* more attractive (the bright colors of some flowers, the fantastic plumage of some birds and their complex birdsong, the daily make-up and weight lifting, and the wearing of perfume, designer clothing, and even university degrees).

At the higher levels of social bonding one encounters various forms of love: the symbolic expressions of cherishing that are expressed in language, touching, and gestures (the gruff handshake between two tradesmen; the cradling of infants in their mothers' arms; the entwining of lovers; the placing of a flower on the grave of a dear friend). At still higher levels of bonding, there is a more expansive experience of love, an experience that grows out of a gradual awareness of how much one depends on the gratuitous generosity of countless people whose work makes social life *possible* (the farmers who produce the food; the builders who build the shelters; the planners who anticipate the complex needs of a modern city; the countless men and women who attend to the daily maintaining of transportation systems, communication systems, financial systems, health systems, and education systems). Added to their fidelity in maintaining the infrastructure of society are the efforts of scholars and artists to probe the mysteries and complexities of the natural, human, and social worlds. They tease out and express the "meaning-fulness" of life and its underlying beauty and terror.

Although the social world we live in is far from perfect, it is this social life that feeds us, that nourishes our sense of our individual and social identities. This social world can be seen as a gift that is gratuitously given to us. There grows a gradual appreciation that deeply embedded in the ambiguity and muddiness of social life is a massive, incoherent, yet clearly spoken collective act of love. All the effort that goes into making social and cultural life (as opposed to the self-seeking efforts of those who manipulate social arrangements to their own benefit at the expense of others) in the present, and even more so during the past centuries of struggle, can be seen as a gratuitous act of love.

We celebrate this collective act of love by remembering the public heroes of the past: the young men and women who gave their lives in battle to defend the country's future; the founding fathers and mothers of the republic; the statespeople, inventors, artists, and saints whose achievements and creations continue to shape our sense of ourselves. Beyond the public heroes is the mass of humanity, whose daily performance of their work in factories and farms, universities and government offices, hospitals and homes, sustained the social and cultural fabric of past generations. These are the ordinary heroes of human history, whose biographies were written in the hearts of friends and families, but who never made it into the official histories of their times. Their lives, however, as well as the lives of public heroes, express a self-giving, a struggle on behalf of human destiny and human dignity against the forces that would destroy us. We live off this inheritance; their self-giving enriches us. They provide us examples of how we might repay the gift by adding the gift of our own lives' work to it, whether that involves raising children whose experience of love enables them to reproduce that love in their adult lives, or fidelity to the highest quality of our craft, or the search for a new medicine, a new symphony, or a new world order.

At these higher levels of awareness of social bonding, one becomes increasingly aware of the gratuitous gift of nature itself in all its variety, complexity, inventiveness, and sheer abundance. Our very bodies are extraordinary creations, the result of millions of years of patient experiment. We are the result of the efforts of cosmic dust reaching for the dream of life, of the struggle of life to become more and more in charge of itself, of the amazing flowering of atoms into human intelligence over eons of cosmic time. Whether our religious beliefs posit a transcendent God or Creator, or whether we leave the existence of some divine force outside of or above the universe as an open question, we are still confronted with the awesomeness of the existence of life and its almost infinite variety as a "natural miracle."

As we saw in Chapter 5, the sciences continue to discover the enormous intricacy of the structures and processes of life forms and the interpenetration and mutuality between levels of life systems, from the biochemistry of DNA to the neurochemistry of consciousness to the social ecology of cultural rituals that create and sustain meaning. What this inheritance points to is a universe that is ultimately benign, despite its apparent indifference to dead-end experiments and despite the chaos and randomness embedded in its very intelligibility. This awareness of a benign universe—a mothering universe, if you will—leads to thankfulness for this patient, mutely eloquent, self-giving process that has given birth to us and to a planet in which we find a home and all the ingredients for a full and rich life. It also leads to a sense of responsible membership in a community of life, so that the gift becomes, not diminished, but enriched by my history, by our history.

THE INDIVIDUAL'S RESPONSE TO COMMUNITY

Through this growing awareness of being bonded to and gifted by successive levels of community, we see how love generates love, how our affective, cognitive, and personal participation in community reveals to us deeper and richer insights into love as the center of these communities. Love, therefore, is a response to community, a reciprocal gift of life, to the welfare of the natural, social, and human communities we inhabit, and in that giving, we more fully realize the meaning, identity, and purpose of our lives as human beings.

From this vantage point, we sense how immature the instinct is for individual survival, how small-minded and self-defeating it is. We also see how immature communities (tribes, cities, states, nations) are that close in on themselves, mistakenly believing all other communities to be inferior to them in strength, intelligence, cultural achievement, or nobility—seeing all other communities as threats to their hegemony or simply to their survival. The more mature community embraces the community of humanity, the community of life, and the community of being, and finds through that bonding an increased wisdom and strength that are the seeds of its own transformation.

THE STRUGGLE FOR THE MATURE COMMUNITY

That is the game, the epic, the meta-narrative, the tragi-comedy that is played out in everyday life. The instinct for individual self-survival pulls us in one direction; the instinct for connectedness, the attraction to loving relationships pulls us in another. Sometimes the two instincts become confused. Often the two pulls are entangled in the same choices and actions. Sometimes one is used to rationalize the other ("the arms race is necessary for world peace"; "we need more prisons to promote the security of the community"; "a healthy economy requires an unemployment rate of 6 percent").

When I speak about administering community, I am not imagining a sugar-coated, utopian reality. I am speaking, rather, of attempting to build an environment where the pulls and tugs between these two instincts provide the very stuff of the social learning agenda, an environment that is noisy, conflicted, filled with ambiguity, muddied by the traditional vices of anger, lust, envy, contentiousness, and greed, and yet an environment that encourages trust, openness, loyalty, integrity, generosity, courage, and love. Nevertheless, this struggle for a community goes on within larger communities where the selfish influences of individualism control vast resources of institutional and political power. The influence of this power will not evanesce simply by our wishing it to. Reinhold Neibuhr criticized this naivete when he observed:

> . . . most. . .social scientists. . .seem to imagine that men of power will immediately check their expectations and pretensions in society as soon as they have been appraised by the social scientists that their actions are anti-social.[23]

Neither can those who administer such a community stand above the struggle in paternalistic self-righteousness. They enter the struggle as wounded healers, as humans who experience and openly acknowledge the pulling and tugging of the two instincts in themselves. In concert with teachers, parents, and students, administrators of community engage in the struggle and pain of calling forth the larger, more generous, more mature instincts.

THE ISSUE OF CITIZENSHIP

The concept of this more mature community requires a rethinking of our notions about citizenship and concomitantly of our notions about education for citizenship.[24] Previously, citizenship was seen as a role made up of limited activities required of isolated individuals who shared responsibility for the social contract. Remember that the individual was seen as the primary unit of society. The duties of the citizen, then, were to see that the social contract was maintained, and that the justice envisioned in this contract was upheld (a justice, primarily of legal protections of private property and constitutional rights and of legal punishments for violators of private property broadly conceived). The upholding of the social contract was achieved through participating in the election of those who would support the social contract thus understood. Since the common good was identified with the freedom of individuals to pursue their own self-interests (limited by the rule not to interfere with the legitimate self-interests of others), it was assumed that the state (and other do-gooders) would not interfere with the natural course of events that would result from everyone pursuing their own self-interests, since that would naturally result in the best arrangements for everyone.

There would be room for charity to be extended to the destitute and mentally incapacitated, of course, but that was a matter of personal choice, not of social policy.[25] Since citizens were only minimally a community, and much more a collection of private individuals with rights that pertained to them as individuals, being "civil" to one another meant extending the minimal signs of a superficial goodwill toward the other.

In contrast, citizenship can be understood in terms of building up the community, in terms of proactive activities that create fellow feeling among people. For example, the proactive citizen gives time and work to a serious discussion of possible solutions to widespread poverty, or to the search for a better public educational system. Within the general culture, however, these activities are not seen as *normal* citizen activities. On the contrary, the individualist would proclaim that one's work, time, and energy belong to oneself and are to be used for one's own betterment. Everybody is responsible for looking after themselves. We should not take that responsibility away from people. If we start that, before we know it those do-gooders will be interfering in our private affairs.

Such a view of citizenship, as the minimum public participation needed to keep the social contract functioning, is based on the faulty premise of the individual as the primary unit of society. As we are coming to understand better, the primacy of the individual over the community or of the community over the individual is a false dualism. It does not have to be an either–or, win–lose relationship. We are coming to understand that communities are stronger and richer when they are made up of individuals of diverse talents and potentials. Likewise, we see that individuals are stronger and richer when they are bonded into networks of people who offer different perspectives on life, when they complement their own talents with the community's cornucopia of other talents, when they associate with others who stretch them beyond the limits of their isolated perspectives. We are also beginning to understand that individuals are sustained at every level by love—the explicit love of family, friends, spouse, and children, and the tacit love behind the generous gift of the work that sustains social and human life made by countless others in everyday life. We are starting to understand that this love, when expressed both explicitly and inchoately, creates community, gives it continuity, consistency, and value.

In this view of community, the individual is enriched simply by membership in the cultural, economic, and political life of the community, and finds even greater fulfillment in responding to the community (now in the person of a beloved friend, now in the person of neighbors, now in the form of a voluntary association, now in the form of his or her career) with loving service. Through that loving service, the community is enriched, and reflexively, the individual re-creates/performs him- or herself. The individual becomes a more expansive being, a more complete being by being more closely bonded to a member or group in the community, or to the community itself. Through engagement with the community, the individual ceases being isolated, alone, unconnected to anyone or anything, and thus becoming, tragically and unnecessarily, extinct.

Civil libertarians argue, however, that the individual has the *right* to choose to be alone; that every person enjoys a fundamental freedom to isolation from community involvement, the freedom to be selfish, the freedom to go off in the woods, like Thoreau, and thumb his nose at the community. This is indeed a constitutionally protected freedom. Sometimes, a separation from the community for psychological or moral or political reasons is necessary, for a while. Such isolation from the community, however, especially on a permanent basis, has never been seen as a desirable state of affairs for humans. Most civil libertarians, while maintaining the right of the recluse to live that way, think of such behavior as odd and eccentric. Even in prisons, solitary confinement is seen as one of the most punitive sanctions against a person who has already been removed from normal social relations.

The normal life of humans is found in community. Even when Thoreau removed himself from his human community, he sought a deep communion with nature. He studied the rhythms and patterns and eccentricities of nature and grounded his own identity within the web of nature's life. Perceiving the gift of nature to humans, he gave nature back to us in his writings, thus connecting us to our natural community of life.

I argue here for a much more expansive view of citizenship. Citizenship should be a proactive involvement in the life of the community, an activity that seeks to give back to the community what the community has already given to the individual: life, talents, capabilities, energy, and love. Citizenship can take many forms—as many forms as there are relationships in the community (volunteering on a neighborhood child care committee, serving on a faculty grievance committee, working in a clothing factory, designing a new highway bridge). In this regard, I differ with Levin, who maintains that we need one kind of education for citizenship and another kind for work. Levin posits citizenship as democratic participation in the pursuit of citizens' rights (note the echo of classical liberalism). The role of worker, according to Levin, requires quite a different set of attitudes, namely, obedience to the owner or foreman, the surrendering of our rights of free speech, free assembly, and so on, to the authority of the employer. Our work and our relationship with fellow workers is carefully spelled out in the contract whereby we sell our labor to the owner, a contract far different from the social contract we enjoy as citizens.[26]

Work is, in my scheme of things, another way of exercising citizenship. I am not simply working for an employer, I am also working for the clients of the company, the customers. Through my work, I join with the others in my company and with those countless other citizens who help to make the institutions of society work. The products or services I render contribute to the well-being of my society. Furthermore, if the products I produce or sell were to harm or disadvantage society (e.g., unsafe automobiles, defectively tested medicines, environmentally contaminating chemicals), I have an obligation *as a citizen* to speak up to my employer. If the employer refuses to respond, then I am obliged to go to the proper authorities and report it.

Another way of thinking about citizenship is to see the individual citizen when he or she is engaged with others as being, in microcosm, the community. By this I mean that in all my relationships I should be acting out the ideals and values of the community. Acting as a "good citizen" means pursuing in all my relationships those ideals which my community stands for. . .at least in the minimum observance of those customs of civility, traditions of etiquette, minimal rules of social exchange, and legal requirements. If I were representing my neighborhood at some regional gathering, I would want the other participants to see me as a good representative of my neighborhood, not as someone who flaunted all the values my neighborhood stands for. That is why members of teams who represent their country at the Olympic competitions are held to exacting standards of sportsmanship and social behavior. For that moment and in that place, they *are* Italy, China, France, or Brazil. The kind of citizenship we need to promote is not a self-centered focus on my rights as a member of such-and-such a community, but rather a citizenship that stands for the values and ideals of his or her community. This, of course, assumes that citizens know what their communities stand for and have come to cherish those values and ideals. When this happens, the individual becomes, in microcosm, the community in action, serving itself, knowing itself, healing itself, celebrating its nobility and its destiny. The individual, in his or her immediate circle of family, neighbors, and co-workers, becomes the community seeking a fuller expression of itself.

Education in this kind of citizenship will involve a discussion of the kinds of meanings embedded in the community's understanding of itself. We list many of these terms in Chapter 6. It will also involve the practice of those ideals and values in specific and concrete ways within the school setting. Teachers can devise learning activities that require exploration and performance, within the school itself, of justice, caring, democratic processes, nonviolent negotiation of conflict, debate on public policy, the sharing of talent for the building up of community, and so forth. Unacceptable behavior will be seen, not so much as breaking a rule imposed by the administration, but as failing to live up to a value that is cherished by the community. This response to deviant behaviors, when reinforced over years of schooling, will change the youngster's perception of the ground for moral action, away from thinking of the obligation imposed on him as an isolated individual to obey this abstract rule or principle, and toward thinking of his connection to his community and how that behavior enhances or diminishes the community's life. We move from a kind of Kantian abstract ethics of duty-to-principle to an ethic of citizenship, of proactive participation in the life of the community.

SELF-GOVERNANCE

One of the fundamental questions facing the individual as well as the community is "How shall I/we govern myself/ourselves?" This question covers a whole host of decisions, from how one controls the schedule of digestive relief, to how one gets a fair share of the family platter of macaroni, to how a school makes out a class schedule, to how a family makes out a monthly budget, to how I respond when an opposing player in the neighborhood basketball game knocks me down from behind. In the formation and building of community within a school, the processes by which a community governs itself, and the corresponding processes whereby individuals govern themselves, is crucial.

I am not referring to the drawing up of a student book of rights, nor of a faculty/parents bill of rights (although that may eventually be treated in a much larger and continuous development of processes of self-government). The formation and building of community should start with questions: "What kind of a community do we want to be?" "What do we value most about the prospect of our life together in this school?" "When a new class comes into our school, what do we want them to know about us as a community?" "What do we want to be thought of by people in the wider community?"

Discussions of these questions will bring to the surface the values that the members of the school community themselves hold sacred. These values will be articulated in stories (precision of philosophical definition is not the goal of these discussions) that provide typical examples of behaviors that reflect those values. These discussions (which should include parents and school board members as well as students and teachers) should produce the choice of two or three central values by which the community wishes to distinguish its life. The school may want to adopt a motto or a coat of arms expressing these values.

These values can be embossed on a school flag, on pins or emblems, and written into a school song or a school pledge. All these symbolic representations become ways for the community to remind itself what it stands for. Membership in the community brings with it general obligations to enact those values in the daily course of the school week or school year. School awards for outstanding contributions to the living out of those values can become a semester or end-of-year occasion.

Encouragement of a generalized, proactive exercise of membership is far more important in the activity of self-governance than a book of rules and prohibitions. The community governs itself by pursuing those human ideals that make living in that community desirable and humanly fulfilling. In reality, the interpretation of these values as justifying or rationalizing certain behaviors will be a daily process of negotiation. There will be a pull toward self-centered behaviors. There will be normal misunderstandings between people and arguments that tear at the fabric of the community. It is the community's daily work and responsibility to heal divisions, to provide space for differences of opinion, and to allow for a plurality of cultural expressions, while at the same time calling the members to honor and pursue those common human values that unite them.

Besides the honoring of central values that unite the community, there will be a need for explicit policies and procedures for handling grievances, arbitrating disputes, and setting community goals. This, of course, will require constituting a body or group that has the authority to set the general frameworks by which the community conducts its business (calendars, budgets, work schedules, delegation of responsibilities, standing committees, etc.). This authority within the school will be exercised in conjunction with the authorities of the local community and state who have jurisdiction over aspects of school life. Hence, if the school establishes a student court, that court's jurisdiction will need to be defined in reference to the civil law as well as to the internal procedures of deciding disputes within the school. For example, the student court may have something to say to a student who is caught selling drugs within the school, but it also has to recognize the civil jurisdictions of law enforcement agencies in the larger community over such illegal behavior. The school may have an internal budget committee, but that committee has to function within the resources and limitations set by local and state agencies. The school budget committee may have little discretion, for example, in limiting expenditures for children in special education programs.

Involving the school community, or representative committees of the community, in *administrative* decisions will help to cement ownership of the practical decisions necessary to run its affairs. Whenever possible, however, these decisions should be related to those large values by which the community wishes to govern itself and not simply to the technical values of efficiency and expediency. Self-governance involves self-administration, but it is not to be equated with it. Governance involves not simply the administration of scarce resources or the restricting of unacceptable behavior; it also involves those proactive choices that go beyond expediency to reach out in more generous ways to our fellows—not so much in the pursuit of some abstract virtue, but simply out of a caring for the person, a desire to share a part of our life more fully with that person or persons.

A community governs itself proactively by seeing to the necessary services required of all or some members of the community. These services include the communication of news and public opinion, assistance to disabled members, health and sanitation services, commercial services, and so on. In the school community, every person ought to be involved in some kind of service activity. This might involve working on the student newspaper, putting out the daily bulletins and announcements, serving as big brothers or big sisters to under-class students, serving as peer tutors, working with maintenance crews on special clean-up projects, serving on peer conflict-resolution teams, or working on the student court. These service activities can be cycled periodically so that students experience serving the community in a variety of ways.

Service activities that reach outside the school into the larger community can be options for the older children as well. Every child should learn the lesson that their quality participation is needed by the community. That lesson, repeated over eight to twelve years of school, can create a life-long habit of community participation.

Self-governing is about self-control, to be sure, but it is also about channeling one's actions in a certain direction, and that channeling may be narrow or it may be expansive. Governance may involve a choice to go beyond what administrative guidelines suggest to the more generous choice of self-giving. Hence a teacher may follow administrative guidelines in providing her class with crayons and colored paper from general supplies. She may also pay out of her own pocket for a pair of eyeglasses for a child in her class whose family cannot afford them. A school may provide administratively for cooperative learning arrangements; a group of students may decide to govern themselves in a way that, besides following the administrative arrangements for cooperative learning, sets up an after-school tutoring service for younger students who are having academic difficulties, or an after-school enrichment program for children whose parents are working. They govern themselves just as surely by choosing to go beyond the normal administrative arrangements of the school as by complying with those normal administrative arrangements. In that case they are exercising their rights to *help* others instead of engaging in a contest against the community to preserve an independent exercise of a right in opposition to the community.

Under the influence of modernity's ideology of individualism, our culture does not see that kind of proactive building up of community as part of "the democratic process." That is because deeply embedded in our notion of democracy is the notion of possessive individualism, which uses democratic procedures to protect this possession, this property of "my life," by which I stand apart from the community of other separate property owners, *by which standing apart* I exercise my basic freedoms. Freedom is not seen as the freedom to share my life and my possessions with others; it is seen as freedom *from* other people, from their interference with my life, from their intruding on my living my life the way I want to live it. The rights of free speech, of assembly, and of owning property, however, can also be understood as necessary rights for building community, as necessary to a form of proactive citizenship on behalf of a democratic community.

SUMMARY

We have seen how administering community involves a refashioning of the term into a much richer and more expansive idea. This more expansive idea of community is called for as we approach the twenty-first century, with its concepts of the global village and a planetary community of life. It is an idea of community that is called for not only by the postmodern critique of individualism, but by the growing contributions of women scholars, by the scholars from our increasingly multicultural citizenry, and by the many scientists who provide a new view of the planet and of the cosmos. Once again, we see that the message of the first chapter has been underscored. Educational administration is not for the faint-hearted. It is not for those who cannot sustain the intellectual effort to understand and to study and to attempt to verbalize a sense of community that is still being formed within our culture. It is also not for authoritarians or rugged individualists. It is, rather, for those who have the courage to make a career in a profession that must find its way in a time of transition, a profession that must embrace a new understanding of community that is only beginning to be dreamed of throughout the world.

Commitment to this dream places a new agenda on the table for educators. It is an agenda to which other scholars are pointing as well. The building of community becomes part of the curriculum of the school. It cannot be ignored on the excuse that there is already too much academic material to be mastered in an already crowded school year. Mastering that academic agenda without preparing youngsters for participating in a new kind of community will render that academic learning problematic, if not dangerous. That is why we have to look at the administration of meaning and the administration of community as inescapably intertwined.

ACTIVITIES

1. In your journal, describe how democracy is understood and taught in your school.
2. Generate five school-wide activities that could be initiated within a month in your school that would increase the sense of community in your school.
3. In your study group, brainstorm administrative initiatives that would improve the sense of community at school.
4. The author presents some fanciful ideas about the individual being situated in a variety of communities—cultural, national, natural, and cosmic. He suggests that a response of bonding and participation, rather than withdrawal and protective isolation, is the more "mature" response. In your

study group, discuss how strongly the cultural understanding and ideology of individualism inhibits your own mature response.

5. In your own words, prepare a statement on the school as a self-governing community. Present this statement to your faculty for their response and commentary.

ENDNOTES

1. Lynn G. Beck, *Reclaiming Educational Administration as a Caring Profession*, Teachers College Press, New York, 1994; Nell Noddings, *The Challenge to Care in Schools*, Teachers College Press, New York, 1992.

2. Ernest Becker, *Beyond Alienation: A Philosophy of Education for the Crisis of Democracy*, George Braziller, New York, 1967.

3. David Bricker, *Classroom Life as Civic Education*, Teachers College Press, New York, 1989.

4. Orit Ichilov (ed.), *Political Socialization, Citizenship, Education, and Democracy*, Teachers College Press, New York, 1990.

5. David E. Purpel and H. Svi Shapiro (eds.), *Schools and Meaning: Essays on the Moral Nature of Schooling*, University Press of America, New York, 1985.

6. Robert J. Starratt, *Building an Ethical School: A Practical Response to the Moral Crisis in Schools*, Falmer Press, London, 1994.

7. Anthony Bryk and Michael Driscoll, *The High School as Community: Contextual Influences, and Consequences of Students and Teachers*, National Center on Effective Secondary Schools, Madison, WI, 1988.

8. Gregory A. Smith (ed.), *Public Schools That Work: Creating Community*, Routledge, New York, 1993.

9. Ralph Peterson, *Life in Crowded Places*, Heinemann, Portsmouth, NH, 1992.

10. Thomas J. Sergiovanni, *Building Community in Schools*, Jossey-Bass, San Francisco, 1994.

11. C. A. Bowers, *Elements of a Post-Liberal Theory of Education*, Teachers College Press, New York, 1987.

12. Charles B. MacPherson, *The Political Theory of Possessive Individualism: Hobbes to Locke*, Oxford University Press, London, 1962.

13. Thomas Popkewitz, *A Political Sociology of Educational Reform*, Teachers College Press, New York, 1991; Smith, op. cit.

14. Popkewitz, op. cit., p. 142.

15. I refer to a panel discussion on schools as communities held at the 1994 annual meeting of the American Educational Research Association, New Orleans.

16. Bricker, op. cit.

17. Bricker, op. cit., p. 97, emphasis added.

18. John Dewey, "My Pedagogic Creed," in M. S. Dworkin (ed.), *Dewey on Education*, Teachers College Press, New York, 1959, p. 22.

19. Ernest Becker proposed this, even though he died before the flowering of the new environmental sciences that have grounded this notion more

firmly. See Ernest Becker, *The Structure of Evil*, The Free Press, New York, 1968.

20. This seems to be a choice advocated by Alasdair MacIntyre in his *After Virtue: A Study in Moral Theory*, University of Notre Dame Press, Notre Dame, IN, 1981.

21. Anthony Giddens, *The Constitution of Society*, University of California Press, Berkeley, CA, 1984.

22. See Erving Goffman, *The Presentation of Self in Everyday Life*, Doubleday Anchor Books, Garden City, NY, 1959.

23. Reinhold Neibuhr, *Moral Man and Immoral Society*, Charles Scribner's Sons, New York, 1932, p. xvii.

24. For a good overview of present work on the theory of citizenship, see Will Kymlicka and Wayne Norman, "Return of the Citizen: A Survey of Recent Work on Citizenship Theory," *Ethics*, **104**: 352–381 (1993).

25. David Bricker would promote the virtue of generosity among students as a way of sharing an intelligence unequally distributed. His generosity, however, would be a form of charity freely dispensed by autonomous and independent individuals who possess/own a greater abundance of intelligence than others. See Bricker, op. cit.

26. See Henry M. Levin, "Political Socialization for Workplace Democracy," in Orit Ichilov, op. cit., pp. 158–176.

CHAPTER 8

Empowerment

In the previous chapter on administering community, we realized that community need not be opposed to individuality (although it is opposed to individualism as an ideology). As a matter of fact, mature communities cannot reach their potential unless they are made up of members with a strong sense of individuality. In this chapter we shall explore this theme further. The thesis is that administering community begins with administering empowerment. That phrase, of course, is laden with all the paradox of the other phases of administering meaning, administering community, and administering excellence. The paradox, again, lies in the apparent contradictions between what is normally understood by "administration" and the other terms, even though administrators are inescapably *obliged* to administer meaning, community, and excellence.

We shall begin with the premise that good communities are made up of good individuals, strong communities of strong individuals, innovative communities of innovative individuals, caring communities of caring individuals, and self-governing communities of self-governing individuals. We assume that schools as communities are made up of both teachers and students. Hence, what applies to teachers in our discussion also applies to students, with, of course, appropriate allowance for their earlier stages of human development. When we speak of administering strong, inventive, caring, and self-governing communities, therefore, we are speaking of growing strong, inventive, caring, and self-governing students as well as teachers.

In order to get a clearer fix on what empowering teachers and students means and how we might attempt a process of empowerment, we need to clean up some misunderstandings, make some distinctions, and get beneath the surface definitions of empowerment and its root word, *power.* Then we focus on three sources of power: the power to be oneself, the power of connected activity, and the power contained in ideas, dreams, and visions.

106

EMPOWERMENT IN SCHOOL REFORM

Empowerment is a term that is frequently used in discussions of school reform, especially discussions that focus on increasing the professionalism of teachers. The term, however, carries a variety of interpretations, not all of them benign. For some of the more assertive teacher union leaders, empowerment means more power in the hands of the teachers to control school policies and practices. In some extreme cases, the union would replace administrators with committees of teachers, leaving administrators with little more than the work of clerks and secretaries. For others, empowerment means the involvement of teachers in major decisions in the school. In this latter interpretation, teachers and administrators would work as peers and colleagues to arrive at appropriate decisions regarding school affairs. In cities like New York, the move toward school-based management has been linked to shared decision making.

Empowerment as a strategic tool of school reform, however, is not the panacea that many initially expected. Those who would place teachers in charge of schools have discovered that the principals and other administrators do not simply fall over and surrender their positions. Administrators have used their collective political power to resist any such wholesale takeover of the schools by teachers. In addition, many teachers have resisted such a move on the grounds that they do not want the responsibility of running the school, saying that they simply want to teach with minimum interference from administrators.

Those who want empowerment through shared decision making are finding that many teacher colleagues resist such initiatives for at least two reasons. First, they are suspicious that the authorities simply want to give them more work to do without any increase in pay. Second, many teachers resent the enormous amount of time required to make shared decision making work. Many meetings are spent simply on procedural and legalistic matters. Even when substantive curriculum matters are taken up, the process of curriculum redesign is tedious and lengthy. Teachers complain of being distracted from their main work, teaching children in classrooms.

Underlying most attempts at these types of empowerment is the issue of trust. Everyone seems to assume a hidden agenda. Everyone fears being manipulated. Again and again one hears cynical interpretations of "the real game."

The previous interpretations of empowerment, however, are too narrow and too absorbed in the politics and technical procedures of participation. A different interpretation of empowerment may offer greater possibilities for both teachers and administrators. This interpretation looks to the human and professional power of each teacher to stimulate learning for all children and, in turn, to empower them. We need to explore where that power comes from and what hinders its free exercise.

WHAT IS POWER?

For many people, power has negative overtones. It is associated with force, coercion, threat, and sometimes violence. Power is often viewed as something only a few people have: "The powerful" are thought to be able to control or influence the affairs of the community. From that vantage point, empowering people implies that those who hold power over others give them some of their power. Yet the reality is that no one has power over another unless that person is allowed to have that power. If everyone refuses to comply with those "in power," then they have no power. We saw that happen in the disintegration of the communist empire in Eastern Europe. Even the power of persuasion implies that the listener assents to the reasonableness of the other person's argument. The power of the judge to impose a prison sentence is based on an assumed prior agreement of people to live according to the law.

Besides power as meaning power over someone or something, we can conceive of power as something each person possesses, a power to be and a power to do. The most interesting power each of us possesses is the power to be ourselves. No one else has the power to be me: Only I can be me. Often I fail to use that power and instead try to live up to an idea that others have of me or to some collective image of what the truly modern, sophisticated, cosmopolitan, urbane woman or man should be.

We are all socialized, to one degree or another, to displace what we want to be or do in order to conform to social norms of propriety and tradition. "Good boys" don't do that! "Good girls" would never dream of doing that! "At Edison School, we simply don't do things like that." We grow up maintaining our fragile sense of self-esteem by what we think others think of us. Often this leads to a suppression of ever being or doing what our spontaneous wishes suggest, out of fear of disapproval.

What "growing up" means, however, is that we learn how to be ourselves and still live, more or less, within the acceptable bounds of social propriety and tradition. Maturity means taking responsibility for ourselves, being the person we want to be and loving the person we are. It means deciding to resist the fads and trends of popular culture when they start to twist what we value. When our own sense of integrity is at stake, we will risk the disapproval of others. In other words, each of us has the power to say yes and to say no. To be sure, that power is heavily circumscribed by the cultural meanings, values, and associations that lead me to censure certain choices; it is further circumscribed by my physical attributes. I cannot be a bird (although some acquaintances may think I am a rare one, indeed), or the Golden Gate Bridge. Nevertheless, the power to be me is a power I never lose. Although we may turn it over to other people, it always belongs to us, and we can take it back whenever we choose. That is the power of freedom, the freedom, especially, to be myself, to sing my own song, dance my own dance, speak my own poetry, the freedom to be true to my best self—to be that unique and unrepeatable being, the likes of which has never been nor ever will be after I am gone.

The paradox about this power is that, although it is mine, I can only exercise it in relationship to my community. Some mistakenly think that the power to be an individual is a power *against* the community, a power that *necessarily defies* the community. Yet that attitude leads to a kind of narcissistic, selfish isolation. That form of self-centeredness is actually self-destructive. I can be myself only in relation to others, to other selves whom I value as they value me. I can only express myself in relation to the world, to another person, to a particular circumstance that at that moment is part of my definition (such as my home, my workplace, my neighborhood, my garden). I express myself by responding to persons and events in my immediate surroundings, and that expression is an expression either of giving or of taking, an expression of gratitude or of greed, an expression of celebration or complaint, or an affirmation or a denial of life. So far as my expression of myself is giving, thankful, celebratory, and affirming, I myself receive life, I grow, and I am nurtured. So far as my expression of myself is taking, hoarding, complaining, and denying, I hurt myself and those around me. The myself I express in negativity is an expression of self-destruction.

It is important, however, to add at this point that some people are so overwhelmed by their circumstances that even the power to be themselves is drastically circumscribed. A sexually abused child can be emotionally crippled in her or his power to be her- or himself. A "crack child" is hampered from saying yes or saying no by internal demons that physicians and psychologists have yet to identify. A teenage Appalachian parent who has dropped out of school and scrapes by on welfare is fighting huge obstacles in trying to make a life for herself and for her child. For an angry, unemployed, African-American twenty-year-old, the power to be himself may find expression in ways that the larger culture censures. The larger culture does not want those on the psychological, economic, or cultural fringe to express themselves, and it has at its disposal numerous ways to censure such expression, from the pink slip to the search warrant, to exclusion from clubs and restaurants, and from neighborhoods and bank loans. Even in very constrained circumstances, however, that power is never totally smothered. Without denying the injustice and the tragedy of wasted human potential, one can find in any outcast community of humans a diversity of characters whose self-expression remains fiercely and humorously, quaintly and outrageously unique.

Hence the power to be myself is a remarkable power. It is an enormously creative power, a power to create myself, so to speak, while adding to the life around me; or it is an enormously destructive power, a power to destroy myself (even though that takes place by barely perceptible, miniscule choices), while smothering and depressing life around me. That is why some people choose not to exercise that power at all: They sense the existential risk involved. Better to leave the choices in the hands of others.

EMPOWERMENT AS A PROCESS AND AS AN ACHIEVEMENT

When we speak of empowerment, we should distinguish between the process of empowerment and the achievement of empowerment. Just as with the word *liberation,* there are two meanings: One deals with the activities in which one engages in order to liberate oneself, while one is not yet liberated; the other meaning signifies that one has reached the state of liberation. Empowerment in a school context is a relational process, in which administrators and teachers engage in a mutual process of bringing to the surface what the power to be and the power to do *means* in this particular school, what positive qualities are attached to the exercise of that power, and what limitations are imposed by the circumstances of the communal effort at schooling. Empowerment is not a process of administrators giving power to teachers. Rather it is a process that involves mutual respect, dialogue, and invitation. It implies recognition that each person enjoys talents, competencies, and potentials that can be exercised in responsible and creative ways within the school setting for the benefit of children and youth.

Empowerment is also an achievement, an arriving at a state of autonomy in the exercise of one's power to be and to teach, using all the talents and wisdom at one's disposal. As an achievement it is always relative, because we never exhaust the possibilities of our power to teach. Empowerment as a policy, then, is a commitment that the school environment will continually nurture teachers' growth in their abilities to promote the growth of students, both through their own modeling of what it means to be an authentic person and through their engagement with the students and the learning material itself.

EMPOWERMENT ON AN INDIVIDUAL AND COMMUNITY BASIS

Empowerment has to happen with each individual teacher. Each teacher must be invited to be authentically her- or himself. Sometimes that invitation can be direct, as when a principal asks: "What would you like to explore in your work as a teacher?" or "What do you need to do better that you already do well?" Sometimes the invitation will be indirect, as when teachers are asked for suggestions for next year's staff development days. Sometimes the invitation is simply an attentive ear when a teacher needs to discuss a problematic situation at the school.

Empowerment, of course, does not mean a flabby acceptance of anything a teacher does. We are not interested in empowering teachers to be mean. Individuals have selfish as well as altruistic motives. Empowerment is not intended to encourage selfishness. Rather, it means encouraging the best that is in each person. It may also mean, at times, the indirect or direct discouragement of the worst that is there. However, I do not need to encourage administrators in their responsibilities to correct teachers. For some reason, administrators seem to learn that skill quickly and with great sophistication. Rather, administrators need to focus their attention much more on the empowering of the best that is in teachers, rather than on controlling their flaws. Accentuating the positive possibilities for people tends to diminish their negative possibilities.

Empowerment has to be individualized. Although all teachers may be invited to develop new skills, such as using computers in classroom instruction or developing debate formats within classrooms, each teacher should be expected to bring his or her own creative insight and intuition to the exercise of those generic skills. If empowerment means the development of a talent—say, the talent to orchestrate a productive class discussion—then the teacher will need time and encouragement to practice that talent and the administrative support to improve, refine, and enlarge it. Power is in that teaching talent—the power to tease out students' insights and understandings and acceptance of differences, the power to stimulate and nourish the new life of expanding minds. Assisting teachers to expand their talents leads necessarily to the spread of those talents in the learnings of the students.

Empowerment as a school policy means recognizing the power that both teachers and students have to be themselves and to express themselves through their talents. It means inviting them to exercise that power with joy and laughter and compassion: joy, because the exercise of their talent brings profound satisfaction; laughter, because in the exercise of our individuality we often catch ourselves acting absurdly or foolishly; and compassion, because the exercise of individuality can sometimes lead to mistakes, excesses, or misunderstandings. The expectation that forgiveness is an everyday necessity is a precondition for any communal exercise of our power to be ourselves.

That leads to a consideration of a fundamental requirement for any effort at empowerment, and that is the requirement of trust. If a teacher is to feel free enough to try more spontaneous activities, he or she must trust that there is room for mistakes, that differences will be tolerated, and that unique insights will be honored. Most teachers have been socialized into relatively limited protocols of teaching. They have not been encouraged to go beyond the textbook and the curriculum guide to think for themselves and to design creative student learning activities. They have to know that they are trusted to try out new possibilities in a responsible and effective manner. If they expect immediate criticism of deviations from standard operating procedures, they will not risk trying something new.

Administrators are often not aware of how critical this sense of trust is. Simply telling teachers to have trust does not work. Trust is something built up over time through the personal relationship an administrator is able to establish with each teacher, through always telling the truth, through encouraging the sharing of ideas and criticisms, through acting on teacher suggestions. Only when trust has been established will teachers believe that administrators' talk about increased teacher autonomy and creativity is genuine.

Empowerment on an individual basis, however, is only a small part of the empowerment agenda. Empowerment must be felt and exercised by the whole staff. When individual teachers who feel empowered work together to respond to school needs, then empowerment is raised to a new strength. An empowered staff comes to believe that it has within its ranks enough talent and insight to respond to most school problems and to create from their own talent an outstanding school. By discussing ideas, sharing experiments, and pooling resources, an empowered staff can generate extraordinary energy and enthusiasm. That should be the ultimate goal of any policy of empowerment. When an administrator has nurtured that kind of empowerment, then the whole staff becomes involved in the exercise of leadership. The united efforts of the staff in sharing their individual visions of the school can result in an overarching vision for the school; mutual problem solving and organizational evaluations can lead to structural redesign and to institutional transformation. That in turn leads the staff to a greater sense of empowerment, to confidence in their own creative talents, and to even greater willingness to pursue the dream of creating an exciting and satisfying school.

From this vantage point, one can view empowerment as a genuine exercise of self-governance and moral fulfillment. Administering community means encouraging a community to take charge of its destiny, and in so doing to achieve the satisfaction of creating something wonderful. Every teacher worthy of the title dreams of a school environment in which youngsters find learning an exciting and awe-filled experience. That is the ideal we all hold. Empowering teachers to work collectively toward that goal is what administering community is all about.

THE POWER OF CONNECTED ACTIVITY

It follows easily from the above that the empowerment of individuals takes place within an empowering community. We can engage in a process of growth, self-discovery, and self-expression in a community of persons who care for us, who respect us and all the ways we are different, who appreciate and embrace our talents as sources of enriching the community. A second important focus in the empowerment process, therefore, is building a supportive and collaborative community. This means building a community culture that supports differences of opinion, differences in teaching protocols, and differences of cultural expressions.

The process of building community encourages creativity and initiative, and discourages the "tall poppy syndrome." The tall poppy syndrome is manifested in a group that cannot tolerate someone in the group excelling at anything. The group cuts down to size anyone whose head sticks up above the commonly approved height of the group. The group assumes that anyone who achieves beyond the group's norms is showing off, trying to impress the authorities, and is thus putting their own performance in a bad light and is a threat to the group's solidarity. When this syndrome is present in a school culture, administrators will need imagination to invent a variety of initiatives for many people in the faculty, so that the whole group may, as much as possible, move away from their routine ways of behaving. By cheerleading the various members of the group who are attempting new responses in their teaching, the administrator can promote the awareness that *many* heads stand above the crowd, making it difficult for the group to gang up on any one individual.

Another way of building a supportive community is to create team projects. Putting two to five teachers together on a project often produces a team that can find a diversity of talents among themselves, all of which are needed to achieve the project's goals. A new networking of individual talents takes place, a connecting of abilities that enables talent to play off and utilize other talent. The results are usually a new awareness and appreciation of the talents of others, and a new sense of bonding that supports the expression of those talents. In turn, the individual teacher gains a new appreciation of his or her own talents and can find new outlets for their expression within the team. This kind of teamwork is perhaps best exercised in "house" teams, where a team of teachers have major responsibility for the education of a limited number of students over a two- or three-year period.

Whatever the arrangements, the experience of teamwork, in which teachers are engaged in meaningful projects that relate directly to improved learning for their youngsters, is electric.[1] Through the work of the team, each individual experiences a new sense of autonomy, of being in a place where he or she can make decisions with the team that will improve the learning of the children. Because a house team usually has the discretion to rearrange its use of time, space, groupings, and sequence of curriculum units, there is the empowering sense of genuinely participating in something whose significance transcends the work of teaching in an isolated classroom. There is an opportunity to explore new relationships among teaching strategies and curriculum topics, new field trips and field projects, new learning activities. There is a feeling that one's own ideas and the ideas of the team are the creative stuff of their work, rather than a passive following of chapter sequences in a textbook or topics in a syllabus.

THE POWER OF IDEAS, DREAMS, AND VISIONS

Finally, I want to argue for the empowering force of ideas, dreams, and visions. Another aspect of empowerment that has been promoted in the literature on empowerment is the notion of teacher professionalism. By that is meant teachers' mastery of a diversity of teaching skills and competencies, as well as a deepening knowledge of the subject matter(s) they teach. In this literature, however, one rarely encounters the encouragement of teachers to connect their work to the world of everyday life, to the world of cultural politics, to current social history.[2]

This lack of involvement in the world of ideas stems in part from our culture's concentration on technical rationality at the expense of substantive rationality. By this distinction I mean the difference between, on the one hand, a rationality that concentrates on how things work, on breaking things down into simpler component parts, on inventing new technologies, on procedures and organizational arrangements, on quantitative analyses of relationships, and, on the other hand, a rationality that seeks the larger *gestalt*, the deeper, complex relationship of parts to wholes that are parts to larger wholes, the multiple relationships that define the significance of moments, places, stories, symbols, and works of art. Technical rationality seeks to answer the questions of how: how to do; how to fix; how to design; how to sell; how to build; how to negotiate. Substantive rationality seeks to answer questions of what and why: What is it we really want? What is it we seek to do, attempt to say, seek to find? Why are we doing this? Why should we choose this rather than that? What does this mean? Why should I believe you? Substantive rationality seeks meaning. Technical rationality seeks efficiency, economy, and procedural logic. Substantive rationality tends to focus on purposes, values, and ends. Technical rationality tends to focus on means, procedures, quantitative relationships, technical invention, and virtuosity.

Proposing that teachers will develop a greater sense of empowerment by increasing their professionalism implies that teachers will develop greater technical virtuosity, a more flexible repertory of teaching protocols, and more technical mastery of the academic disciplines. Indeed, teachers who grow in this kind of professionalism will experience empowerment.

In addition to administrators supporting and nurturing this enhanced professionalism, there is the work of engaging teachers in the exploration of powerful ideas, ideas that are capable of mobilizing the energies of teachers with a greater sense of purpose and value. We can see this kind of power at work in alternative schools. As teachers organized their school around one, two, or three themes, they found that they had discovered a new logic and meaning to their everyday work with students. The meaning of what they were doing took on a new significance. Fired by the excitement of the newly discovered significance of what they were doing with youngsters, they found within themselves resources of creativity, intuitive insight, and sheer physical energy that had gone untapped in their more traditional roles in more traditional schools. As they explored the generative themes that grounded their school's identity and attempted to translate those themes into learning units, they often had to confront the social and economic realities facing their students with a new understanding. They had to make new connections to the world outside the school. They had to see the consequences of their ideas, and relate their thinking more explicitly to the students and to their parents.

One might say that these teachers created a dream or a vision of what their schools could become. These dreams and visions brought them to new levels of activity, well beyond the passive conformity to the bureaucratic arrangements of traditional schools. They overcame the enervating resentment toward school policies and practices formulated long ago on the factory metaphor of schooling.[3] When teachers are captured by exciting possibilities, by a new vision for their schools, they are empowered with a deep sense of meaning and a new energy to work for its realization. Administrators who work with teachers to create alternative schools are offering teachers a chance to regain their own sense of mission as teachers. That sense of mission gives them a renewed sense of the power and significance of their work.

WHAT ABOUT STUDENTS?

All that we have said about the empowering of teachers also applies to the empowering of students. The empowering work with teachers should be directed toward translating *their* sense of empowerment into their work with students.

Students should feel empowered by their teachers. The sources of this empowerment can be found in encouragement to be themselves and to express their talents; in the support that a community of students and teachers can give to the inventive exploration of the connections between learning and the project of creating themselves; and in the source of ideas and dreams for the creation of themselves as a community of strong, inventive, caring, and self-governing individuals. The empowering work for teachers can play itself out in their empowering work with students. In the process, administrators will find the community beginning to "administer itself." The work of the administrator is to get the process rolling, and then to support its unfolding.

STRUCTURAL IMPLICATIONS OF EMPOWERMENT

This kind of empowerment does not take place simply by wishing for it. Besides the personal involvement of the principal with individual teachers, and of teachers with individual students, there have to be structural arrangements in place that nurture and support the process of empowerment. Empowerment themes must be tied to the process of curriculum development and embedded in the curriculum itself. The design and implementation of teacher professional development and accountability have to be placed largely in the hands of teachers. A variety of award and recognition schemes needs to be in place so that a variety of different talents and initiatives can be honored. Other structural arrangements might include a weekly and monthly schedule that allows for a wide variety and frequency of small-group staff workshops and seminars, perhaps a design studio with computers and visual media with which to design new curricular units, perhaps retreat opportunities where teachers can explore the appropriate integration of their life stories with their teaching. Similar opportunities must also be created for students.

Schools and school systems are notoriously impoverished environments. Some administrators expect teachers and students to be empowered because they circulate a photocopy of a speech about it. Empowering teachers and students, however, requires schools to enrich their environments with opportunities for empowerment, to make the place of work so exciting and full of ideas and stimulating discussions of new possibilities that it would be impossible not to grow. Administrators sometimes blame teachers for becoming stale after their first few years of teaching. They blame the students for lack of motivation and responsibility. That is to blame the victims of a disempowering environment that smothers enthusiasm in routine and that punishes inventiveness by subtle demands for conformity and uniformity.

This kind of leadership is what we are all called to. It is an ideal, but unless we see the ideal, there will be nothing on which to build a vision. Administrators will always need practical administrative techniques, but they need much more the dream of what it is possible for the school community to create together. The payoff, of course, is for the youngsters in the school. The drama of their lives will be enriched because of what teachers do. More new songs will be sung; more new inventions will be tried; more compassion will flow between people; the community will feel greater confidence in its ability to govern itself; students might even discover a benign universe.

ACTIVITIES

1. In your journal, cite three instances in the past month when you clearly exercised your power to be yourself. What was going on at these times? Then cite three instances in the past month when your power to be yourself was diminished, thwarted, or threatened. What was happening at these times? Do you experience the power to be yourself often or rarely in your present work? What are you doing to become more empowered?
2. Ask yourself whether teachers and students in your school are empowered in the way we speak of it in this chapter. Give several examples of people who are. Explain why this kind of empowerment is absent in some people in your school. With specific teachers and students in mind, suggest various kinds of specific empowering things you could do with them.
3. At the policy level, ask yourself how teacher and student empowerment might be nurtured in your school. Write five specific policy proposals. Discuss them with administrators in your school system and report back to your study group on their reactions.
4. Identify as many disempowering practices and aspects of your school's culture as you can. For each instance, design a counter practice that would increase empowerment. Discuss the results of these findings with your classmates, and then come up with a class proposal for creating more empowering experiences for teachers and students.

ENDNOTES

1. See the examples cited in Gregory Smith (ed.), *Public Schools That Work: Creating Community*, Routledge, New York, 1993, and in Thomas Sergiovanni, *Building Community in Schools*, Jossey-Bass, San Francisco, 1994.
2. There are exceptions, of course, among whom one can find feminist scholars, scholars of color, those espousing the critical theory framework, and sociologists of education. To get a flavor of the diversity and depth of this thinking, see Henry A. Giroux, *Teachers as Intellectuals*, Bergin & Garvey, Granby, MA, 1988; C. A. Bowers and David J. Flinders, *Responsive Teaching*, Teachers College Press, New York, 1990; William F. Pinar and William M. Reynolds (eds.), *Understanding Curriculum as Phenomenological and Deconstructed Text*, Teachers College Press, New York, 1992; Thomas S. Popkewitz, *A Political Sociology of Educational Reform*, Teachers College Press, New York, 1991.
3. See Raymond Callahan, *Education and the Cult of Efficiency*, University of Chicago Press, Chicago, 1962.

CHAPTER 9

Organic Management

In Chapter 8 we spoke about administering community through the process of empowering people. We spoke of the energy of the community to govern itself when the individual members of the community feel empowered to be themselves, when their work is connected to the work of others in the community, and when they feel energized by core ideas and values of the community. In this chapter we consider more structural ways of administering community. Assuming that we want the school to become a self-governing community, we want to put in place administrative structures that facilitate the primary work of the community and at the same time enhance the ability of the community to govern itself. In other words, the self-governance of the community should be exercised in and through its work. We will first look at the need for a culture of commitment in the school. We will then turn explicitly to organic management and its focus on the primary work of the school, student learning. Two aspects of organic management, the principle of subsidiarity and the dynamic of job enrichment, will further develop our understanding of the administration of a self-governing community.

BUILDING A CULTURE OF COMMITMENT

Brian Rowan offers a helpful distinction between two ways of administering a school: through control or through commitment.[1]

Administering a school through control implies an adherence to the principles of scientific management, including the following.

- Decide on the goals and objectives of the school, and then arrange everything else to serve those goals.
- Design the courses by carefully defining the desired learning outcomes of the course and then designing learning units that closely or exactly correspond to those learning outcomes.

- Consult the latest research on teaching and learning, and design teaching and learning arrangements based on that research.
- Construct assessment instruments to closely or exactly correspond to the learning outcomes.
- Evaluate results of assessment and place underachieving students in remediation loops and ineffective teachers in corrective supervisory process.
- Design staff development programs around the acquisition of teaching effectiveness protocols.
- Conduct teacher evaluations based on criteria of teaching effectiveness and consistent pursuit of the learning outcomes of the class and curriculum unit. Feed results of teacher evaluations into plans for staff development.

Note the linear logic behind this kind of management. It is a rational system guided by goals and clearly defined outcomes. If the system does not produce the desired results, then administrators need to work on the parts of the system that seem to be causing the problem.

Administration by control, however, makes several assumptions that are not warranted by the conditions of schooling. Although some of the principles of "effective instruction" derived from research on "classroom effectiveness" may apply some of the time for some students at some grade levels—especially when the learnings involved are concerned with rote memory or the repetition of simple skills—an increasing body of research is showing that learning, and teaching, are complex phenomena.[2] When teachers are responsible for twenty to thirty children in a class, it is impossible to motivate and communicate with all of them simultaneously given the diversity of talents, interests, prior learning experiences, home situations, and so on.[3]

Furthermore, learning outcomes are not a uniform series of outcomes. Learning to work imaginatively in art class is a different kind of learning than memorizing vocabulary lists, which is a different kind of learning than debating a political party's platform on civil rights. These learnings require different approaches by the teacher. Teaching strategies that work with one child will not work with another; teaching strategies that work on Monday sometimes do not work on Wednesday.

The goals and objectives of schools, moreover, are general, and allow for many interpretations in specific circumstances. A school objective may be the learning of principles of good citizenship. There is no one classroom technique, however, that has been shown in all cases to result in the learning of citizenship. In any given school, there will be ten or fifteen interpretations of what citizenship means, let alone interpretations of the best way to teach it. Even with goals that appear clearer on the surface, one can find substantial differences of opinion among teachers and parents. For example, a school goal may be to graduate students who are knowledgeable in the natural sciences. For some, that means knowledgeable especially in the methodologies of scientific research; for others, it means a knowledge of the central metaphors of science; for still others it means being knowledgeable about the interfacing of the sciences in a more synthetic understanding of the complex systems that sustain life on the planet.

Administration by control—the application of a means–end rationality that assumes uniform agreement on goals and uniform methodologies to achieve these goals—appears to many to be an inappropriate application of the factory metaphor to schooling. The activities of teaching and learning are not easily captured in a reductionistic formula of inputs and outputs and feedback loops. The objectives of schooling are not easily boiled down to three or five outcomes. They are numerous, and they are open to numerous interpretations. Hence the process of teacher evaluation and supervision is fraught with simplistic assumptions about what constitutes effective or good teaching.[4] Similarly, assessment of student learnings by standardized testing is of limited usefulness because it encourages a simplistic understanding of learning and promotes an equally simplistic practice of teaching when all the efforts of the teacher are focused on preparation for these tests.[5] The flaws in the assumptions of administration by control are numerous. The counterproductive effects of practice are serious.[6] Brian Rowan suggests that there may be a more effective strategy for administering a school, which he calls *administration through commitment*.[7] In schools that run by commitment rather than control, there is an entirely different dynamic at work. In these schools there is still a concern with school-wide goals, as well as with learning outcomes. However, the assumptions and beliefs behind administration by commitment are quite different. Within the teaching faculty there is a much greater awareness of diversity and difference among the student body. Teachers assume the need for flexibility in teaching protocols, pacing, and the performance of the learning that will be accepted as indicators of mastery. There is a belief that one can teach many things simultaneously, that on any given day students may be more disposed to learn than on others; that cultural pluralism in the classroom requires sensitivity to a variety of meanings generated by classroom activities; that there are many social lessons to be learned in the classroom as well as the academic lessons suggested by the textbooks (learning to respect racial, ethnic, and sexual differences); learning how to negotiate disagreements; learning how to control antisocial impulses; learning how to listen to and appreciate another point of view).

In schools administered by commitment, there is no attempt to monitor each teacher's classrooms according to a predetermined, uniform set of expectations. Rather, there is the expectation that each teacher, carefully reading the talents and interests in her class, is responding to both the curricular objectives and the complex chemistry of the human beings in her class as she designs a variety of learning activities to assist their appropriation of the material and their creation of knowledge through those activities. Administrators do not control what goes on in the classroom; instead, in their visits to classes they listen to teachers explain how they are using their professional talents and skills to create exciting learning possibilities for the children. Administrators promote and reinforce the teachers' commitment to make learning exciting, interesting, and fulfilling.

How does a school nurture this kind of commitment? There is a growing awareness in the research literature that a school's culture can be enormously influential on the quality and degree of commitment of teachers. By concentrating on building a culture of shared purposes, a sense of mission, and a sense that in their work teachers are making a significant contribution to the lives of their children, administrators and teachers develop a deep motivation to make the school experience successful for youngsters.

In a culture of commitment one finds a kind of shared covenant, an unspoken rule that the school won't work unless everyone is fully involved. There is a feeling of being responsible to each other, a sense of the bonds of loyalty and common ideals, a sharing of common beliefs about teaching and learning, about how children grow, about the social purposes of schools, and about what it means to be a full human being.

In such cultures teaching is a reflective activity. It is the work of the professional who continually tests theories and intuitions about what will work in *this* circumstance by attending closely to the immediate results. This kind of reflective teacher is always looking at the student, at what is going on, engaging the student in a dialogue so the teacher has a sense of what is happening inside the student's head and heart. That is difficult to do with twenty or thirty children in a class, or with 120 children in the course of a school day. Good teachers find ways to keep close to the work that students are doing. Even a brief review and comment lets the students know the teacher cares about their work.

In cultures of commitment, it is not so much the administrators who hold teachers accountable, it is the teachers who hold themselves accountable to create genuine learning opportunities for their students. Their sense of accountability is passed on to the students. Teachers work on motivating the students to take responsibility for their learning.

ORGANIC MANAGEMENT

One builds such a culture of commitment by a process of organic management. By *organic management* I mean that the administrator continually tries to focus on the core or central work of the school and brings others' attention to that central work. Other forms of management, such as the bureaucratic management of traditional schools, begins with an organizational arrangement. The school day is divided into seven or eight periods of forty- to forty-five-minute segments. The school day ends at 2:30. School bus schedules are arranged so that most of the students are expected to go home at 2:30, whether or not they have finished their work at school for that day. Teachers are assigned textbooks and specific classes; they are expected to fill out report cards formatted the same for everyone. The curriculum is parceled out in forty- to forty-five-minute periods. In other words, the core work of the school—student learning—is arranged to fit an organizational structure that is already in place, even if that organizational structure impedes the core work of the school.

The core work of the school is the work of learning. That is the work that students do. The work of students is not to produce a uniform product as workers on an assembly line do. The work of students is the creation of knowledge appropriated from the culture and from the academic resources available in the school and in the community in the form of books, films, computer data banks, electronic switchboards, and communication networks. That work will also involve applying knowledge to the interpretation of personal experience, and to the interpretation of community issues and problems. It will also involve invention and creative expression in which the student takes his or her learning and makes something new out of it—a poem, a song, a political statement, a computer application, a design, an interpretation, or a suggestion for recycling plastics. It also involves social learning, the appreciation of other points of view, learning how to disagree, and learning teamwork.

By keeping always in mind that the students' work is the core task of the school, the administrator employing organic management engages the staff and the students in exploring ways to make that work more felicitous, more productive, and more effective. The administrator and staff periodically have to take the present organizational arrangements and imaginatively throw them all away. Assuming no schedule, no classroom, no weekly and monthly calendar in place, how can they better organize their resources of space, time, money, and personnel so as to improve the core work of the school, namely, student learning? The work should dictate how the day is scheduled and how teachers work with students. Perhaps some of that work can be done more effectively outside the school building, at some location in the community at large. Some of the work may best be done individually, some in teams of students. Some of the work may require intensive teacher involvement at the beginning and minimal involvement as the project matures. Some work may involve sophisticated computer hookups to major data networks that can only be done within the school; some, however, may be done with a computer at home. Some work will best be achieved in apprenticelike relationships with resource people in the community; some may involve participating in evening political meetings in the community.

The point of organic management is to keep teachers and students focused on the core task of the school: the promotion and enhancement of student learning. Organic management of schools continually evaluates how that work is managed so that institutional arrangements do not get in the way.

THE PRINCIPLE OF SUBSIDIARITY

An important part of organic management is the principle of subsidiarity. According to this principle, the authority to make discretionary decisions concerning the work is placed as close to the work as possible. This means that operational decisions about the work are not made at the superintendent's level, or even at the principal's level. They are made where teaching and learning take place. The persons closest to the task are given the authority and responsibility for carrying out the task. Subsidiarity unites authority with responsibility. If

students have the responsibility to produce the learning, then as much authority as possible should be placed in their hands to decide the details of its production. The teacher, as the next closest to the task, should likewise have the authority to negotiate the production of learning with the student.

This does not mean that superintendents and principals should have no say
in what goes on. Clearly, their voices will need to join with the voices of the
teachers as discussions are held about the school-wide and district-wide goals
of the school. As educators with overall responsibility for a K–12 system or for
a whole school in the system, they have a broad perspective on the large goals
of schooling. Furthermore, there will be occasions when essential decisions
have to be made in the face of divided opinions on a particular matter, when no
consensus is available. Administrators, while listening to both sides of the argument, will nonetheless have to make the decision. The state will also have a
voice in setting general graduation requirements, as well as determining legal
constraints on school systems to prevent illegal activities and to provide special
services to underrepresented populations. This is all taken for granted.

Nevertheless, the essential work is done at the student level, through the
coaching and teaching of teachers. This work cannot be micromanaged from a
distance, because the number of variables needed to be taken into account in
the production of learning only can be dealt with at the micro level, not at the
system or state level. If learning involves the production and performance of
meaning, then ultimately the meaning has to be the student's. The culture provides the ingredients for constructing meaning, the state and local school board
set the curriculum to be covered, the teacher, as the closest *other* person to the
student's production and performance of learning, strongly influences what
and how that learning is to be through his interpretation of the cultural ingredients and curriculum material, but the student is the one who by her or his autonomous activity *does* the learning.

THE PROBLEM WITH CORRECT ANSWERS

The system of rewards and sanctions in schools assumes that the student is responsible for learning. The *what* of learning, however, is often mistakenly assumed *not* to be the student's, but the state's or the scholarly academic community's or the teacher's, when educators make judgments about whether that
learning produces "the right" or "the correct" answer. The "what is learned" in
any instance is still produced by the student, even though that learning may
produce the "wrong answer." The student may need to correct that learning
with new information; then the previous learning becomes realigned with a
new learning that brings the previous and the new information into a new
gestalt.

When we learn, we make meaning. We do not learn information; we learn
from information to make meaning. We extract the meanings encoded in information and align that meaning with previously constructed meanings. Along
the way, we make many "mistakes," making things and relationships mean

123

something that later experience and new information shows us they do not mean.

Teachers help speed up the process of making meanings about the physical, social, and human world. They enable youngsters to participate in those worlds as agents whose destinies are entwined with the destinies of those worlds. Teachers help students correct learnings that hinder participation in those worlds. Teachers normally do not, however, do a good job of teaching students that this realignment, broadening, deepening, transformation of earlier meanings is a never-ending process. We hear encouragement for the principle of "learning how to learn." We do not hear enough emphasis on the equally important principle, "learning how to un-learn." Emphasis on this principle promotes the understanding that our making of meaning as individuals *and* as communities is always a provisional enterprise. Our meanings always have to be revised for a deeper and broader understanding. When they teach the importance of un-learning as a necessary component of life-long learning, schools avoid the mistake of turning out young people who believe that the world really conforms to what their tenth-grade textbooks said it was.

The making of meaning is bound up with the community's self-identification in relationship to the physical, social, and human worlds. The immature individual's making of meaning cannot pursue its course independent of the community's sense of its relationship to the physical, social, and human worlds. Hence, schools present the community's meanings as the school's curriculum. However, schools also need to teach that these meanings are not frozen and totally exhausted in their current cultural expression. Hence, the work of the school also needs to promote the exploration of alternative expressions of standard cultural meanings or new applications of traditional meanings to different problems or questions. For example, feminist ways of framing questions now challenge traditional cultural meanings that previously framed those questions. Likewise, environmental concerns require the reframing of issues previously thought to be firmly understood (and settled) by other meaning frames. The reshaping of issues related to the conduct and economics of warfare—and the warfare of economics—may be required by new global alignments, by the international community's need to suppress the production of nuclear and biological weapons, by the redistribution of global sources of economic power, and by the emerging global consensus on human rights. The realities of global scarcity and global environmental deterioration require a re-formation of the meanings traditionally associated with market economics. A society whose schools do not equip its younger generation with the expectation that its current understanding of itself in relationship to the physical, social, and human worlds are limited and continually need to be reimagined, refashioned, reformed, is preparing itself for a dysfunctional future. It is placing itself more at risk than it was a generation ago, when a panel of national leaders thought the nation was at risk for not teaching enough students enough of the correct answers.[8] Hence, when we speak of the work of the school as involving the student in the making and performing of meaning, we need to recognize the full measure of that task.

FOUR REQUIREMENTS FOR SUBSIDIARITY

The principle of subsidiarity as the centerpiece strategy of organic management requires four elements if it is to work. Subsidiarity requires (1) trust, (2) knowledge of what the task is, (3) the capacity to carry out the task, and (4) a sense of the whole. If any one of those elements is missing, the strategy will not work. Teachers and students may know what the task is, but lack the trust of the school board, and hence lack the discretionary authority to effect the work. Teachers may know that the student has to be actively involved in the production and performance of meaning, but they have been socialized into a way of teaching that blocks such active involvement by the student. Students may want to study only science and math, and have no interest in the rest of the curriculum; teachers may want to work only with bright students. In either case we have people who do not want to work with the larger whole, which is necessary if subsidiarity is to make sense. Let us explore what these four requirements mean.

Trust

One of the difficulties that newly appointed administrators have is dealing with their authority and their sense of accountability to their superiors. In popular understanding, administrators are supposed to be in charge. They are supposed to make things happen. When things go wrong, administrators are blamed. Yet most administrators know, at least at a subconscious level, that they cannot control all the details of a school, even a small school. Apprehension over what the public or the school board might think of them if something were to go wrong, however, can lead them to suppress this knowledge that they cannot control things (even while that same knowledge subconsciously fuels their apprehension) and to establish tight reins of control. No decisions will be made unless cleared with the principal; no expenditures of funds will be allowed unless first cleared by the principal; no letters to parents will be sent home unless first cleared through the principal; no deviation from the assigned curriculum will be allowed unless the principal explicitly grants an exception. Mandate follows upon mandate. New rules are constructed to account for yet another unforeseen situation. Not only will the administrator end up continuously frustrated by her inability to anticipate every mess (messes are a daily, ontologically guaranteed certainty in schools), but teachers and students will resent her attempts to control every facet of school life. This resentment, in turn, will lead to noncompliance, or at best minimal compliance with all the control strategies. Messes will be invented, just to see the principal turn apoplectic. Of course, complaints will filter up to the principal's superiors, who in turn will send queries back down to the principal that, to this now half-crazed unfortunate, will be interpreted as complaint about his inability to *control* things at the school.

    The beginning principal has to learn, often the hard way, that one cannot control every facet of school life, and furthermore, that one should not attempt to control *any* facet of school life. Rather, the administrator's job is to get people to take responsibility for their own work. This does not mean that, once everyone has agreed to take responsibility for their own work, messes will disappear. People will still make mistakes, will still misunderstand each other, will still descend to selfish concerns. If they have agreed to take responsibility for their work, however, the administrator can ask them to take responsibility for cleaning up their own messes.

The lesson to be learned here is that when people know that you rely on them, they will do the job more energetically than you would have imagined possible. Perfection eludes us all. There will be problems, bruised egos, petty jealousies, and plain childishness, from time to time. In a climate of trust and mutual responsibility, however, these things can be worked through. Furthermore, when individual teachers feel trusted, they more easily develop a sense of team, a sense that together they can collaborate on the resolution of nagging problems, on the redesign of programs, on the deepening and broadening of students' learning. In a climate of trust, individual teachers and groups of teachers can approach administrators with their concerns. They can indicate that they need some help in working out a problem. They can openly address school-wide issues that are negatively affecting student learning. In other words, one administers by encouraging the self-governance of which we spoke of in the last chapter.

People will more readily take charge of their work when they perceive that they are trusted to do so, when they understand that they are expected to do so. A parent will hold the spoon and feed an infant. As the child grows older, the parent expects the child to feed itself. Parents may correct a child's manners and etiquette, but the expectation is that the child can feed itself. Adults know that they are responsible for feeding themselves. Their sense of responsibility ensures that they will indeed feed themselves. When adults are trusted to do a good job, the quality performance of that job becomes habitual. No one has to give them permission to do the job. Doing a good job is simply the way one works.[9]

If teachers have formerly not been trusted to do a good job, then it will take some time to convince them that you really trust them. There will be disappointments along the way, as some betray your trust by cutting corners. Some teachers will accuse the trusting principal of naiveté, of wimpishness, and of indecisiveness. Principals will be told by superiors to "come down hard" on certain teachers. Nonetheless, persistence in trusting is the answer. Most people can be motivated to doing a decent job by trust.

Knowledge of the Task

Trust alone will not guarantee that teachers manage their work well. They need to understand what the task is for which they are responsible. One of the difficulties of teaching is that the tasks for which teachers are responsible are multiform. Many of these tasks are not spelled out in the teachers' contract. Many of the tasks are never "covered" in preservice courses in teacher education.

What does one do, for example, when a youngster throws up all over his desk? Of course one must protect oneself and the other children from possible contamination by viruses or bacteria, and get the child to the school nurse. But should one provide prior instruction to the children about the procedures to be followed in this situation, or is it better to make light of it and not create unnecessary anxieties? What if the ill child has, not chicken pox, but AIDS? Or consider the question of what to do when a teacher suspects that a child is suffering physical abuse at home. How is one to proceed so that the rights of the parents as well as the rights of the child are respected? How does a teacher break up a fight in the school yard? How does a teacher speak to a child whose lack of social sensitivity leads to her ostracism by the other children? How does a teacher help a child develop study habits when her home life is totally chaotic? How does a teacher respond to a very assertive parent who is convinced that his second-grade child is a budding Fulbright scholar, when all indications are that the child has rather average academic talents? These concerns may not be treated in the formulas for effective instruction in the teacher education textbooks, yet teachers are expected to deal with all these contingencies as a "professional."

Organic Management and Administering Meaning

Administrators need to work with the teachers, both individually and in groups, to encourage them to identify their major tasks. Teachers initially may identify these tasks by highly particularized examples, such as teaching students how to work out equations with fractions, or how to use the subjunctive voice, or learn the names of the major rivers in the United States. Teachers need to be asked why these learning tasks are included and others are not. They need to talk about the larger purposes and values that ground particular learnings. Through these conversations, they can be led to a clearer definition of the task that encompasses the many small things they do. They may come to understand that they are attempting to develop in their students habits of life-long learning, habits of learning how to learn, habits of applying their learning to real-life problems and issues, habits of using their learning to define themselves, habits of continually refashioning themselves in relationship to their physical, social, and human worlds. These larger definitions of the task of teaching enable the teacher to bring a larger sense of purpose and mission to the daily work with the students.

Capability to Accomplish the Task

In the course of these conversations, administrators and teachers will need to discuss what they need in order to do the work more effectively. In some instances, the discussion may lead to the realization that the teacher needs to know a lot more about child development, or about learning disabilities. In other instances, they may come to the conclusion that there are certain academic areas where the teacher is weak—say, physical science, or history. In other instances, the teacher may come to the realization that he or she simply does not understand the cultural backgrounds of the children. This may be due to differences between the race or ethnicity or class of the teacher and the students. The teacher may need workshops in multicultural sensitivity, or a course in the history of the children's culture. This academic enlargement of the teacher's cultural horizons may need to be supplemented with more direct conversations with the parents of the children so that they may work out ways of collaborating together in the children's education.

A SENSE OF THE WHOLE

The principle of subsidiarity also requires a sense of being part of a larger whole. If teachers and students are to have the authority to make discretionary decisions about their learning, then they have to make those decisions with the realization that they have responsibilities, not simply to do this specific task, but to the working of the larger community and its variety of tasks. Students may be encouraged to take the necessary time to complete a project, but this project may be only one of many projects. If the student is a member of a team that is working on another project, then the team has some claim on the student's time as well. Teachers may want to provide an abundance of colored construction paper to their children, but they have to leave enough in the supply closet for the other classes to have their fair share. In other words, the discretion to make decisions necessary to carry out the work is not a license to disregard the needs of everyone else in the school.

Ground rules and explicit agreements about the use of space, time, and resources are a necessary component of organic management. However, they should be worked through by the people most involved with the work, rather than dictated from a remote administrative office. At the beginning of every school year, teachers and students need to review these agreements. More than likely, meetings will need to be called from time to time to work out imbalances in the way resources are shared in the various learning tasks. The work of the administrator is to monitor the self-governance of the teachers and students and to facilitate and arbitrate when the parties cannot work out their disagreements on their own.

The brief examples mentioned above are intended to illuminate the requirements of trust, knowledge of the task, capacity to accomplish the task, and a sense of the whole. We can see, at this point, that all four requirements feed on one another. Organic management requires an ongoing learning of the task, developing greater strength and versatility to tackle the various dimensions of the task. As greater concentration on learning tasks develops, teachers and students have to balance the demands of those tasks with the whole curriculum and with the limited resources at their disposal. As they honor the demands of the whole, teachers and administrators will develop greater trust in their ability to address the practicalities of the learning tasks.

It is also evident that one of the major investments of an administrator's time is in conversation with teachers, including both informal and formal conversations about their work. Regular conversations will ensure clear lines of communication, both vertically and horizontally. Through regular conversations, problems will be identified and possible responses tested; conflicts between teachers and students, teachers and parents, teachers and other teachers, and teachers and administrators can be raised and addressed. The commitment is to making the school work for youngsters, for their enhanced learning. Hence the conversations should continually raise and encourage the common commitment to this work and the awareness of each person's responsibility to engage in that work.

As teachers and administrators discuss the nature of the task—the promotion of the student's enhanced understanding of herself in relationship to the physical, social, and human worlds and her involvement in those worlds—it may become evident that teachers will want to and need to work more in teams. In other words, the work of the school is a multifaceted and complex one, a task that is larger than the ability of one teacher to achieve. Teachers working in teams can accomplish significant units of the task, or indeed the whole task. In teams their talents and areas of expertise complement one another; collectively they can make a qualitatively richer response to the work of students' learning.

In some instances, this may mean a team of teachers working with a group of, say, 100 students over the course of three or four years. In contrast to the tendency toward specialization, where the work of teachers is narrow, repetitive, and separated from the sense of the larger task, teachers working in teams can work on a variety of facets of the large task with a sense of how their work fits together. This, of course, will enhance the students' sense of the connectedness of their learning to the large unities of the physical, social, and human worlds. When teachers work in teams, the authority and responsibility for the work is clearly located as close to the work as possible. The work is managed organically, because the decisions made flow from the intrinsic demands of the present contingencies of the work of learning, rather than from an artificially constructed administrative structure built on the assumption of uniformity of learning, learners, daily readiness for learning, cultural backgrounds, and learning performances.

Whether talking with individual teachers or with teams of teachers, the administrator will be concerned with another sense of the whole: the larger school curriculum. Teachers who are working with a particular grade level need to keep in mind how the work at that level fits within the overall curriculum. Usually, their work is so focused on the immediate learning tasks that they seldom refer to the larger curriculum framework. Administrators can provide the opportunity for teachers to make those connections in their conversations while on their rounds.

JOB ENRICHMENT

Besides the principle of subsidiarity, the theory and research of job enrichment provide further insight into the dynamics of organic management. The work of Hackman and Oldham is especially informative.[10] Although their studies involved workers in the industrial and corporate world, the dynamics they describe apply as well to the dynamics of organic management we have been proposing for schools.

Hackman and Oldham found that workers were motivated to high-quality work that they could be proud of by a consistent set of job dimensions. These dimensions led to an internal experience of the job that was highly satisfying and meaningful. These internal experiences of the job, in turn, led to high-quality performance of the work. They summarized their findings as reproduced here in Table 9-1.

Hackman and Oldham found that five core dimensions on the job made all the difference between work that was considered highly satisfying and work that was not. Three of those dimensions had to do with the task or work itself: skill variety, task identity, and task significance. Workers prefer variety in their work, rather than a fixed routine of the same tasks. They enjoy using a variety of skills on the job, rather than narrowly specialized, single skills. The variety of skills a teacher needs in her work with students qualifies the work of teaching as potentially highly satisfying. Task identity refers to the clarity of understanding what the work entails. Workers need to know that the task has a core and that it has boundaries. They do not want to be held responsible for work that is not assigned to them. They want to know clearly what it is they are expected to do. They want to have a clear understanding of *the what* of the work. Conversations between the principal and teachers by which they identify the meaning of what they are doing is an example of an attempt at task identity.

Task significance refers to the value attached to the work. What does the

TABLE 9-1 The Dynamics of Job Enrichment

Core Job Dimensions	Critical Psychological States	Personal and Work Outcomes
Skill variety Task identity Task significance	Experienced meaningfulness of work	High internal motivation; high-quality work
Autonomy	Experienced responsibility for results	High satisfaction and pride
Feedback	Knowledge of actual results of the work	High satisfaction and high enthusiasm

Source: Adapted from J. R. Hackman, G. Oldham, R. Johnson, and K. Purdy, "A New Strategy for Job Enrichment," *California Management Review*, **xvii**(4): 64 (1975), © 1975 by the Regents of the University of California, used by permission of the Regents.

work mean in relation to a large framework of value? Teachers get little feedback from parents or administrators that their work with students is valuable, that it has significance in the ongoing life of the community. Many beginning teachers start out with a sense of mission, but the traditional culture of bureaucratic schools quickly drains it away, replacing it with a pragmatic or cynical political perspective of survival. Exposure to the daily routine of the teachers' room is enough to defeat most ideals. "Ideals?! God forbid we should get caught with such a social disease! Ideals, you say! Better for you to guard against the stupidity of superiors and the incorrigibility of children and simply get on with the next five pages of the textbook, thank you. Enough about ideals, already. We don't need any more do-gooders around here."

To combat these attitudes, principals need continually to remind their teachers of the value of their work. Even though it may sound like motherhood and apple pie, principals who believe in the social and humanistic value of education need to employ inspiring imagery in their attempts to remind teachers of the nobility and sacredness of their work. What could be more sacred than participating in the reflexive and inventive process of the universe in its continuing creation of itself? What could be more sacred than nurturing the values and idealism of the country's next generation of leaders? What could be more noble than nurturing the imagination and intelligence of the next generation of artists, musicians, builders, astronomers, police officers, architects, farmers, doctors, judges, geophysicists, poets? What could be more worthwhile than expanding the humanity of the new generation of parents and citizens? What could be more exciting than exploring the boundaries of knowledge with young minds? The work is so sacred it is scary. Perhaps that is why teachers cover it over with the ritual of routine. Ordinary people could never do such extraordinary things. Ideals. God forbid.

The two other job dimensions which Hackman and Oldham highlight are autonomy on the job, and feedback of results. Obviously, autonomy does not mean total latitude to do whatever you want in your work. It does mean that the worker has enough discretion to respond to situations that are beyond the routine guidelines for getting the job done. It also means discretion to pursue an insight about how the work could be improved. Where the work goes beyond the assembly-line production of uniform widgets, where the work involves selling or marketing or designing, or negotiating an organizational conflict between two competing groups, the worker has the autonomy to channel the work in a way that makes sense to him or her. If the decision turns out to be inappropriate, the worker learns from that and stores that learning in the bin labeled "Avoid in the future."

Although teachers enjoy a fair amount of autonomy, it is not an autonomy granted to a mature professional. It is an autonomy granted by indifference and expediency. Many administrators are indifferent to the specific ways teachers nurture learning. If most of the children are getting passing grades, the assumption is that the teacher is doing a good job. There is no effort to explore with the teacher how student learning could be qualitatively enhanced by the introduction of new approaches. "Good enough" is a judgment often made with little understanding of whether that means the teacher has done a spectacular job with youngsters of very limited talents or a mediocre job with students of high talents. Given the way school systems interpret the task of instructional supervision, the lack of stimulating collaboration with teachers is neglected from a sense of expediency; there is only so much time available for a once-or-twice-a-semester "observation."

Feedback or knowledge of results is important to job satisfaction and enrichment because it enables the worker to gain confirmation that he or she is doing a good job, or needs to attend to some things in order to improve the work. Feedback complements autonomy. The more autonomy one has to use inventive discretion in one's work, the more one needs some way of getting feedback about the results of the work. Unfortunately, for many teachers the only official feedback they receive is the collective results of their children on standardized tests. A much closer, criterion-referenced form of performance assessment in which at least two other knowledgeable people are involved would serve this feedback process better.

Moreover, the nature of *what* is assessed needs to be examined. How many teachers get feedback on their efforts to teach youngsters to appreciate the opinions of others, or to resolve their disputes in nonviolent ways? Normally, the only time teachers receive feedback on these efforts is when something unpleasant happens between students, and teachers are blamed for not attending to it. If the building up of community is important to the school, then teachers should receive feedback on the results of their efforts. Knowledge of results of standardized tests is good, as far as it goes, but there are many more things that teachers attend to, the results of which are rarely assessed.

SUMMARY

In this chapter we have explored how one can administer community through a process of organic management. Organic management means management by commitment rather than by control, and therefore implies attention to the development of a culture of commitment. We saw that organic management begins by identifying the core work of the school—the active learning of students—and the facilitating work of teachers in promoting this active learning. With a clear sense of the core work of the school, organic management involves designing all administrative procedures and structures to enhance and facilitate this core work. We then explored the principle of subsidiarity as providing the strategic orientation to aligning administrative procedures with the core work of the school, by placing the authority to do the work as close as possible to those who have the responsibility to do the work: teachers and students. The requirements of trust, knowledge of the task, capacity to do the task, and a sense of the whole were seen as essential to subsidiarity. Finally, Hackman and Oldham's job enrichment theory shed further light on the dynamics of organic management. As in earlier chapters, we have not developed a list of "how-tos." That is the work that lies before us as we take the general ideas of organic management and study how the school workplace can be organically managed.

ACTIVITIES

1. Study your workplace. Is the school governed by control or by commitment? If by control, what are the undesirable and desirable results of this in terms of morale, professionalism, inventiveness, and productivity of the staff and students? If by commitment, then what are the values that explicitly or implicitly ground that commitment, and how are they sustained? In either case, make three policy recommendations that would improve the way your school governs itself.
2. In your workplace, what is the definition of the core work of the organization? How does this core work relate to the organizational structures and administrative procedures that channel and direct the work? What needs to be done about the situation, if anything? Do you have any policy recommendations?
3. Use the job enrichment schema in Table 9-1 to analyze the level of enrichment that people experience in your workplace. What policy recommendations would you make to improve work enrichment?
4. Discuss your results with others in the class and come up with some system-wide policy recommendations that would encourage organic management in all the schools of the district. Develop a short- and long-term plan for implementing these policy recommendations.

ENDNOTES

1. Brian Rowan, "Commitment and Control: Alternative Strategies for the Organizational Design of Schools," in Courtney B. Cazden (ed.), *Review of Research in Education, Vol. 16,* American Educational Research Association, Washington, DC, 1990, pp. 353–389.
2. See, for example, Linda M. McNeil, *Contradictions of Control: School Structure and School Knowledge,* Routledge, New York, 1988; and Eleanor Duckworth, *"The Having of Wonderful Ideas" and Other Essays on Teaching and Learning,* Teachers College Press, New York, 1987.
3. See Tracy Kidder, *Among Schoolchildren,* Avon, New York, 1989; and Phillip Lopate, *Being with Children,* Poseiden Press, New York, 1975.
4. See Robert J. Starratt, "After Supervision," *Journal of Curriculum and Supervision,* **8**(1): 77–86 (1992); Susan Stoldowsky, "Teacher Evaluation: The Limits of Looking," *Educational Researcher,* **13**: 11–19 (November 1984).
5. See Lorrie A. Shepard, "Why We Need Better Assessments," *Educational Leadership,* **46**(7): 4–9 (April 1989).

6. See Joseph Blase, "Some Negative Effects of Principals' Control-Oriented and Protective Political Behavior," *American Educational Research Journal*, **27**: 727–753 (Winter 1990); Arthur E. Wise, "Two Conflicting Trends in School Reform: Legislated Learning Revisited," *Phi Delta Kappan*, **69**: 328–333 (January 1988).

7. Rowan, op. cit., pp. 353–389.

8. See the National Commission on Excellence in Education, *A Nation at Risk*, U. S. Government Printing Office, Washington, DC, 1983.

9. See Max DePree, *Leadership Is an Art*, Doubleday, New York, 1989, for examples of this kind of commitment to quality work. See also, the earlier work of Douglas McGregor, *The Human Side of Enterprise*, McGraw-Hill, New York, 1960.

10. J. R. Hackman and G. Oldham, "Motivation through Design of Work: Test of a Theory," *Organizational Behavior and Human Performance*, **16**(2): 250–279 (1976).

CHAPTER 10

Governing by Design

THE MEDIUM IS THE MESSAGE

The sign that something is made by humans is that they add to the material elements and natural forms of wood and stone, fabric, and food, a fingerprint of human intelligence, imagination, playfulness, and inventiveness. A branch may have a natural bend and curve as it leaves the tree trunk that would make it suitable for use as a ladle or scoop. The human sees the design of the ladle already in the bend and scoop, so he takes the branch and fashions it into a human instrument. Yet he will often add to the natural curve and scoop design by carving the image of a serpent, a flower, or a face on the handle. Animals build nests and burrows out of natural materials, and many add distinctive designs to these materials as they build. One species will weave the straw with mud, another with small pieces of wood. When humans build homes, they use natural materials, but they design and decorate the spaces so that they are both functional and pleasing. More often than not, the design carries symbolic value as well: One room is clearly a woman's room, one a man's; a family coat-of-arms decorates the parlor; a religious shrine sets off an interior room.

The way humans design their living environment communicates the values they attach to those environments. The austere, uniform, and simple design of a boot-camp barracks communicates the value of the spartan single-mindedness of the soldier/warrior preparing for mortal combat, the value of everyone doing exactly as ordered, the value of thinking only in terms of the group, the platoon, the regiment, and the company. Prisons are designed to communicate other values. The design of factories, cathedrals, banks, and other kinds of social institutions reveals core values that those who commissioned the design wanted to communicate. Think of the design of a present-day bank. Ordinary customers stand in line and wait their turn to approach a high counter, where their business is transacted very expeditiously. Normally the teller does not even call the customer by name. More valued customers—the prospective homeowner seeking a mortgage on which the bank stands to realize a substantial profit, or the executive who represents a company whose business with the bank will generate sizable profits—sit in another part of the bank, with walls hung with works of art, with fine drapery and carpeting and upholstered furniture. The medium carries the message.

THE DESIGN OF SCHOOLS

The layout of a school will often reveal the educational philosophy of those who commissioned its construction. I usually look for the central space of the school, for that usually tells me what activity is considered most important. If the principal's office sits at the center of the school, then I get a sense that the designers assumed the principal's office would be the control center of the school, providing roughly equal access to the office from all directions. If, on the other hand, I find the library at the center of the school, or at least in a more prominent location than the principal's office, then I assume that the designers of the schools value learning and storytelling more than administrative control. Sometimes I find the cafeteria at the center, or an auditorium, a gymnasium, or even the boiler room. What is at the center and the periphery of buildings often conveys the symbolic order of importance of the activities conducted in those spaces. I also like to visit the teachers' room, staff lounge, or whatever it is called. Where it is located and how it is fitted out often tells me a lot about how the administration thinks of its teachers and how they think of themselves.

I also look for what is displayed in the corridors, especially in those closest to the front door. In many schools, there are cabinets containing athletic trophies; in some, there are bulletin boards covered with student art work; in others, there are displays of photographs of student groups involved in a variety of projects and special events; and in others, there is nothing but walls.

Look at the way classrooms are arranged. Are they clustered by grade levels, with common rooms designated for that cluster's use, or are they all of the same size? Do they all manifest the same configuration of desks in rows, or are the seating arrangements in a variety of configurations? Is the building an egg crate of classrooms, or are there various sizes and shapes to the work spaces, some curved, some two-tiered, some triangular, some simply rearrangeable into a variety of shapes?

All of these spatial design features reveal values and perspectives about the work of educating youngsters. In a uniformly arranged series of identical classrooms with identical seating arrangements, it is difficult to introduce variety into the instructional methods of teaching, and into the performance of the learning tasks. Not impossible, but difficult. Access to books, computers, and audio-visual resources is also a measure of the difficulty of varying the learning tasks. If these resources are half a school away, then it becomes more difficult to use them. Not impossible, but difficult. The way a room is wired and lighted will likewise add to or subtract from the possibility of variety in the teaching and learning activities. Clearly, the way a school is designed communicates the kind of work that is expected to go on in the various spaces of the school.

A LARGER VIEW OF DESIGN

We often think of design as being involved exclusively with the design of space. Yet design includes much more. Choreography can be seen as the design of bodily movements to the flow of the music. Composing a musical score is designing sound into melodies and harmonies and patterns. Clothes are designed to communicate a feeling or impression. Jewelry is designed to highlight form and texture and color. Graphic design communicates feelings of energy and excitement or contemplative harmony or delicate fragility. In choosing the kind of lettering for a business card, an executive wants to communicate a sense of who he or she is. Packagers of commercial goods will attempt, through the attractiveness of color and the printing design, to draw prospective buyers' attention. Gardens, landscapes, neighborhood street patterns, computer software and hardware, book covers, and record album covers—these and so many other things in our lives are products of design.

When we think of administering a community, therefore, we ought to think of how that community wants to design its work, its work spaces, its sequencing of the work, its use of sound and silence, its use of color and light, its communication processes, its disciplinary processes, and its personnel procedures. The design of all of these aspects of the community's life will reveal, or ought to reveal, the essential values espoused by that community. In other words, the values revealed by all of these aspects of the community's life, taken collectively, ought to be clearly expressive of the community's values and purposes.

EXAMPLES OF DESIGN FEATURES IN SCHOOLS

Consider something as prosaic as a report card. Most often they reveal a rather simple design: name and identification number; date; marking period; subjects listed down the left side; grades for achievement and effort in the middle columns; and terse, judgmental comments on the right. Why not add the school motto at the top and intersperse quotations from various sages about the value of effort, the joy of learning, and the significance of education for the building up of civil society? Perhaps a humorous short poem or ditty could lighten up the doomsday heaviness of report cards. Perhaps a cartoon of a Charley Brown-like character talking to his teacher about his homework could be placed in the bottom corner. At the bottom of the card, some information about upcoming school events could be added as a way to encourage parents to participate more in the life of the school. In other words, report cards can be designed as a more personal communication between the school and the home. Of course, performance assessments should also affect the design of report cards, with prose analyses of the student's work replacing or at least supplementing the perfunctory numbers and letters.

Memos from the principal or some other administrator is a weekly occurrence in most teachers' lives. Normally, these memos are not joyously and eagerly received by the teachers. Usually the memo brings news of added work on an up-coming event, warnings about the need to attend to something or other in the school rule book, complaints about teachers not doing something they are supposed to do, communication of parents' concerns (or complaints), news about some new regulation by the state department of education, or family services, or whatever. Granted that sometimes these announcements are necessary, often the whole faculty appears to be accused of something one or two teachers have done, or even that one or two students have done. Besides the substance of the message, there is the style of the message, the impersonal, bureaucratic language, the officiousness of the format. Administrative memos could begin with a humorous limerick, or a cartoon, or a joke, or a thought-for-the-day. After that, every memo should carry some good news, some congratulations or gratitude for something a student or teacher or parent has done. Then the bad news can be received in a way that balances the burdens of the job of an educator with its satisfactions. Why can't the format of memos have some decorative (but unpretentious) edge to them, something that communicates a care for the esthetic and human sensibilities of the recipients? Sometimes even such a small gesture communicates that the administrator cares enough about his or her teachers to go to the trouble of designing memos to be personal communications.

Much the same can be said about administrators' letters to parents. A touch of humor, an encouraging word, a thank you for their trust in the school, an invitation to participate on a school committee, a funny story—these can go a long way toward establishing connections between the home and the school. The esthetics of the format, a touch of color, a symbol of parent–child relationships, a saying about the significance of parenting—all these can create a tone of respect and caring.

As one approaches the main entrance to the school, one can get a sense of the school. Are there flowers and shrubs around the entrance, or is it barren, even dirty? Is there attention to landscaping and to creating a natural space where things grow, where squirrels and birds are visible? Schools communicate how they feel about nature by the way they ignore or feature it. If everything is covered over with asphalt and surrounded by high fences, the school makes a statement by how it designs its exterior spaces.

Within the building, the walls can make a statement about art, about the natural and social environment, about the school's pride in student achievements, or they can be barren and functional. Are there plants and fish tanks in classrooms? Lack of color and light contribute to the drab impersonality that some schools communicate; other schools communicate a vibrant sense of energy and excitement with bright colors, mobiles, student art work, differentiated lighting that highlights different spaces and contours of the rooms or hallways. The design of color and light can make some buildings decidedly friendly and others decidedly unfriendly.

Getting closer to the bone, we have to look at the design of time and space. Is the daily schedule broken up into uniform time blocks, or is it flexible, more under the control of teachers and students? Is the weekly schedule always the same, or does it vary from week to week, allowing for intensive learning units here and for more steady, uniform learning units there? Are learning spaces all the same, or are some more congenial to group work, some more to individual work, some more to whole-class activities, and indeed, some outside the school building itself?

In the design of learning activities themselves, do we find variety, creativity, flexibility? Or do we find teachers' lesson plans fairly uniform, conforming to one model? A uniform design of learning activities communicates a sense that all learning is the same, that all subject matter requires the same approach, and that every hour of the school day will be filled with the same student energy and interest. The design of the learning activities influences what is learned as well as how it is learned. A learning activity that requires exact measurement of the weight and mass of a rock cannot teach the same thing as a learning activity that considers the geological conditions that formed the rock, or a learning activity that explores the shapes a sculptor might chisel out of the rock, or a learning activity that requires the student to demonstrate six different uses of a rock. Each of these learning activities requires a design of sequential steps to approach the learning. Each learning requires a different performance assessment design. The design will come from the teacher's understanding of the connections of this learning activity to the larger conceptual frameworks in which the learning is nested, as well as the teacher's understanding of the developmental readiness of the student to deal with more or less abstract thinking, and the student's past learning experiences that would support the drawing out of relationships. Perhaps the most essential talent of teachers is involved with the way they design learning activities, for it reveals their own understanding of the subject matter, their understanding of the child, and their understanding of the complexities of the learning process.

The design of learning activities by teachers will also reflect their sense of the larger design of the curriculum. Teachers' involvement in the design and continuous redesign of the curriculum reveals the depth and breadth of their own scholarly grasp of the disciplines of knowledge. Administrators who encourage teachers working continually on the larger design of the curriculum promote the sharpening of the teachers' intelligence, the deepening of their understanding of the conceptual material embedded in the disciplines. In other words, administrators' support and encouragement of teachers at this level, through staff development and program development activities, nurture the very life blood of teachers' growth.

DESIGNS IN CONFLICT

Sometimes the designs of various aspects of the community's life work at cross-purposes to each other. For example, it may be expected that students in class will engage in debate and heated discussion over the questions posed by the learning assignment. Students are encouraged to question the teacher. The design of the give and take of the classroom has established an accepted pattern of interaction. However, the assistant principal in charge of school discipline may have in mind a different design of the interaction between students and himself. The design of the disciplinary system may be quite authoritarian; no debates are allowed about detention after school. Students pick up two different messages. When it comes to exploring academic issues, they enjoy a certain freedom of speech and inquiry. When it comes to questions of school discipline, such freedoms are suspended. But no reason for the difference in design of the relationship is given.

As another example, the school may try to promote individualized learning packages as well as group learning projects. Yet the design of the grading system may be a holdover from an earlier time, with allowance only for individual achievement. The design of the grading system with its concentration on ranking of students, grading on a curve, and so on, may communicate negative judgments about common learning outcomes.

The more the design of aspects of school life are disjointed or even contradictory, the more fuzzy becomes the messages the school communicates. Nancy Lesko's portrait of a Catholic girls school provides a good example.[1] The school stressed two primary values throughout the life of the school. The value of community was related directly to the religious purposes of the school. The value of competition was tied to the larger American culture. The way the school designed its religious ceremonies, its assemblies, and its after-school activities communicated a valuing of community. The way the school leaders designed their grading system, their exams, their college guidance system, and indeed their pedagogy all communicated the value of competition. No one realized, however, that these two values were in conflict with each other. The design of various aspects of school life were sending contradictory messages. In contrast, the more the design of the various aspects of school life are in sync with each other, the more powerful and lasting will be the message the school communicates. Sarah Lawrence Lightfoot hints at this harmony of design in her portraits of good schools.[2] We find even more explicit attention to design in the stories of "schools that work," in Gregory Smith's recent book on that topic.[3] Similarly, Fred Newmann's account of schools that redesigned themselves to promote student engagement in the learning task underscores this lesson.[4]

DESIGNS FOR COMMUNITY

Design is a subtle carrier of value and a shaper of culture. When we speak of administering community, we must attend to the ways we design the life and the work of the school. The point is to bring the *way* we communicate, the *way* we learn, the *way* we celebrate, the *way* we govern ourselves, the *way* we evaluate our progress into greater harmony and consistency, so that we promote the value of community, of individual and collective empowerment, in all these aspects of the school's life. If we are committed to building a community, then the design of the many ways we live and work as a community has to promote that value, not simply as a pleasant add-on to the more serious work of academic achievement, but as an essential characteristic and purpose of the school. We want, in short, to become an excellent community. This theme leads us to the final fundamental of educational administration, the administering of excellence, to which we shall turn in the next part of this book.

RECAPITULATION

In the chapters of Part Three, we have explored the rationale behind administering a school as a community. We looked at some of the dynamics of administering community, such as the process of empowerment, organic management, and managing by design. The intent in Part Three was to explore how one administers a self-governing community, to see how one sets up an environment where the spirit of community enables people to govern themselves by focusing on the work at hand and the decisions it requires, by sharing ideas and solutions to problems, by collectively empowering ourselves in the process of involvement in the main work of the school, which is the student production of knowledge. These self-governing processes are enhanced and channeled through the design features that facilitate and shape them. Thus it becomes clear that administering community means arranging the conditions and reinforcing the understandings by which the community governs itself. Lest this appear too facile or simplistic, it must be remembered that this means a substantial change from the way schools are run now. To get from the present way of running schools to a self-governing, communal way of running schools requires a patient and intelligent involvement in the process of change. Change will require redefinition of roles and responsibilities, considerable staff development and curriculum development, and institutional redesign. The activities at the end of each chapter were intended to suggest some of the areas requiring substantial overhaul. The study group conversations were intended to generate a variety of possible frameworks and procedures for carrying on these changes. It is assumed that additional courses dealing with curriculum development, staff development, organizational change, program evaluation, and political and community relations will flesh out further frameworks and processes for carrying on the work of restructuring the school and the school system. In this fundamentals text, we hoped to establish the focus on these essentials that should frame the whole restructuring effort. We turn in Part Four to the third fundamental concern of educational administration, administering excellence.

ACTIVITIES

1. Let us construct a hypothetical school and play out the design issues a little in order to make our point. Suppose that, after a year of discussions among the faculty, students, and parents, it was decided that they wanted to promote three central values: academic learning, community, and the enrichment of diversity. Let us assume that this school is housed in a traditional school building in a multicultural neighborhood. The promotion of

community amidst diversity and the enrichment of diversity within a bonded community are seen as two mutually intertwined values. Let us assume that this community also wants to move the teaching–learning work of the school toward a much greater sense of the student as the producer and performer of knowledge.

Now, imagine how the school would work if, having agreed to these three values, the principal simply left it up to each teacher to incorporate those values into his or her work with the children. Imagine that the design of space, of the class day and week, and of the report cards and grading system remained the same. Imagine yourself as a teacher in that school. What would be some of the difficulties you would encounter as you tried to incorporate in your own classroom the central values decided upon by the school community? The textbooks are the same, the curriculum guidelines are the same, the class periods are the same, and the technology available is the same. Write your reflections in your journal.

Next, imagine yourself in the same school during the year following the decision to promote the three core values. Assume that you had an intuition that you needed to redesign many aspects of your school to bring them more consistently into line with the core values. Sketch out five or six features of the school that you would redesign. Share these with the members of your working group. Have the group come up with a comprehensive redesign of the school.

2. Identify design features in your school that seem to be in conflict with each other. What are the consequences? How would you redesign to gain greater consistency with the mission of your school?

ENDNOTES

1. Nancy Lesko, *Symbolizing Society*, Falmer Press, London, 1988.
2. Sarah Lawrence Lightfoot, *The Good School: Portraits of Character and Culture*, Basic Books, New York, 1983.
3. Gregory A. Smith (ed.), *Public Schools That Work*, Routledge, New York, 1993.
4. Fred M. Newmann (ed.), *Student Engagement and Achievement in American Secondary Schools*, Teachers College Press, New York, 1992.

PART FOUR

Administering Excellence

In attempting to administer excellence, we come again to a paradox. One cannot administer excellence, in the sense of orchestrating its appearance at will. Excellence in education will result primarily from the individual and collective efforts of students, and secondarily because of the efforts of teachers and parents. One of the things administrators *can* do is establish institutional conditions favorable to its development, and furthermore, refashion the criteria by which excellence is defined and measured. In the following chapters we explore a more expansive understanding of excellence, one that includes but goes beyond the narrow band of excellence that is currently promoted in schools. We will see that this more expansive understanding of excellence includes moral excellence and an expanded notion of effectiveness. As the chapters unfold, it should become increasingly apparent that administering excellence is inextricably intertwined with administering meaning and administering community. The final chapter tries to underscore these connections among the three fundamentals and point the reader to some of the implications of holding for these three as *the* fundamentals of educational administration.

CHAPTER 11

Administering Excellence

One of the problems with talking about education for excellence is that almost everyone has a different idea of what that means. Prakash and Waks provide helpful distinctions among four conceptions of excellence.[1] One definition of excellence refers to a high level of proficiency in basic skills and units of knowledge that are measured on standardized tests. Another view of excellence considers excellence to be a high level of mastery of disciplines of knowledge by which the world is made intelligible, and whose modes of investigation, thought, and argument enable the learner to further pursue the public intelligibility of the world. Yet a third understanding of excellence refers more to the personal development and rounding out of the individual. The development of proficiency in basic skills and the mastery of the disciplines of knowledge contribute to this self-development, but the self-actualization of the individual is something more personal and internally creative. Hence the excellence sought in the educational process has more to do with opening up the freedom of the individual from the constrictions of the socialization process. Finally, the fourth conception of excellence places it within a communitarian setting: excellence as social responsibility. This form of excellence features self-actualization within community and for community, because it assumes that each person's fulfillment depends on the community's fulfillment. Each person's achievement of personal excellence is "governed by a principle of active concern and responsibility for the common good."[2]

While I tend toward the latter notion of excellence, I prefer to conceive of excellence as a complex and all-embracing term for what one finds in an excellent community. I use Socrates as my mentor here. In Plato's account in *The Republic,* Socrates was trying to probe the meaning of justice with his friends. Despite much rhetorical pulling and tugging at the term, they could not agree on a good example of justice. Only when they considered justice writ large, as it could be seen in an ideal just society, could they begin to understand it in its fullest sense. We might, on our part, think of education for excellence as an education for a community or a society that could be called excellent.

AN EXCELLENT COMMUNITY

Excellence is what people produce who *excel*. To excel means to go beyond the ordinary, the average, the routine, and the mediocre. Excellence signifies high-quality performance; more than that, it signifies a high quality of living. Of all the terms used to contrast with an excellent performance—ordinary, average, routine, mediocre—I would choose *mediocre.* Something ordinary can still be excellent. Bird song is ordinary in the sense that it is something we take for granted. But sometimes our neighborhood bird gives an excellent perfor-mance—when we stop to listen. A leaf on an oak tree is ordinary, but it can also be valued as an excellent performance, a marvelous creation. Similarly, the av-erage or the routine can contain qualities of excellence. An average snowflake is nonetheless an extraordinarily beautiful thing. Mediocrity, however, seems to convey the idea of a half-hearted performance, a satisfaction with a minimum of effort. In contrast with mediocrity, excellence takes on the meaning of a full pouring of talent and attention into an activity.

Can we get some sense of what education for excellence means by consid-ering an ideal community of people who excel? I suggest that we can. What, then, would a community of people who excel look like? There are five quali-ties we would find in such a community.

1. An excellent community would be made up of people who are wide awake, alert to what is going on around them, and responsive to the human and natural context in which they find themselves. They would not be drugged by routine. They would not be so engrossed in their own concerns that they could not attend to the circumstances that surround them. They would be aware of the feelings, the colors, the shapes, the tones, and the hues of interpersonal re-lationships, the drama that is being played out in front of them and by them.

2. An excellent community would be made up of people who hold them-selves to a high standard of work. What they made—baskets, telescopes, build-ings, paintings, boats, telephones, kidney pies, jumpers, parks, computers, or cities—would all be made with care. They would take pride and satisfaction in their work. Their work would carry the stamp of their personality. It would also carry the stamp of their respect for one another; that is, they would not disre-spect their patrons by making a shoddy product. Their work would also ex-press a certain inventiveness: It would be responsive to the needs of specific persons or situations, as well as to the materials they were working with. There would be a certain custom-made feel about their work. Their products would not be boring; there would be a spontaneity, a style or understated flair about their work, sometimes even a hint of mischief. Clearly, their work would be one important way that they would make a contribution to their world.

3. An excellent community would be caring about relationships. Such a community would value friendship, openness, trust, and honesty. People would enjoy being with each other; they would be able to let others be them-selves. They would have the ability to love, to forgive, to empathize, to accept imperfections. They would also have the ability to argue and disagree without fracturing relationships. Their sensitivity to context, and the caring about work

would have an interpersonal and social dimension derived from a conviction that others deserve their best. In such a community, people would bring the best that is in them to their encounters with others. People would believe that others will respond with the best that is in them when they are accepted as and for what they are: If I give you the best in me, I call forth the best in you.

4. An excellent community would care about the quality of its public life, in its cultural, political, economic, and environmental dimensions. This caring would be based on the conviction that a healthy and vigorous public life provides the context for a healthy and integral private life. Aware that the contemporary world tends to encourage a self-centered privatism absorbed in the pursuit of private recreation and leisure time to the neglect of public involvement, such a community would call one another to public responsibilities and to public service. An excellent community would know that there will always be work ahead to create a fairer, more humane community.

5. Finally, an excellent community would support individual expressions of and journeys toward excellence. Such a community would recognize that its own health requires diversity, new ideas, and inventiveness in all areas of life as a way of responding to new challenges and as a way of rediscovering and reinterpreting core community values. With respect for individual expressions of excellence, the community would avoid the extremes of extraordinarily high rewards for some talents and very meager rewards for other talents. Without replacing market influences on salaries and other rewards, the community would seek ways of rewarding all expressions of excellence, including previously taken for granted expressions of excellence such as parenting, community service, a variety of healing and helping talents, and artistic talent. This community would see, furthermore, that its cultural diversity is a great treasure for enriching its life. Hence it would promote the preservation of diverse cultural traditions and heritage, as well as the mutual enrichment that can come from cross-cultural inventiveness.

SCHOOLING FOR EXCELLENCE

By describing such an ideal community, we can begin to understand the ingredients of excellence. Excellence, when isolated as the perfection of one human quality, divorced from a rich human context, can become an aberration. We can have excellent concentration camps, superior methods of torture; we can have psychotic poet laureates and lunatic world-class soccer players. Excellence is not a single, extraordinary talent in itself, but that talent exercised on behalf of a human purpose, within a richly diverse community that values the full range of human excellence. In such a community, therefore, schools will have a special place of importance, as places that nurture a rich diversity of talent to high levels of excellence. One lesson above all will be taught in these schools: The quest for excellence in the exercise of talent is a quest for a way to contribute to the life of the community. One's fulfillment and satisfaction in the pursuit of excellence is not to be found primarily in the material rewards reaped by the individual, but in the satisfaction of the quality of the performance or activity it-self, and the satisfaction of contributing to the quality of life of other people.

More specifically, what would schools that focused on this kind of educa-tion for excellence look like? Without going into great detail, we can briefly sketch some elements.

Schools concerned with a sense of wide-awake awareness of the context of one's life would take the time for specific learning episodes to develop such sensitivity. There would be group activities for developing self-esteem and for gaining a sense of being centered. Exercises in gaining an empathetic awareness of what others are feeling and experiencing would complement the centering exercises, so that, as they come to know themselves as sources of their own ac-tions, they would appreciate others as persons in their own right. Students would write their own biographies to gain a sense that they are a source of his-tory both individually and collectively. They would be encouraged to experi-ence the drama of their lives and to examine the scripts by which they engage in that drama. Such inquiry would include the exploration of alternative scripts and of improvisations within the scripts. The school would also provide a wide variety of expressive artistic opportunities, encouraging the students to re-create their experience of their world in music, poetry, paint, clay, and other media, including computer graphics. Humanities and studies of current events would heighten their awareness of the various dramas being played out in the lives of people all around them. These activities and others like them would de-velop in the students that foundational sense of alertness, connectedness, re-flection, awareness, and confidence that is critical to any quest for excellence. In other words, they would experience their world as alive with possibilities and challenges to heroic endeavor, and would experience the satisfaction of a wide-awake participation in that world.

The schools would also be concerned with high standards of performance. Students would come to understand that the academic program is not an end in itself or a relentless series of trivial activities demanding attention only as long as they are useful to passing tests and getting grades. Rather, academics are *for* something. That is, academics are ways of creating knowledge that can be used to serve, to solve, to discover, and to create new knowledge. Hence, in every semester, students would be expected to employ their knowledge in pro-ducing a product of some kind. Teachers would help students explore the var-ious possibilities of student productions. Halfway through any course, students should have a sufficient grasp of the material to chose a project to complete the course. The measure of achievement would be the product itself and its useful-ness to the community. Students would come to understand science, not as a fictionally pure and uncontaminated way of knowing, but rather as a pursuit of knowledge that can be used to serve human and social purposes. Similarly, social sciences will be seen as ways to create understandings about how society "works" and ways to explore alternatives toward a more just and humane community.

The pride one learns to take in one's work would be nourished by a reward system that honors a wide variety of achievement, a broad exercise of talent.

Through cooperative teamwork on large projects, students would learn to appreciate the special talents that each brings to the task and how those talents assist their collective inventiveness and productivity. These group projects would include but go beyond academic projects. They might involve various expressive learnings, for example, publishing a book of student poems, creating a new banner every month to hang in the school cafeteria, designing and silk-screening T-shirts for special school events, building floats for a town parade, producing a clown show for preschoolers, setting up displays for parents' nights, and painting a corridor with a new design. Some projects would have more practical learnings in mind—building a shed, fixing equipment, solving a conflict. Other projects might be oriented toward community service, such as addressing a local environmental problem, staging Special Olympics, organizing a picnic for senior citizens, organizing a neighborhood clean-up, making a quilt for a homeless person, and producing children's theater for foster-home children.

Schools for excellence would take the necessary time to promote learnings about relationships. Exercises in group communication, discussion, and debate would nurture those skills so necessary for establishing and maintaining healthy relationships. The focus would not be on intimate, "I–thou" relationships, but on more general, public relationships. Multicultural explorations, not only of the cultural traditions of various peoples, but open discussions of the injuries that various groups have suffered at the hands of dominant cultural groups, would create greater openness to and understanding between differing cultural groups. Academics would not be the source of competition but the stuff of conversation, collaboration, community building, problem solving, and for exploring relationships themselves. Student government would hold an important place in the school, and learnings from mistakes would be as common, if not more common, than learning from successes in this area. Real experiences of governing themselves must be part of the experience of all students. Moreover, the function of paracurricular activities would be twofold: (1) the pursuit of excellence in the activity; and (2) the building of relationships and habits of teamwork and cooperation. One important lesson that would be pursued throughout the school years is the expectation that human imperfections will always require compassion and forgiveness; hence, skills of healing, conflict resolution, and forgiving would be taught expressly.

Schools pursuing excellence would teach the importance of a healthy and vigorous public life. Besides the critical study of public life as it is currently conducted, other parts of the academic program would contain explicit references to public life, whether that has to do with the formation of public policy, with some long-standing conflict between factions in society, or with structural elements in society such as the legal or economic systems. Academics would be related to employment when appropriate, especially insofar as one's employment is a way of making a contribution to the community. Academic topics would be explored as ways to discuss public issues intelligently, as ways to engage in cultural activity, as ways to debate and decide and to bind and heal. The quality of public life at the school itself would be a major learning opportunity.

Hence, the activities of the student government and of all other student activities and clubs would be seen as carrying lessons far beyond the immediate goals of the week, or semester.

Finally, schools for excellence would support individual expressions of excellence. While traditional mastery of a common core of skills and understandings would be emphasized, as much as one-half of the semester or final grade would be based on a project, or a series of projects, that expresses the student's individual talent and genius. While these projects might support the common learnings of the curriculum, the way those common learnings are expressed would be a matter of individual synthesis and creativity. Furthermore, students would be given a chance to study the products of other students as a way to gaining a deeper appreciation of the many ways excellence can be expressed. Promotion and graduation requirements would allow and encourage alternate projects as substitutes for some of the standard requirements. In these ways the school would overcome the traditional apathy and rebellion toward school subjects imposed from above, which allow little or no personal involvement with the material.

IMPLICATIONS FOR ADMINISTRATORS

Having explored what attention to the ingredients of excellence would look like in a school, we can turn to the administrators of such schools. A moment's reflection raises the obvious corollary to what we have been discussing, namely, that school administrators would need to be models of such excellence. A requisite for leadership is that one should live or exemplify what one calls others to do. A principal who demands that all teachers respond to each child as an individual learner but who treats all his teachers in an impersonal, uniform way is sending conflicting messages. In administering excellence, administrators should ask themselves whether they practice what they preach. If they do not practice it, they will not have much credibility when they preach it.

Administrators need to evaluate their own performance and, more important, their own desires for excellence. They should ask themselves whether they arrive at work alive to each new day's possibilities for teachers and youngsters, believing that new and wonderful breakthroughs are going to happen for youngsters at their school. Do they take pride in the kind of school they are building, always seeking to instill that pride in the work of their teachers and students? Do they promote a sense of community in the school, a community that fosters respect and caring for the talents of everyone? Are children from all cultures honored at their school? Do they devote sufficient time to the quality of the public life at their school, encouraging youngsters in the dynamics of self-governance and encouraging teachers' participation in the setting or shaping of school policies? Are parents part of this public life at the school? Finally, do they put into practice, through their grading and promotion system and in other organizational arrangements, their belief that schools should nurture a variety of expressions of excellence? Are variations in excellent approaches to teaching honored? Are they comfortable being themselves, letting the stamp of their personality be part of the overall excellence of this community?

Those are difficult questions to answer, because most of us, if we are honest, recognize occasions when we let bureaucratic routines replace more altruistic choices; occasions when we do not practice what we preach; and occasions when our self-righteous judgment about the failure of others to pursue excellence could be turned against ourselves. Some administrators conduct this kind of self-evaluation every other month or so, and write down one or two things they want to attend to in the next few months in order to bring their performance closer to their ideals.

This self-examination, of course, assumes that there is a version of excellence already formulated. Many administrators have not yet spelled that out sufficiently, even though they may be acting on some intuitions about excellence. It is always good to try to put such intuitions into words, so that they will be more open to scrutiny. Once an administrator, or a team of administrators, has expressed their version of education for excellence, they need to encourage teachers, students, and parents to create their version, and then to work toward a version that the whole community can own. This creation of a common version of excellence is one of the primary activities of leadership in which an administrator can engage.

Once the community's statement about education for excellence is completed, further leadership involves administrators and teachers discussing ways to bring that statement close to the everyday realities of the school. Such discussions may be very well ordered, as in a three-year school-improvement effort that involves assessment of present practices and programs, design of new practices and structural arrangements, and a phased implementation of improvements. However, the discussions may be more developmentally exploratory, letting the conversations with individual teachers mature over a few years to the point where they eventually lead to individual teachers trying out new approaches, and then, after increasing teacher involvement, to more collective changes in school-wide arrangements.

The point is not to help teachers feel satisfied with their efforts, but on the contrary, to feel dissatisfied with their efforts to promote excellence. By stimulating that dissatisfaction, administrators can encourage teachers to explore more imaginative and responsive teaching strategies that nurture the kind of excellence they propose in their school-wide goal statements. As opposed to a one-dimensional formula for "effective teaching," teachers will need to develop a wide variety of approaches that engage the students in the pursuit of a variety of rich learning experiences.

The important thing for administrators to understand is that their leadership will be exercised with the teachers; the teachers will be the ones who do most of the design of learning activities and who will reorganize the curriculum to nurture the kinds of student growth toward excellence that the school-wide goals call for. The leadership role of the administration is to engage the teachers in discussion about what needs to be done—not from the vantage point of the administrators knowing the answers, but rather from the vantage point of the teachers possessing the collective wisdom to come up with workable answers. Administrators often need to start these discussions, simply because that is the way such discussions are legitimated in the current culture of the school.

In conducting these discussions, administrators will help by asking specific questions. The first question is: "How do we identify excellence in this subject area?" The question may have to be repeated in various forms (e.g., "Is that the only example of an excellent performance in this subject? Could there be five or six other ways to pursue excellence in this subject? Could there be alternate projects or products that are acceptable for mastery of the unit?), so that the teacher and administrator develop greater clarity about *what the task facing the student is,* and hence what the task facing the teacher is. In the course of exploring these various tasks in the pursuit of excellence, it may become apparent to the teachers that other teaching strategies might be called for, strategies in which that teacher or group of teachers lacks competency. This could lead to staff development efforts that will enable teachers to develop a rich repertory of teaching approaches. Such development will enhance the teachers' sense of professionalism and self-efficacy.

Another set of questions deals more with values. Administrators and teachers need to discuss such questions as "Why is this important?" "What significance does this activity have for the varieties of excellence we are encouraging here?" "What relationship does this unit have to real life?" "What does this task have to do with developing students' critical awareness of the quality of public life, or with understanding people different from themselves, or with improving their sense of self esteem?" In other words, besides identifying *what* the task is, the educators and students should know *why* that task is important in some larger scheme of things. Grappling with these kinds of questions forces educators to move beyond the mindless routines of everyday life so often criticized in schools. Furthermore, insights into the significance of the task at hand increase both student and teacher motivation.

Viewing the teacher as the primary professional responsible for encouraging students' pursuit of excellence, administrative leaders will go on to ask another set of questions, about resources needed to do the teaching job. Hence the principal will ask such questions as "What do you need to get better results with your students?" One of the most important resources in learning is time—time on task. Administrators will have to become wizards in fashioning flexible time schedules that enhance teachers' availability for their students as well as students' work time for specific projects. Sometimes a new piece of equipment will enable a teacher to devise a whole series of quality learning experiences for the youngsters. Sometimes it will simply be an opportunity to plan and coordinate learning units with one or more teachers. The important point behind the question, "How can I help you do your job?," is that it reinforces for the teacher his or her sense of being responsible for the outcomes of teaching. Such questions also help teachers reflect on how they might restructure their teaching arrangements to facilitate greater student productivity.

Finally, administrators can set up and facilitate feedback systems by which teachers and students have an opportunity to appraise their work, to acquire a sense of accomplishment, to have a notion that the community is taking notice of their work. A rich reward system that honors diversity in achievements within a monthly schedule of displays, assemblies, newsletters to parents, pieces in the local newspaper and radio station provide a sense of excitement and satisfaction and leads to greater pride in the quality of the school's performance. The danger, of course, is that only certain kinds of achievement will be singled out or that only the "top" 10 percent of the students will be honored. Administrators will need to employ imagination in devising creative ways to honor all students. They should consider that they have failed their students if even one of them graduates without having once been praised for some special achievement.

SUMMARY

Only when we place our discussion of excellence within the context of a community that honors excellence in a variety of expressions that serve human purposes can we devise an appropriate education for excellence. The brief sketches of some elements in schooling for excellence indicate a need to restructure our current curriculum and reward system. That will be a long-lasting challenge to school administrators. It will be achieved by working with and through the teachers and parents, for the day-to-day nurturing of excellence will ultimately be in the hands of teachers and parents.

I have not gone extensively into the pursuit of excellence for vocational and economic purposes. Educators have received and will continue to receive advice and exhortation on that score, so I wanted to talk about other, equally important aspects of excellence that provide the broad context in which these more narrow concerns for excellence make sense.

The pursuit of excellence in its larger sense is indeed necessary as we face the twenty-first century. Our survival requires excellence of character, as well as excellence of technical virtuosity, excellence in courage as well as excellence in technological invention, excellence in fidelity to values and agreements as well as excellence in commercial productivity. We have for too long focused primarily on productivity, invention, technical virtuosity, as though that was all we needed. We continue to neglect the development of character, courage, honor, and fidelity to our peril. Hence discussions about schools for excellence, whether at the state level or the local level, need to include the exploration of moral excellence. Finally, we will always need excellence in the arts, for we always need to sing and celebrate the human adventure, to illuminate our follies, and to create a new form of hope to embody our yet unfulfilled dreams.

ACTIVITIES

1. What do you think of the five ingredients of Excellence? What would you add to the list, or subtract?

2. In your own school or school system, analyze the kinds of excellence that are rewarded and the kinds of excellence that are ignored. Share your analysis with your study group.
3. Design at least ten new awards that could be added to the graduation awards. Design monthly awards that could be announced at school assemblies. Indicate how the curriculum and extra-curricular programs could be restructured to promote a greater diversity of excellences.
4. In your school, who would receive the following awards, and how would you word their citations:
   a. The Martin Luther King Award
   b. The Eleanor Roosevelt Award
   c. The Vince Lombardi Award
   d. The Galileo Award
   e. The Charlie Chaplin Award
   f. The Helen Keller Award
   g. The Tom Dooley Award
   h. The Edward R. Murrow Award
5. Dream up five other awards, given in the name of famous people who exemplified various forms of excellence.

ENDNOTES

1. Madhu Suri Prakash and Leonard Joseph Waks, "Four Conceptions of Excellence," *Teachers College Record*, **87**(1): 79–101 (Fall 1985).
2. Ibid., p. 88.

CHAPTER 12

Administering a Moral Community

In the previous chapter we recognized the need to promote a variety of excellences in the school. One form of excellence is moral excellence. This chapter examines the complex issue of promoting moral excellence. We take up the possibility that there are premoral human qualities that predispose persons to act morally, and we imagine how schools might legitimately nurture these foundational qualities. We then consider explicit ethical frameworks within the curriculum, the extra-curriculars, and the institutional support programs of the school. As we can see, this chapter opens up a variety of possibilities for developing moral excellence.

It will be helpful at the outset to state my fundamental understanding of ethics and moral practice. Ethics is the *study* of moral practice. As a study, it attempts to understand concepts such as obligation, virtue, justice, and common good, and to explore the epistemology of moral judgments and the psychology of moral acts. As a scholarly inquiry, ethics tends to dissect human actions, thinking, and choices in order to understand when they are ethical or unethical. Often the study of ethics can lead us to think that being moral is primarily a question of thinking and making moral judgments. Morality, however, *being moral*, involves more than thinking and making moral judgments. Morality involves the total person as a human being; it involves the human person living in a community of other moral agents. Morality is a way of living and a way of being. Individual activities, such as telling the truth or giving money to a beggar, or telling a lie or insulting a beggar, have to be seen in the context of an individual and communal way of living and of being. We cannot understand an action's true moral significance unless we see it as expressing a way of living or as an exception to a way of being. When we speak about morality in education, we can speak of it as teaching a way of thinking, or as teaching a way of being. If we teach morality as a way of being, we can get at a more encompassing kind of moral education. We begin to see teaching itself as a moral way of being with students. We can then see administration as a moral way of being with teachers and students.

From this perspective we can begin to probe the essential morality involved in the act of learning, and therefore in the act of teaching. Learning and teaching, when situated in a community of learners, take on additional moral qualities, for they imply relationships of cooperation, sensitivity to and negotiation of differences, being responsible to the group task, and so on. When administrators engage teachers in exploring the nature and meaning of their work, that conversation necessarily touches upon the moral qualities that attach to the activity of teaching: respect for the integrity of the learner, caring for the truth that emerges in the act of learning, caring for the intricate complexity of what is being studied, appreciation for the individual expressions of what was learned, and gentle support for the vulnerabilities of the learner.

While it includes conversations with individual teachers, the larger work of administration involves calling all the teachers to the building of an ethical school. This involvement provides the administrator and the teachers with a large moral task, one that will never be finished, but one that will enable them to integrate many of the specific moral and professional components of teaching into a larger, meaningful whole. One might benignly interpret all or much that teachers presently do as tacitly involved with nurturing an ethical school. In the best of schools that may certainly be true. I suggest that they do this work more intentionally, discussing explicitly the fundamental components of the task and seeking through explicit programmatic elements to offer an intentional environment for moral learning.

A VISION OF AN ETHICAL SCHOOL

If we assume that the school promotes a moral way of being, as well as a moral way of thinking, we have to ask ourselves what constitutes a moral way of being. Plato and Aristotle explored this question and began a tradition of philosophical inquiry into the nature of the moral life that engaged secular, Hebrew, Islamic, and Christian scholars for many hundreds of years. Each succeeding generation, however, while grounded in this tradition, has to answer the question anew, for the historical circumstances keep changing, and the language of moral discourse develops new images and metaphors for the moral life.

Discourse about the moral life may embrace two fundamental perspectives. One perspective encompasses what I will call the foundational qualities of the moral life. The second perspective embraces what I will call a framework for explicit moral understanding and action. The first perspective implies a grounding of a moral way of being in fundamentally human qualities that are tacitly or implicitly moral. The second perspective implies a conscious awareness of the moral landscape as illuminated by schools of ethical thought, a maturing ability to reflect on human action as implying moral responsibility, an understanding that one's life inescapably implicates one in moral responsibilities to oneself and to one's community. Moral education needs to attend to both of these fundamental perspectives. We first take up the perspective of the foundational human qualities for a moral life and then the framework for explicit moral action. Once we develop some familiarity with these perspectives, we look more particularly at how administrators and teachers can build a moral community.

FOUNDATIONAL HUMAN QUALITIES FOR MORAL LIVING

A moral way of being is a moral way of being human. Hence, one's morality will flow from one's humanity.[1] Three qualities of a fully human person are *autonomy, connectedness,* and *transcendence.* These are the foundational human qualities for a moral life; it would be impossible to be moral without developing these qualities.

Being autonomous means owning oneself, being one's own person. It does not mean acting in isolation from one's culture, one's socialization into that culture, or from the specific social context in which one finds oneself. Being autonomous means that, once these cultural and contextual influences are taken into account, one takes responsibility for what one does. The moral choices an autonomous person makes belong to him or her; they carry a personal signature and are clearly distinct from choices due to mindless routine, fear of reprisal, or unquestioning obedience to external authorities. Ironically, an autonomous person cannot express his or her autonomy except in relationship to another person, to a culture of meanings and traditions, as a male or female in this historical social moment. This leads us to the next foundational quality.

Being connected means being-in-relationship with someone or something and accepting the responsibilities implicit in the relationship. Every human being is involved in a network of relationships and with obligations and privileges that attend to these relationships. Human life implies social living, and social living implies a moral code by which the contingencies of social living are conducted. To be sure, culture determines how these moral codes are expressed and interpreted. Specific contexts also provide clues for moral expectations. Nevertheless, there appear to be certain universal demands in relationships and in communal living that define us as human beings. Every culture has categories that define "inhuman" treatment of other people.

Being connected, moreover, means being connected to a tradition, a cultural heritage that provides the language and world view for defining oneself and the human and natural world. There is a sense in which that connection to a cultural heritage brings moral obligations to honor the heroes of that tradition, those who have played a part in the ongoing regeneration of human ideals and visions of greatness by which the people of that tradition have been able to transcend their selfish concerns for the preservation and renewal of the community.

Being connected also means being connected to nature and the natural universe. The recognition that humans are members of an eco-community brings a

sense of obligation toward the environment. Recognizing that we are benefi-
ciaries of a bounteous nature brings a sense of obligation to preserve the integrity of the air, the soil, the water, and the various forms of life.

Finally, an essential quality to living a fully human life is the quality of what
I call transcendence. Transcendence is what leads us to turn our life toward
someone or toward something greater than or beyond ourselves. One form of
transcendence is reaching for a form of excellence, whether in athletics, the creative arts, scholarship, professional expertise, the founding of an organization,
or a craft. Another form of transcendence involves turning toward some kind
of ideal embodied in collective action, such as an association concerned about
the environment, or about child care or political freedom or legal protection or
the preservation of historical sites.

Every culture has some way of expressing the heroic impulse in humans.
That heroic impulse, however modest and understated, underlies most expressions of altruism in society. Humans apparently need something heroic to vali-
date their own identity, either through their individual striving or through
identification with something heroic in their associations, their culture, their religion, or their national origins.

When transcendence is joined with the qualities of autonomy and connectedness, we begin to see how the three qualities complement and feed each other
in the building of a rich and integral human life.[2] Autonomy makes sense only
in relation to other autonomous persons, when the uniqueness and wealth of
each person can be mutually appreciated and celebrated.

Connectedness means that one is connected to someone or something other
than oneself. Hence it requires an empathetic embrace of what is different from
the autonomous actor to make and sustain the connection. Community enables
the autonomous individual to belong to something larger; it gives the individual roots in both the past and the present. However, the community is not automatically self-sustaining. It is sustained by autonomous individuals who
transcend self-interest in order to promote the common good, who join with
other individuals to re-create the community. This transcending activity includes, for example, offering satisfying and mutually fulfilling services for one
another, services of protection and support, care and help, joint action on a common project, celebration of a common heritage, honoring a community tradition by connecting one's own story to the larger story of the community. This
give-and-take of life in the community simultaneously depends on and feeds
the heroic imagination of individuals, whose actions, in turn, give new life to
the community.

Although we speak of these three foundational qualities of a moral life
somewhat abstractly, we do not want to think of them as a list of virtues we set
out to acquire. These qualities are never achieved as an acquisition. They are always to be found in the action of a specific person in this moment, in these circumstances, with these people, and hence are never perfectly or fully expressed.
They are achieved only in the doing and in the doing-constantly-repeated.

If these qualities are foundational in a developing ethical person, then an
ethical school will be concerned to nurture those qualities and discourage the

development of their opposites. Hence, teachers need to reflect on how they can use the everyday activities of youngsters in their classrooms and other areas around the school to nurture these qualities. Of course, youngsters develop in recognizable patterns, so what might be appropriate for a ten-year-old may not be appropriate for a sixteen-year-old. How one nurtures the sense of transcendence in kindergarten would differ from an approach taken in seventh grade. But the three qualities can be supported in every grade, in ways that are suitable for the children.

It would be a mistake, however, to expect all the children to manifest these qualities in the same way. Sex, race, culture, and class will all nuance the child's expression of autonomy, connectedness, and transcendence. Class-bound and ethnocentric teachers will have difficulty with such varied expressions. Sensitive teachers will observe the different expressions and listen to youngsters explain their behavior. Over time such teachers will be able to promote these qualities within an appropriate range of plurality and diversity.

In any event, a major agenda of administrators promoting the vision of an ethical school is to encourage teachers throughout the school to design explicit learning activities which will involve the developing of these foundational qualities. This agenda provides the foundation on which the next level of ethical education can develop.

At this juncture, however, we should realize that the promotion of these foundational qualities should not disturb those parents and teachers who worry about religion inserting itself into the curriculum of the public school. While one would hope these qualities would not be perceived as antithetical to religion, it would be difficult to point to any religious institution or church as claiming these qualities as their exclusive doctrinal property. They belong, rather, to the human race.

FRAMEWORKS FOR EXPLICIT MORAL UNDERSTANDING AND ACTION

The next perspective on moral living is concerned with frameworks for explicit moral understanding and action. This perspective deals with attempts to explain what constitutes certain actions as ethical and other actions as not ethical, and explores how they might be useful for moral education. In the field of ethics we can find a variety of frameworks that provide a rationale for a form of moral education.[3] Some stress an ethic of justice as an overall framework; others stress an ethic of care; still others criticize those ethics as politically and culturally naive, preferring an ethic of critique. I suggest that we consider a large framework that embraces all three schools of thought in a multidimensional framework. That is, each of these schools of thought provides direction for an important part of an ethical education, but no one of them taken alone is sufficient. When combined, they complement each other to provide a richer response to the complex ethical challenges facing contemporary society.

What follows is not an attempt to develop a full-blown ethical theory. We discuss core ethical values, going somewhat into the arguments that support them, but without delving into the comprehensive philosophical blueprint that undergirds them. Each theme is developed consecutively. While attempting to remain faithful to the theory, or body of theory, from which the theme was selected, the exposition is guided by the ethical demands of the educating context. Underneath these three ethics, of course, are the irreducible assumptions and cultural beliefs about what is valuable in human life, in which every theory is grounded.

THE ETHIC OF CRITIQUE

Since the historical moment appears to be one of transition and of transformation, as we move into a global market, a global information age, a global awareness of ecological catastrophe, it seems best to begin with the ethic of critique. Because it goes well beyond the functional critique of contemporary reformers such as Goodlad and Boyer, the ethic of critique developed here draws its force from "critical theory," that body of thought deriving from the Frankfurt school of philosophers and of others sympathetic to their perspectives.[4] These thinkers explore social life as intrinsically problematic, because it exhibits the struggle between competing interests and wants among various groups and individuals in society. Whether considering social relationships, social customs, laws, social institutions grounded in structured power relationships, or language itself, these thinkers ask questions such as: "Who benefits by these arrangements?" "Which group dominates this social arrangement?" "Who defines the way things are structured here?" "Who defines what is valued and disvalued in this situation?" The point of this critical stance is to uncover which group has the advantage over the others, how things got to be the way they are, and to expose how situations are structured and language used so as to maintain the legitimacy of social arrangements. By uncovering inherent injustice or dehumanization imbedded in the language and structures of society, critical analysts invite others to act to redress such injustice. Hence their basic stance is ethical, for they are dealing with questions of social justice and human dignity, although usually not with particular, individual ethical choices.

Examples of issues confronted by critical ethics include sexist language and bias in the workplace and in legal structures; racial, sexual, and class bias in educational arrangements and in the very language used to define social life; the preservation of powerful groups' hegemony over the media and over the political process; and the rationalization and legitimation of institutions such as prisons, orphanages, armies, nuclear industries, and the state itself. The point the critical ethician stresses is that no social arrangement is neutral. Every social arrangement, no matter how it presents itself as natural, necessary, or simply "the way things are," is an artificial construct. It is usually structured to benefit some segments of society at the expense of others. Even the institution of marriage is structured in many cultures in favor of males and places the unmarried in a less privileged social status. The ethical challenge is to make these social arrangements more responsive to the human and social rights of all the citizens, to enable those affected by social arrangements to have a voice in evaluating the consequences and in altering them in the interests of the common good and of fuller participation and justice for individuals.

This ethical perspective provides a framework for enabling the school community to move from a kind of naïveté about "the way things are" to an awareness that the social and political arena reflect arrangements of power and privilege and interest and influence, often legitimized by an assumed rationality and by law and custom. The theme of critique, for example, forces educators to confront the moral issues involved when schools disproportionately benefit some groups in society and fail others. Furthermore, as a bureaucratic organization, the school exhibits structural properties that may promote a misuse of power and authority among its members.

From a critical perspective, no organizational arrangements in schools "have to be" that way; they are all open to rearrangement in the interest of greater fairness to their members. Where unjust arrangements reflect school board or state policy, they can be appealed and restructured. The structural issues involved in the management of education, such as the process of teacher evaluation, homogeneous tracking systems, the process of grading on a curve, the process of calculating class rank, the absence of important topics in textbooks, the lack of adequate due process for students, the labeling criteria for naming some children gifted and others disabled, and the daily interruptions of the instructional process by uniform time allotments for class periods—all these and others imply ethical burdens because they contain unjustifiable assumptions and impose a disproportionate advantage to some at the expense of others.

The ethic of critique, based as it is on assumptions about the social nature of human beings and on the human purposes to be served by social organization, calls the school community to embrace a sense of social responsibility—not simply to the individuals in the school or school system, and not simply to the education profession, but to the society of whom and for whom the school is an agent. In other words, schools were established to serve a high moral purpose, to prepare the young to take their responsible place in and for the community. Besides the legal and professional obligations, yet intertwined with them, the moral obligation of educators is to see that the school serves society the way it was intended.

THE ETHIC OF JUSTICE

One of the shortcomings of the ethic of critique is that it rarely offers a blueprint for reconstructing the social order it is criticizing. The problem for the school community is one of governance. How does the school community govern itself while carrying out educating activities? The ethic of critique illuminates unethical practices in governing and managing organizations and implies in its critique some ethical values such as equality, the common good, human and civil rights, democratic participation, and the like. An ethic of justice provides a more explicit response to the question of self-governance, even though that response may itself be flawed. We govern ourselves by observing justice. That is, we treat each other according to some standard of justice that is applied uniformly to all our relationships. The theory of justice we employ to ground those standards itself requires a grounding in an anthropology and epistemology. Socrates explored this grounding in *The Republic*; his search was to be pursued by a long line of philosophers up to the present day.

Currently there are two general schools of thought concerning the ethic of justice. One school can trace its roots to Thomas Hobbes in the seventeenth century and can find a contemporary expression in the work of John Rawls.[5] In this school, the primary human reality is the individual, independent of social relationships: The individual is conceived as logically prior to society. Individuals are driven by their passions and interests, especially by fear of harm and desire for comfort. According to this theory, individuals enter into social relations to advance their own advantage. Individual will and preference are the only sources of value. Therefore social relationships are essentially artificial and governed by self-interest. The maintenance of social life requires a social contract in which individuals agree to surrender some of their freedom in return for the state's protection from the otherwise unbridled self-seeking of others. In this school of thought, human reason is the instrument by which the individual can analyze in a more or less scientific fashion what is to his or her advantage and calculate the obligations to social justice called for by the social contract.

The second school of thought on the ethic of justice finds its roots in Aristotle, Rousseau, Hegel, Marx, and Dewey. They placed society as the prior reality within which individuality develops. Furthermore, it is through experience, through living in society, that one learns the lessons of morality. Participation in the life of the community teaches individuals how to think about their own behavior in terms of the larger common good of the community. In this school, freedom "is ultimately the ability to realize a responsible selfhood, which is necessarily a cooperative project."[6] Ethics is grounded in practice within the community. Hence the protection of human dignity depends on the moral quality of social relationships, and this is finally a public and political concern. Citizenship is a shared initiative and responsibility among persons committed to mutual care.

From this perspective, a communal understanding of the requirements of justice flows both from tradition and from the present effort of the community to manage its affairs in the midst of competing claims of the common good and individual rights. That understanding is never complete; it is always limited by the inadequacy of tradition to respond to changing circumstances and by the impossibility of settling conflicting claims conclusively and completely. But the choices will always be made with sensitivity to the bonds that tie individuals to their communities.

Kohlberg, whom some associate with a Rawlsian framework, also believed that moral reasoning and choices were best made in a communitarian setting.[7] Kohlberg carried this belief into the formation of "just community" schools.

Hence, it can be argued that an ethic of justice, especially when focused on issues of governance in a school setting, can encompass in practice the two understandings of justice, namely, justice understood as individual choices to act justly, and justice understood as the community's choice to direct or govern its actions justly. In a school setting, both are required. In practice, individual choices are made with some awareness of what the community's choices are (school policies), and school community choices are made with some awareness of the kinds of individual choices that are made every day in school.

It does not take much imagination to perceive the close relationship of the ethic of critique to the ethic of justice. In order to promote a just social order in the school, the school community must carry out an ongoing critique of those structural features of the school that work against human beings.

THE ETHIC OF CARE

One of the limitations of an ethic of justice is the inability of the theory to determine claims in conflict. What is just for one person might not be considered just by another person. Hence, discussions of what is just in any given situation can tend to become mired down in minimalist considerations. (What minimal conditions must be met in order to fulfill the claims of justice?) In order for an ethic of justice to serve its more generous purpose, it must be complemented or fulfilled in an ethic of love. While earlier discussions of the incompleteness of the ethic of justice took place in a theological context,[8] more recent discussions have tended to ground the ethic of love and caring in a philosophy of the person.[9] Scholars such as Gilligan and Noddings have promoted these ethical directions from a vantage point of psychology, especially women's moral development, in the current literature on the ethic of caring.[10]

Such an ethic focuses on the demands of relationships, not from a contractual or legalistic standpoint, but from a standpoint of absolute regard. This ethic places the human persons-in-relationship as occupying a position for each other of absolute value; neither one can be used as a means to an end; each enjoys an intrinsic dignity and worth, and, given the chance, will reveal genuinely lovable qualities. An ethic of caring requires fidelity to persons, a willingness to acknowledge their right to be who they are, an openness to encountering them in their authentic individuality, a loyalty to the relationship. Such an ethic does not demand relationships of intimacy; rather, it postulates a level of caring that honors the dignity of each person and desires to see that person enjoy a fully human life. Furthermore, it recognizes that it is in the relationship that the specifically human is grounded: Isolated individuals functioning only for themselves are but half-persons; one becomes whole when one is in relationship with another, and with many others.

A school community committed to an ethic of caring will be grounded in the belief that the integrity of human relationships should be held sacred, and that the school as an organization should hold the good of human beings within it as sacred. This ethic reaches beyond concerns with efficiency, which can easily lead to using human beings as merely the means to some larger purpose of productivity, such as an increase in the district's average scores on standardized tests or the lowering of per-pupil costs.

Educators can promote an ethic of caring by attending to the cultural tone of the school. Often the use of language in official communiques will tell the story: Formal, abstract language is the language of bureaucracy, of distance; humor, familiar imagery and metaphor, and personalized messages are the language of caring. Some schools clearly promote a feeling of family and celebrate friendship, loyalty, and service. Laughter in the halls, frequent greetings of each other by name, symbols of congratulations for successful projects, frequent displays of student work, hallways containing pictures of groups of youngsters engaged in school activities, and cartoons poking fun at teachers and administrators—these are all signs of a school environment that values people for who they are.

A LARGER ETHIC

One can argue for the necessary interpenetration of each ethic by the others if one is to argue for a fully developed moral person and a fully developed moral community. Even a superficial familiarity with these ethics suggests that each implies something of the other. The ethic of critique assumes a point of view about social justice and human rights and about the way communities ought to govern themselves. The ethic of justice assumes an ability to perceive injustice in the social order as well as some minimal level of caring about relationships in that social order. The ethic of caring does not ignore the demands of community governance issues, but claims that caring is the ideal fulfillment of all social relationships, even though most relationships among members of a community function according to a more remote form of caring.

Moreover, each ethic needs the strong convictions embedded in the other: The ethic of justice needs the profound commitment to the dignity of the individual person; the ethic of caring needs the larger attention to social order and fairness if it is to avoid an entirely idiosyncratic involvement in social policy; the ethic of critique requires an ethic of caring if it is to avoid the cynical and depressing ravings of the habitual malcontent; the ethic of justice requires the profound social analysis of the ethic of critique in order to move beyond the naive fine-tuning of social arrangements in a social system with inequities built into the very structures by which justice is supposed to be measured.

BUILDING A MORAL COMMUNITY[11]

One way administrators can build a moral community is to encourage individual teachers to nurture the foundational qualities of autonomy, connectedness, and transcendence in their classrooms, as well as communicate the large ethical framework of justice, critique, and care. Relying on the imagination and professional talent of the teachers, the administrator can simply suggest that they bring these perspectives into play in their individual classrooms. I suggest, however, that the administrator's responsibilities go beyond working with individual teachers. Rather, the administrator should bring a large vision of a moral community to engage the whole school community in a conversation about how they might more intentionally and programmatically create a moral learning environment.

Most schools shy away from a proactive approach to nurturing morality. There is a wariness of self-righteous posturing and of appearing to espouse a religious kind of preachiness. There is concern about respecting the freedom and conscience of the students, to avoid superimposing a moral creed that might conflict with the values held at home. However, never to engage youngsters in discussions about moral issues is to communicate, by default, the message that moral issues are irrelevant to the public life of the community and that the lessons learned in schools exist in some impossible, fictional moral vacuum. It can be argued that one of the major lessons of an educating process is the importance of the *discussion* of moral values as they are embedded in the circumstances of everyday life. Indeed, this is the position we take here: An excellent community is one that struggles with the ethical ambiguities and tensions in contemporary life, which engages its members with the burden of the effort to live morally in community.

INITIAL STEPS

As with any undertaking this important, administrators need to pause at the outset and try to gain clarity about what it is they are trying to accomplish. Conversations with colleagues, and perhaps with consultants who have worked in this area, will help to clarify those essential goals one wants to set before the community, or even those essential characteristics of a moral community one wishes to nurture in the learning process. This initial step may also involve reading and building up a small library of references that others may dip into, once the conversations begin. Another concern of major importance is the trust levels that exist in the school. If the teaching faculty is not trusting enough to engage in conversations about matters that they may not be articulate about or about matters where legitimate differences need to be respected, then the effort to build a moral community will have to start right there, by attending to the lack of trust and to the reasons why they are not more trusting. Such an apparently simple foundation may take two or three years to develop; without it, however, the enterprise will not move forward. Finally, the members of the teaching faculty will need to have some confidence in their ability to develop a moral community. Some initial seminars or workshops can settle many of their anxieties, since, collectively, they already possess the abilities to carry out the enterprise.

In most schools administrators will find a relative absence of formal and programmatic attention to moral education, and it will be necessary to start from the beginning. Or *almost* from the beginning, for in every school one can find numerous examples where the members of the school community do, in fact, teach or at least discuss moral values.[12] Hence, the effort to build a moral community should start there, with stating explicitly the many moral lessons the school already teaches. Although it will be easy to focus on the moral prohibitions in the school's rules and in the student handbook, the conversation should concentrate on the positive things the school is trying to teach by enforcing those rules.

Working with a steering committee made up of teachers, parents, and students, administrators can begin the task of identifying the major foundational qualities the school wants to promote. These conversations may take a year or more before they result in a focus that the whole community can understand and accept. Once the general framework of foundational qualities (such as autonomy, connectedness and transcendence, or similar qualities, with, perhaps, different labels) has been identified, some assessment of current practices in the school can be initiated.

The steering committee may want to subdivide the assessment into three areas: the academic curriculum, institutional supports and procedures, and extracurricular supports. The assessment ought to include space for two responses, one dealing with what currently exists in each of the three areas, and a second, more intuitive part, which suggests additional learnings that could be easily developed in each of the three areas. Based on the initial assessment, the steering committee can summarize the findings into areas of strength and areas for improvement.

Summer workshops can be devoted to teacher-constructed learning activities in the areas for improvement. The steering committee can begin to design a developmental progression of essential learnings, moving from the lower grades to the upper grades and indicating how various activities throughout the academic curriculum and activities in extracurriculars and institutional supports mutually reinforce one another, and moving from the simpler to the more complex moral behaviors.

Involvement of parents should be considered essential at this point. A parent committee should be charged with the task of developing learning activities in the home and neighborhood that will echo the learning activities in the school. Communication with every parent about these initiatives should be established as a regular occurrence. Parental opinion should be sought at every major step along the way. When the school and the home work together to nurture the moral growth of the youngsters, the impact will be very substantial— at least that is what all the research on parental involvement in academic achievement shows.[13]

Over the course of a year or fifteen months, the school should be able to generate its first implementation plan. By selecting a modest number of new learning activities to strategically target the development of foundational moral qualities within the school community, the implementation plan can be organized in such a way that the lessons learned in the academic curriculum are reinforced by additional lessons in the extracurriculars, and in the institutional supports such as the guidance and counseling system, in student government, and in the discipline system. In the second year of implementation, adjustments can be made in the light of an end-of-year summative assessment, and some new learning activities can be added to the ones implemented the year before.

After two years of experience promoting the foundational moral qualities, the school should be ready to move into the next phase, that of incorporating expressly ethical frameworks to promote moral understanding and action. Again, the faculty of the school will need to go through seminars that explore the ethics of caring, justice, and critique, and the application of these frameworks to learning experiences in the normal life of the school.

Armed with a clearer appreciation of the moral focus of each of these ethical frameworks, teachers can again undertake an assessment of the current practices in the school. The steering committee can once again gather the findings into a statement of areas of strength and areas for improvement. The process followed earlier can more or less be followed again in designing new learning activities, putting them into a coherent implementation plan, and then phasing in the new learning activities over a two-year period. Parental involvement will continue to be an essential element in this school-wide effort.

In the interests of brevity, I may have made the process sound simple and easy. In one sense, the overall plan is simple. However, the working through of disagreements, the massaging of sensitivities, and the energy drain on people already overworked—this will be hard work, requiring patience and a long-range view of the change process. Furthermore, the emergence of a more intentionally moral community will be slow and imperfect. However, the slow development and the occasional lapses actually constitute precisely the "stuff" that moral communities have to deal with. That's what moral communities do—reach out for ideals that are always out in front of them, confront their own and others' shortcomings, and heal the rifts that inevitably occur among the members.

Excellence in any aspect of living and learning is always something only partially achieved; moral excellence is no different. The morally excellent community is a community that knows it is on a journey, a journey that is never complete; the excellence is in the striving much more than in the definitive achievement. The point is that there is a sense of direction for the journey, a journey toward the fulfillment of their own humanity.

ACTIVITIES

1. In teams of three, discuss the foundational qualities of autonomy, connectedness, and transcendence as they relate to your own sense of a moral life. Give examples from your own life where those qualities came into play in your own moral growth. Are there other foundational human qualities that you think should be added to these three?
2. In teams of three, design three learning activities that you think would nurture each of the three foundational qualities. Share these activities with two

other teams, who will share theirs with your team. Each person in this nine-person group should choose one of the nine learning activities and try to adapt it for use in his or her own educating context during the coming week. Each person can then report back the following week on the results of the experiment.

3. Of the three ethical frameworks, perhaps the most difficult one to deal with is the ethic of critique. As a way of exploring that framework, ask yourself the questions asked in the chapter and relate them to your work environment. "Which group dominates the social arrangements around here?" "Who defines what is valued and disvalued in situations around here?" "Does my school disproportionately benefit some groups in society and fail other groups?" "Are the practices of teacher evaluation, homogeneous tracking systems, grading on a curve, calculating class rank, the labeling criteria of gifted and handicapped, the absence of topics in the curriculum inherently unfair to some?" After you have written your reflections in your journal, share them with the members of your study group.

4. Repeat the steps of Activity 2 for the three ethical frameworks.

5. Rate your own work environment on a scale of 1 to 10 for its intentional promotion of a moral community. What are the major obstacles to its becoming a better moral community? If you were the leader of your organization, what would you do to overcome these obstacles?

ENDNOTES

1. Rather than distracting the reader with a blizzard of references for each of the particulars in the text, I list here some of the main sources for this material. First, hovering over this whole chapter is the figure of John Dewey. As I reread his writings, I keep stumbling across pieces of his work that have influenced my thinking, even though I have forgotten the precise source of the influence. Beyond Dewey, the work of John MacMurray, the Scottish ethician, has been crucial for understanding the complementary demands of autonomy and relationship; see his *Persons in Relation*, Faber & Faber, London, 1961. The more recent work of Charles Taylor echoes much of MacMurray's themes; see *The Ethics of Authenticity*, Harvard University Press, Cambridge, MA, 1991. Others who influenced the theme of connectedness have been Robert Bellah and his colleagues R. Madsen, W. Sullivan, A. Swidler, and S. Tipton, in their two books, *Habits of the Heart*, University of California Press, Berkeley, 1985; and *The Good Society*, Alfred A. Knopf, New York, 1991. Other influences have been David Bohm, *Wholeness and the Implicate Order*, Routledge & Kegan Paul, London, 1980; Gregory Bateson, *Steps to an Ecology of Mind*, Ballantine, New York, 1972; Elise Boulding, *Building a Global Civic Culture*, Teachers College Press, New York, 1988; Donald Oliver, *Education, Modernity and Fractured Meaning*, State University of New York Press, Albany, 1989; Danah Zohar and Ian Marshall, *The Quantum Society*, Flamingo/Harper Collins, London, 1994. For the theme of tran-

scendence I have been influenced by John Gardner's *Excellence*, Harper & Row, New York, 1961; Joseph Campbell in his commentary on his work, *Hero with a Thousand Faces*, as found in P. Cousineau (ed.), *The Hero's Journey: Joseph Campbell on His Life and Work*, Harper & Row, San Francisco, 1990; and C. Pearson's *The Hero Within: Six Archetypes We Live By*, Harper & Row, New York, 1989.

2. The material in the following paragraphs is adapted from R. J. Starratt, *Building an Ethical School*, Falmer Press, London, 1994, pp. 40–41.

3. Much of the material dealing with these three ethics is adapted from ibid., Chap. 4.

4. See, for example, T. W. Adorno, *Negative Dialectics*, Seabury, New York, 1973; Jurgen Habermas, *Legitimation Crisis*, Beacon Press, Boston, 1973; Robert Young, *A Critical Theory of Education*, Teachers College Press, New York, 1990; Paulo Freire, *Pedagogy of the Oppressed*, Continuum, New York, 1970; Michael Apple, *Education and Power*, Routledge and Kegan Paul, Boston, 1982; Richard Bates, "Corporate Culture, Schooling, and Educational Administration," *Educational Administration Quarterly*, **23**(4): 91–115, 1994; Henry Giroux, *Schooling and the Struggle for Public Life*, University of Minnesota Press, Minneapolis, 1988.

5. J. A. Rawls, *A Theory of Justice*, Harvard University Press, Cambridge, MA, 1971.

6. William Sullivan, *Reconstructing Public Philosophy*, University of California Press, Berkeley, 1986, p. 22.

7. L. Kohlberg, *The Meaning and Measurement of Moral Development*, Clark University Press, Worcester, MA, 1981.

8. R. Neibuhr, *An Interpretation of Christian Ethics*, Harper & Brothers, New York, 1935.

9. J. MacMurray, *Persons in Relation*, Faber, London, 1961; M. Buber, *I and Thou*, Scribner's, New York, 1970.

10. C. Gilligan, *In a Different Voice: Women's Conceptions of Self and Morality*, Harvard University Press, Cambridge, MA, 1977; N. Noddings, *Caring: A Feminine Approach to Ethics and Moral Education*, University of California Press, Berkeley, 1984.

11. A more elaborate change process is suggested in Starratt, *op. cit.*

12. See the insightful study recently completed by Philip Jackson, Robert Boostrom, and David Hansen, *The Moral Life of Schools*, Jossey-Bass, San Francisco, 1993.

13. See the work of James Comer and Joyce Epstein on the effects of parental involvement. J. P. Comer, "Educating Poor Minority Children," *Scientific American*, **259**(5): 42–48, 1988. J. L. Epstein, "Home and School Connections in Schools of the Future: Implications of Research on Parent Involvement," *Peabody Journal of Education*, **63**(13): 18–41, 1985.

CHAPTER 13

School Effectiveness: Revised Version

In the 1970s the term "school effectiveness" grew into one of the major themes of school reform. The interest in school effectiveness grew out of numerous studies, especially in urban elementary schools, where students' performance on tests of basic skills in reading and mathematics were higher than might have been predicted based on the socioeconomic and cultural backgrounds of the students.[1] Although all the early studies on school effectiveness in the United States concerned elementary schools, Michael Rutter and his associates found similar findings in their study of twelve inner-city London high schools.[2]

The enthusiasm of educators over these reports contrasted with their discouragement over a study of school effects conducted by James Coleman a decade earlier.[3] In his study, Coleman concluded that school characteristics such as size, per-pupil expenditures, science and library resources, and student–teacher ratios had little significant influence on tests of student achievement. Instead, the social class of the student and the home environment were found to be far more significantly related to higher achievement on those tests. These findings led many to conclude that schools make little or no difference, unless they provide an opportunity for youngsters of various social classes to mix.

The new studies on effective schools looked at different variables than Coleman's input–output variables. They looked at internal organizational variables such as the press for and rewarding of academic achievement and the sense of order and security in the school; pedagogical variables such as direct instruction, and time to practice the assignments; and school climate variables such as a caring attitude toward students. They found that these internal variables were associated with higher levels of student achievement on tests of basic skills. These studies provided the good news that schools could indeed make a difference. Schools that were shown to make this kind of a difference in the lives of youngsters whose background had led earlier to predictions of low achievement were called effective schools.

Corcoran and Hansen provide a handy summary of the characteristics of effective schools as they were understood a decade ago. These characteristics are summarized in Tables 13-1, 13-2, and 13-3.

CRITIQUE OF THE CONCEPTUALIZATION OF SCHOOL EFFECTIVENESS

The early definitions of school effectiveness, and the criteria by which schools were labeled as effective, have come to be seen as simplified and narrow.[4] The basic measure of effectiveness was a school's average scores on standardized tests of basic skills. Teaching that aims at improving scores on these tests stressed drill, practice, memory, and practice in test taking. Effective teaching became identified with a simplistic five- or seven-step formula of direct teaching. While direct teaching is appropriate at some times, at other times the teacher should stay in the background and facilitate peer coaching or student team collaboration only indirectly. The shortcomings of concentrating only on lower-order cognitive achievements has been pointed out, in favor of a more balanced approach to promoting both basic skills and higher-order thinking.[5]

Another criticism of the earlier definition of school effectiveness was the almost exclusive reliance on test scores as indicators of effectiveness. For basic skills, where one is seeking some standard usage, the use of these tests is understandable. In other areas of learning, a standard "right" response might be

---

TABLE 13-1 Organizational Characteristics of Effective Schools

1. Typical of effective schools is a high degree of consensus around clearly articulated goals. The goals help shape the allocation of time and other resources and provide focus for the daily operations of the schools.

2. In effective schools, learning time is highly valued. Efforts are made to reduce disruptions, improve scheduling, reduce student movement, reduce the number of nonacademic events, increase the length of school days, and improve classroom management.

3. The formal curriculum, the curriculum that is taught, and the content of tests are highly aligned in effective schools. There is careful articulation from one grade level to the next.

4. In effective schools, the staff have considerable autonomy to determine their policies and programs within the framework of district policy and to solve the problems they encounter in attempting to raise academic achievement.

5. Effective schools have high academic standards and monitor pupil performance frequently. Staff use sound assessment practices, participate in the analysis of test data, and use test data to identify program weaknesses.

6. Effective schools maintain frequent communications between the home and school. The evidence concerning the influence of parental involvement on school effectiveness is growing. It also seems self-evident that parental support is needed to create the conditions necessary for school effectiveness and that parental involvement in their own children's academic work is essential to success.

Source: Thomas B. Corcoran and Barbara J. Hansen, *The Quest for Excellence: Making Public Schools More Effective,* New Jersey School Boards Association, Trenton, 1983, p. 8.

TABLE 13-2 Management Characteristics of Effective Schools

1. The principals are assertive leaders; they set clear goals and provide direction to their staff. They offer a vision for the school based upon values which can be, and are, publicly articulated.

2. The principals are achievement-oriented. They stress academics; their personal use of time and their allocation of resources and rewards reflect this priority. Their goals tend to be expressed in terms of student learning.

3. The principals emphasize evaluation of the school and its programs; they hold the staff accountable for results. They lead a process of problem identification and analysis to improve the performance of the school.

4. The principals are active supervisors, spending considerable time in classrooms and in discussions with staff about curriculum and instruction. Their expertise in the technical processes of schooling is respected by the staff.

5. The principals respect the professionalism of their staff members. Strong accountability is balanced by optimal autonomy for the teaching staff. They maintain effective communications with staff and provide frequent feedback to teachers.

6. The principals provide for staff participation in the development of school policies and plans, the design and implementation of staff development, and other decisions affecting work in the school. They reward efforts of teachers to work together cooperatively.

Source: Thomas B. Corcoran and Barbara J. Hansen, *The Quest for Excellence: Making Public Schools More Effective,* New Jersey School Boards Association, Trenton, 1983, p. 9.

the least desirable outcome. In a conflict-mediation simulation, for example, one might want to encourage divergent thinking and creative brainstorming to explore various possible solutions. In an art class there is no right way to color a mood; the choice will be different for each child. In science classes, besides seeking exact answers in laboratory experiments, students should also be encouraged to understand the significance of failed experiments. Anchoring the evaluation of learning to standardized tests alone will automatically exclude some of the most important kinds of learning.

Finally, the research on effective schools tended to overemphasize the direct influence of the principal. Although the leadership of the principal is important, the leadership of and collaboration among teachers is even more important. The principal's job is to design and nurture an environment in which teachers can more readily take charge of their work, as has been suggested in Chapters 7 and 8.

REAL ADVANCES FROM EFFECTIVE SCHOOL RESEARCH

As we look back on the 1970s and 1980s, we can appreciate that the research on effective schools helped us to understand that school improvement is not the result of fixing one or two elements in the school (say, teacher supervision or improved in-service programs). Rather, we began to see that school improvement involves changing the culture of teacher isolation, changing the use of time and

TABLE 13-3 Climate Characteristics of Effective Schools

1. High expectations of success and school-wide recognition of academic achievement and progress are attributes of effective schools. High expectations extend to effort and cooperation as well as to performance. School-wide recognition may take the form of honors, ceremonies, publications, announcements, rewards, posters, and other means of demonstrating the importance of achievement. The school staff take visible pride in the academic accomplishment of their students.

2. Order, discipline, and a businesslike atmosphere are features of effective schools. Rules are fairly enforced and discipline procedures are uniform throughout the school. The resulting sense of security and order builds responsibility and a sense of pride.

3. Effective schools have a cooperative and friendly atmosphere. Administration and staff work closely together and there is a strong sense of community. Teachers share materials and talk to each other frequently about curriculum and instruction. There is low turnover and the resulting stability builds commitment to school goals and high levels of trust, cooperation, and motivation.

4. The physical facilities may not be new or modern but they are safe and clean. And they provide adequate work space. Attractive and pleasant working conditions contribute to higher levels of staff and student motivation and achievement.

5. The faculty of effective schools take responsibility for the outcomes of the educational programs and treat poor results as problems to be solved.

Source: Thomas B. Corcoran and Barbara J. Hansen, *The Quest for Excellence: Making Public Schools More Effective,* New Jersey School Boards Association, Trenton, 1983, p. 10.

space, changing authority relationships, changing assessment procedures, changing the way schools work with parents, changing long-standing assumptions about teaching and learning. Based on these insights from the research on effective schools, we went on to explore how schools became that way.

In the United States, the school effectiveness movement became swept up in the larger national concern in the 1980s for restructuring schools. Many of the earlier findings from research on effective schools became incorporated within the policy recommendations of the national commissions that sprouted up during the 1980s. This national groundswell for school renewal generated a number of regional and national coalitions of schools and school systems that committed themselves to restructuring. The Coalition of Essential Schools,[6] the League of Professional Schools,[7] and the School Development Program[8] were three examples of groupings of schools whose individual members felt supported in their efforts to restructure themselves by their membership in a network of ideas, encouragement, and shared research. These efforts at school renewal also generated research studies that are compiling impressive evidence about what it takes for a school community to restructure itself.[9]

The point of reviewing these recent events is not to launch an extensive review of the ingredients and processes that seem to go into successful restructuring efforts. That is being done by others and is for another book and another course. Rather, I want to point out the link between these schools and the earlier effective schools and to explore the underlying dynamic that identifies them. The earlier "effective schools" and the more recent "essential schools," "professional schools," "developed schools," or "restructured schools" have this in common: They created a strong consensus that they had to do something about their schools and committed themselves to do it. They stayed with it long enough to work out satisfying solutions to the problems they had identified.

That, to me, is the definition of effectiveness. An effective group is one that identifies a problem or a goal, marshalls its resources, and establishes a process by which the problem can be solved or the goal achieved. The group does what it set out to do. The underlying dynamic that identifies the schools referred to previously is that they became and are effective.

I want to revisit the notion of effectiveness because it offers a helpful framework for thinking about the ongoing work of administrators in administering meaning, community, and excellence. As should be obvious by now, this book assumes that educational administration in the present and the future will inescapably involve ongoing restructuring of the school, and this in ways, perhaps, that current reform champions have as yet articulated only imperfectly. For the purposes of our discussions in this part of the book, namely, administering excellence, I want to emphasize that an excellent school community is an effective school community. Administering excellence implies that one is continually inviting the community to the ongoing clarification of the forms of excellence they want to support, and to the problematic nature of some current practices that run counter to the support of excellence. Once that problem has been named or that form of excellence identified, the administrator mobilizes action from the top and from the bottom. That is, the administrator looks at the available systemic and institutional supports that are available to support the decisions for action. This might include finding some discretionary funds in the budget, getting the maintenance staff to alter some classroom space, or mobilizing school board members to solicit support from community agencies and corporations. Simultaneously, the administrator arranges for ad-hoc or standing committees of teachers, parents, and students to devise specific implementation strategies for the action. The administrator, in short, mobilizes the community resources to do what it is they have decided to do.

Administering an effective community implies a *cultural* activity by the educational administrator, namely, developing a communal sense of self-efficacy. In Chapter 8 I suggested that a feeling of empowerment emerges from the experience of shared activity, of collaboration. Although I was referring primarily to the empowerment of the individual teacher who feels supported in the collaborative effort and is energized by being part of something larger than herself or himself, it is easy to see how shared activity leads the group to a sense of empowerment as well. With the experience of success in collaborative efforts, teachers develop a group sense of "can do." This is what I mean by a communal sense of self-efficacy. The faculty and, indeed, the students and parents, grow to believe that they can solve their problems. They grow to believe that if they set a goal for themselves, they can achieve it.

Administrators can play a part in developing this communal sense of self-efficacy by expressing sustained belief in the power of the community to deal with its problems and to achieve its goals. Publicizing successes, praising initiative, calling people together to discuss common concerns, engaging in problem naming and problem finding, and providing institutional support for group initiatives will help to create a culture of self-efficacy. This culture can be further reinforced by a consistent emphasis on organic management. When individuals and groups in the schools are able to exercise the discretion necessary to get the job done, they grow in confidence that they can solve their problems and achieve their goals.

When we tie this into the core focus of the school—the student as the worker—we begin to grasp the power of this enlarged sense of an effective school community. Students who believe that, with the help of their school community, they can achieve what they collectively set out to do are learning perhaps the most powerful lesson that schools can teach them.

THE EFFECTIVE RESTRUCTURING OF LEARNING

Revisiting this notion of effectiveness enables us to bring to the focus on academic achievement the foundational frameworks for nurturing the learning of meaning developed in earlier chapters on the administering of meaning. If school communities believe that they have to bring foundational concerns to the academic enterprise, concerns such as the social production of knowledge, the need to relate learning to human concerns of the life world, the need to relate learning to the larger cultural projects facing society, the need to relate learning to the everyday experience of students, and the need to relate learning to participation in the life of the civic community, then the effective community will set about devising ways to do this. We recall, however, that historically the effective school began with the basic skills of literacy and numeracy. We recall, as well, that later educators added to that concern for basic skills a concern for higher-order thinking skills and problem-solving skills, and the use of imagination in expressive skills. By bringing the foundational frameworks for meaning to the learning of basic skills and the high-order skills, we create a richer blueprint for an academically effective school. We rescue the valuable concept of the effective school from its earlier limitations and marry it to the emerging concerns for new frameworks for meaning. Table 13-4 summarizes this blueprint.

EFFECTIVE RESPONSES TO PROBLEMS

An effective school is able to name its problems and clarify the underlying causes or sources of problems. Many school problems are not based in the formal curriculum. The response of the school community to its problems is, however, a significant part of the informal curriculum. On the way to supporting a variety of excellences, schools have to deal with problems of the institution, which through its practices fails to support the kind of excellences it wants. The

TABLE 13-4 Foundational Frameworks for Meaning to Enhance the Mastery of Basic Skills and Higher-Order Learning

Foundational Frameworks for Engaging the Curriculum	Effects
The social production of knowledge	Feeds into and expands the mastery of basic skills
Relationship to the life world as well as to the world of mass administration	Feeds student's interest in learning
Relationship to the large cultural projects facing society	Feeds into and expands higher-order learning and creativity
Relationship to the students' everyday experiences	Enhances students' sense of self-efficacy
Relationship to participating in civil society	

problems might be the grading system, the teacher evaluation process, the weekly and semester schedules, or the poor quality of communications with parents. The effective school identifies these problems and initiates action from both the top and the bottom to respond to them.

Problems within the student body may also inhibit support for the excellences the school wants to promote. These problems might include interracial stereotyping, vandalism of school property and theft of student belongings, fights in the schoolyard and corridors, or open defiance of classroom teachers. The effective school identifies these problems and brings them before the whole community, or at least before those involved with the problem. Again, student, parent, and teacher committees can be established to suggest ways to deal with these problems. Institutional support should be brought to bear on the problem. A series of responses should be agreed upon and tried. Their effects can be evaluated and adaptations made.

In one school I know of, a group of female students asked that the school ban the "bathing-suit" issue of a popular sports magazine from the library. The principal and the librarian listened to them and decided to bring the problem before the school community. The student government was invited to sponsor a seminar on the issue of sexism in the media. Homeroom sessions for the preceding week were devoted to the same discussion. The problem turned into an opportunity for the female students to educate their male counterparts about a variety of issues in heterosexual relationships. Parents also were invited to discuss the matter with their sons and daughters at home. The effective dealing with the problem resulted in the female students acquiring a new voice in the school, the banning of that issue of the magazine from the library, and the developing of a more mature attitude on the part of many of the male students.

Problems, whether personal or institutional, will always emerge. We will solve one problem, only to find another one right around the corner. Failures, either institutional or personal, will always be part of a community striving for excellence. Their presence can lead to an erosion of the striving for excellence, or they can be an opportunity for the community to remind itself of the excellence it is seeking. The promotion of excellence will always entail the healing of failures and the processes of rebuilding and renewing. That is life. Messes happen. Effective communities clean them up as best they can, learn from them, and then get on with their work and their lives.

SUMMARY

In administering excellence, administrators want to develop a communal sense of self-efficacy, the sense that the community can achieve pretty much whatever it sets out to do. The building up of a culture of self-efficacy is seen as an essential part of generating energy and openness to a variety of excellences in the school community. This sense of effectiveness permeates both the ongoing work of transforming the curriculum and the continuous work of repairing the institution as it deals with its ongoing problems.

ACTIVITIES

1. In your journal, reflect on the attitudes of the people in your school. Do they have a "can do" attitude that enables them to tackle difficult school renewal projects, or do they expect the principal and superintendent to provide the direction and to solve their problems?
2. Examine your own sense of self-efficacy. Do you frequently respond, "That's a good idea, but they would never allow that to happen here."? Or do you respond, "That's a good idea; how could we make that happen here?"? What do you need to do to increase your confidence in yourself to effect significant change?
3. In your study group, devise three strategies or activities that will help to build a collective sense of self-efficacy in your schools.

ENDNOTES

1. Thomas B. Corcoran and Barbara J. Hansen, *The Quest for Excellence: Making Public Schools More Effective,* New Jersey School Boards Association, Trenton, 1983; Ronald R. Edmonds, "Schools Count: New York City's School Improvement Project," *Harvard Graduate School of Education Association Bulletin,* **25**:33–35 (1980); David A. Squires, William G. Huit, and John K. Segars, *Effective Schools and Classrooms: A Research Based Perspective,* Association for Supervision and Curriculum Development, Alexandria, VA, 1984.
2. Michael Rutter et al., *Fifteen Thousand Hours: Secondary Schools and Their Effects on Children,* Harvard University Press, Cambridge, MA, 1978.

3. James Coleman, *Coleman Report: Equality of Educational Opportunity*, Technical Report M 66, U.S. Government Printing Office, Washington, DC, 1966.
4. See Linda M. McNeil, *Contradictions of Control: School Structure and School Knowledge*, Routledge, New York, 1988.
5. See Robert J. Marzano, *A Different Kind of Classroom: Teaching with Dimensions of Learning*, Association of Supervision and Curriculum Development, Alexandria, VA, 1992; Lauren B. Resnick and Leopold E. Klopfer (eds.), *Toward the Thinking Curriculum: Current Cognitive Research*, Association of Supervision and Curriculum Development, Alexandria, VA, 1989; Norah Morgan and Juliana Saxton, *Teaching Questioning and Learning*, Routledge, London, 1991.
6. Theodore Sizer, *Horace's School: Redesigning the American High School*, Houghton Mifflin, Boston, 1992.
7. Carl Glickman, *Renewing America's Schools*, Jossey-Bass, San Francisco, 1993.
8. James Comer, "A Brief History and Summary of the School Development Program," Unpublished Paper, New Haven, CT, 1992.
9. See Karen S. Louis and Matthew B. Miles, *Improving the Urban High School, What Works and Why*, Teachers College Press, New York, 1990; Michael Fullan, *Change Forces: Probing the Depths of Educational Reform*, Falmer, London, 1993.

Epilogue

I hope that by now the interconnectedness of the various parts of this book is apparent. The social construction of meaning and the performance of knowledge do not make sense unless one lives in, with, and for a community. The learning community does not make sense unless there is a drive toward excellence, a concern to rise above mediocrity. Moral excellence is impossible without a self-governing community. Where there is no community, attention to the life world can more easily fall by the wayside. A community without a sense of its history, its meta-narratives, lacks the glue to hold it together in times of crisis.

Because of this interconnectedness of themes throughout the book, I assume that when one attempts to administer meaning it will necessarily spill over into administering community and administering excellence. As is implied in the new science, the whole dictates the unity of the parts; these fundamentals make a whole.

It is important to repeat what I have said earlier: This book is intended for a beginning course for beginning administrators. There is much to be learned after finishing this book: many technical aspects that deal with personnel, legal boundaries to action, the honing of communication skills, the skills of coalition and consensus building; deeper philosophical and psychological studies; deeper studies of multicultural realities; and considerations of how organizational cultures work and of the change process itself. The list of things one needs to know to be a good administrator is indeed long. Most of us will not begin to master the subject until we are close to retiring. My hope is that this approach to the fundamentals will keep you focused as you learn all the other necessary components of this challenging career.

In one sense, writing this book was a huge gamble. It was written on the gamble that graduate schools of education are ready to overhaul their teacher education programs as well as their administrator preparation programs. For administrator preparation programs this will mean moving out of the uniform, three-credit course arrangement into more intensive concentrations on themes, some of them carried out in the field with practitioner/mentors and some of them held in intensive fourteen-hour weekends. Classroom pedagogy will exhibit much greater variety—moving from lecture, to simulations, to debates, to independent reading assignments, to team projects, to case studies, and to site visits for action research. Besides the changing procedures, I am assuming that these preparation programs will go into questions concerning the purposes of schooling more deeply, and that they will explore the relationship of schooling to the larger changes and challenges in society and in culture. I am assuming, as well, that there will be changes in the internal dynamics of the school, especially in the teaching–learning process.

This book will make sense only if these changes are taking place, or at least are being imagined. Then an invitation to consider new fundamentals of educational administration may have appeal.

Index

Premodernism, 93
Principal:
  job of, 172
  as manager, 5
Progress,
  engines of, 45
  myth of, 44, 45
Purpel, David E., 5, 12, 88, 104

Rationality, 27
  in administration, 4, 5, 40, 51,
  118
  bounded, 4
  and modernity, 19, 42
  substantive, 113–114
  technical, 113–114
Rawls, John A., 162, 169
Readiness, 8
Reality, 18
  and meaning, 28
Reconstruction, of the educational
  process, 1
Reductionalism, 43, 91
Reflexivity:
  in assessment, 61
  in evolution, 51
  in humans, 51
Religion:
  and curriculum, 71
  and ethics in schools, 159
Renzulli, Joseph, 12
Rituals, 27, 57
Rowan, Brian, 117, 119, 132, 133

Scholarly community, 71
School:
  core task of, 121
  design of, 135–138
  district officers, 6
  learning agenda, 7, 49, 70
  management, 10
  mission of, 69, 89
  public program of, 10
  redesigning of, 46
  reform, 10, 39
  reinventing of, 6, 85, 89, 172

renewal, 8, 25
  restructuring, 6, 81
    teacher involvement in, 6
  system reform, 8
School effectiveness, 170–175
  characteristics of, 171–173
  critique of, 171
  definition of, 174
Schumacher, E. F., 36
Science:
  meaning of, 28
  and modernity, 19, 40, 42, 44
  and rationality, 42
  and specialization, 51
Scientific management, 4, 11, 117
Scientism, 4
Self:
  –actualization, 145
  –efficacy, 174, 177
  as filter, 18
  –governance, 100
    of community, 117, 179
    of students, 149
  –knowledge, 18–20
  –reflection, 17
  –transcendence, 53
Sergiovanni, Thomas J., 3, 11, 88, 104
Shared decision making, 107
Shills, Edward, A., 21
Simon, Herbert, 4, 11
Socialization, 14, 92, 108
  freedom from, 145
  of teachers, 111
Society, theory of, 40
Special interest groups, 10
Spending, for schools, 10
Standardized tests, 13, 29, 119, 131,
  171–172
Starratt, Robert J., 82, 88, 104
State:
  accountability to, 71
  jurisdiction of, 101, 122
Status quo:
  of administrator, 10
  of economics, 19
  in schools, 1, 31